THE BUTTERFLY DEFECT

Previous books by Ian Goldin

Is the Planet Full?

Divided Nations: Why Global Governance Is Failing,
and What We Can Do about It

Globalization for Development: Meeting New Challenges

Exceptional People: How Migration Shaped Our World
and Will Define Our Future

The Case for Aid

The Economics of Sustainable Development

Economic Reform, Trade and Agricultural Development

Modelling Economy-wide Reforms

Trade Liberalization: Global Economic Implications

Open Economies

The Future of Agriculture

Economic Crisis: Lessons from Brazil

Making Race

THE BUTTERFLY DEFECT

How Globalization Creates Systemic Risks, and What to Do about It

❦

IAN GOLDIN

AND

MIKE MARIATHASAN

PRINCETON UNIVERSITY PRESS

PRINCETON AND OXFORD

Library of Congress Cataloging-in-Publication Data

Goldin, Ian, 1955–
The butterfly defect : how globalization creates systemic risks,
and what to do about it / Ian Goldin, Mike Mariathasan.
Pages   cm
Summary: "Global hyperconnectivity and increased system integration have led to vast benefits, including worldwide growth in incomes, education, innovation, and technology. But rapid
globalization has also created concerns because the repercussions of local events now cascade
over national borders and the fallout of financial meltdowns and environmental disasters affects
everyone. *The Butterfly Defect* addresses the widening gap between systemic risks and their
effective management. It shows how the new dynamics of turbo-charged globalization has the
potential and power to destabilize our societies. Drawing on the latest insights from a wide
variety of disciplines, Ian Goldin and Mike Mariathasan provide practical guidance for how
governments, businesses, and individuals can better manage risk in our contemporary world.
Goldin and Mariathasan assert that the current complexities of globalization will not be sustainable as surprises become more frequent and have widespread impacts. The recent financial
crisis exemplifies the new form of systemic risk that will characterize the coming decades, and
the authors provide the first framework for understanding how such risk will function in the
twenty-first century. Goldin and Mariathasan demonstrate that systemic risk issues are now
endemic everywhere—in supply chains, pandemics, infrastructure, ecology and climate change,
economics, and politics. Unless we are better able to address these concerns, they will lead to
greater protectionism, xenophobia, nationalism, and, inevitably, deglobalization, rising conflict,
and slower growth. *The Butterfly Defect* shows that mitigating uncertainty and systemic risk in
an interconnected world is an essential task for our future."—Provided by publisher.

Includes bibliographical references and index.
ISBN 978-0-691-15470-1 (hardback)
1. Risk management.   2. Crisis management.   3. Globalization.
I. Mariathasan, Mike, 1982–   II. Title.
HD61.G643   2014
658.15′5—dc23
2013039405

British Library Cataloging-in-Publication Data is available

This book has been composed in Aldus with Gill Sans display by
Princeton Editorial Associates Inc., Scottsdale, Arizona.

Printed on acid-free paper. ∞

Printed in the United States of America

1 3 5 7 9 10 8 6 4 2

To Tessa, Olivia, and Alex

Ian Goldin

To Mechthild and Jos, to Vincent and Patrick, and to Sophie

Mike Mariathasan

Contents

Boxes, Illustrations, and Tables

BOXES

ILLUSTRATIONS

TABLES

Preface

I decided to write this book because I believe that globalization, by which I mean the process of increasing global integration and cross-border flows, has been the most powerful driver of human progress in the history of humanity. The tidal wave of globalization that has engulfed the planet over the past two decades has brought unprecedented opportunity. But it also has brought new risks that threaten to overwhelm us. This book focuses on the threat of systemic risk. Systemic risk cannot be removed because it is endemic to globalization. It is a process to be managed, not a problem to be solved. This book aims to provide a better understanding of technologically enhanced globalization with a view to making it more resilient. It seeks to overcome the benign neglect of systemic risk, which is not sustainable, and promote a more resilient and inclusive globalization. To this end, it considers different dimensions of the problem, offering a number of conceptual tools and lessons for managing the challenges of globalization and systemic risk.

The butterfly effect has become widely known to signify systems in which a small change in one place can lead to major differences in a remote and unconnected system. The name of the effect has origins in the work of Edward Lorenz, who illustrated how a hurricane's formation may be contingent on whether a distant butterfly had, days or weeks before, flapped its wings.[1] The effect was subsequently taken up in chaos theory, which draws on a long tradition of examining the unexpected consequences of changes to initial conditions in physics. Our title draws on this evocative concept and focuses on the negative unintended ripple effect of individual or unrelated developments. We are particularly concerned with those that have systemic effects and with the high-level changes in the structures of society that have occasioned new risks. Our title, *The Butterfly Defect*, draws attention to the new nature of systemic risk, which is such that small perturbations now have much greater effects and permeate all dimensions of society. Due to globalization, the butterfly of change has lost its innocence and globalization has produced structural defects that propagate new forms of risk.

Societies ignore systemic risk at our peril. Long before the shocks rip through our societies, the political pressures that seek to reverse globalization build. When citizens feel that openness and connectivity bring more bad things than good, they will seek to close off the flows that bind us. Xenophobia, nationalism, and protectionism are three well-known manifestations of the drive toward more inward-looking politics. A cosmopolitan or international perspective is under threat. The financial crisis of 2007/2008, terrorism, cyberattacks, perceptions of excessive migration, and the ever-present fear of pandemics are among the threats that are seen to arise from cross-border movements of people, goods, and services. Even virtual flows—through the Internet—are seen as sources of threat.

Politicians, business people, and civil society have done a bad job in explaining the wide-ranging benefits of international connections and why these connections imply more, not less, joined-up global action. But we face not only a political backlash. We face the real threats posed by systemic risks. Financial crises, pandemics, and cyber and other threats could overwhelm the ties that bind us. Deglobalization and slowing global growth would be the consequences. These would be disasters for the global economy, particularly for poor people, who are always the most vulnerable. Everyone stands to gain through better management of systemic risk. Poor people suffer most when there are shocks. They also have the most to gain through greater connection. This is particularly the case for those who are not yet connected due to their geographical or social isolation.

This book is the fourth in a series of books I am writing on globalization. Each seeks to make specific arguments, and together I hope they will provide insights into how better to manage globalization. *Globalization for Development: Meeting New Challenges* (coauthored with Kenneth Reinert) demonstrates that globalization can be a powerful force for poverty reduction but that this is not automatic. Specific policies are required to ensure that the potential is realized. That book covers the flows associated with finance, trade, aid, migration, and ideas. The significance of migration, which is one of the most misunderstood of the global flows, is brought out in my book *Exceptional People: How Migration Shaped Our World and Will Define Our Future* (coauthored with Geoffrey Cameron and Meera Balarajan). My most recent book, *Divided Nations: Why Global Governance Is Failing, and What We Can Do about It,* shows that the existing global institutions are unfit for twenty-first-century purposes and suggests a way forward. The failure of global governance has greatly aggravated the risks identified in this book, *The Butterfly Defect.*

This book for the first time identifies the systemic nature of risk in the twenty-first century in finance and other sectors as an endemic feature of globalization. It provides interdisciplinary perspectives from which to examine the sources of systemic risk and possible solutions in terms of mitigating and building resilience against the negative dimensions of the cascading consequences of globalization.

Among the solutions that my coauthor, Mike Mariathasan, and I propose are changes in competition and regulatory policies to take better account of the geographical concentration of risk. We show that simpler and more widely understood and enforced rules are required to manage the growing complexity and instability that underpin globalization. Because systemic risk transcends national borders, it is vital that the governance of these risks also become more coordinated internationally. For business, we have specific recommendations regarding the need to overcome the excessively short-term bias in management accounting and to rebalance incentives toward longer-term valuations. The adoption of commercial principles that drive out resilience in society is also seen as a major shortcoming. "Lean and mean" management principles that seek to "sweat all assets" result in excessively brittle and vulnerable systems. The tension between individual rationality and collective outcomes is another theme that runs through the book. What may be rational for an individual may be disastrous for individuals collectively. Antibiotic resistance or the collapse of fisheries and other failures of the global commons are examples of such failures. They highlight the limits of the market when addressing the risks arising from inadequate accounting for the systemic effects of individual actions.

Ian Goldin, Oxford, UK

Acknowledgments

In writing this book I have been fortunate to be able to collaborate with Mike Mariathasan. Mike has assimilated a vast amount of material and explored numerous concepts that were half cooked in my mind. Fresh from his doctorate in economics, Mike has put aside his equations to immerse himself in interdisciplinary research into the complexities of systemic risk. The initial development of the central thesis of this book benefited greatly from my collaboration with Tiffany Vogel. Tiffany brought fresh insights, and her rare ability to pollinate ideas is reflected in the paper we coauthored, titled "Global Governance and Systemic Risk in the 21st Century: Lessons from the Financial Crisis," the echo of which is particularly evident in chapter 2, which is the reason that she is credited on that chapter.[1]

Mike and I have benefited greatly from the summer employment of Ely Sandler, an outstandingly talented undergraduate at Oxford. Despite his relatively short engagement with the book, his imprint is reflected in improvements in our narrative and the clearer exposition of a number of arguments. Ely also deserves credit for the title of the book. In the final stages, Co-Pierre Georg made a vital contribution in ensuring that the manuscript reflects the latest thinking on the interface of complexity, systemic risk, and economics. We are most grateful to him for devoting weeks to helping us clarify a number of complexities in the literature and to adding a number of fresh insights and perspectives. His imprint is greatest in chapter 2, focusing on finance, where he is deservedly cited as a coauthor.

My ability to embark on these book projects, and indeed the source of the underlying ideas, arises from my position as director of the Oxford Martin School at the University of Oxford. The school is a truly remarkable and unique interdisciplinary community of well over three hundred Oxford scholars drawn from over 20 disciplines. Its institutes and programs are seeking to provide fresh perspectives from which to resolve a number of the greatest challenges facing humanity. Many of the issues covered in this book—finance, pandemics, migration, cybersecurity, climate, and biodiversity, as well as complexity and global governance—are the focus of teams of scholars that are among the most able in the world. I have been most fortunate to be able to draw on their expertise and indulgent tolerance of what inevitably must have been naïve questions about their areas of life-long expertise.

The Institute for New Economic Thinking in the Oxford Martin School (INET Oxford) aims to develop the concepts and tools for more sustainable and equitable global economic development. It was established due to the vision and generous support of George Soros and with funding from the Institute for New Economic Thinking Foundation. This institute has enabled the Oxford Martin School to establish a number of research programs, including a program on complexity, as well as one on risk and resilience, jointly supported by the Rockefeller Foundation and directed by Felix Reed-Tsochas, whom I have to thank for his very constructive comments on parts of the manuscript. The INET program on economic modeling has brought Mike Mariathasan to Oxford, and I am indebted to Professor Sir David Hendry and Professor David Vines for recruiting Mike and supporting his involvement in this project.

The smooth running of the Martin School, and also my research, owes much to the effective operational leadership provided by our administrator, Laura Lauer. Lindsay Walker has provided much-needed expert help with the manuscript and, through superb management of my schedule, has carved out the time I have needed to think and write. Claire Jordan has ensured that in our attempt to "stand on the shoulders of giants" we secured the necessary legal permissions.

Princeton University Press (PUP) has once again lived up to its excellent reputation. I was fortunate that the publisher, Peter Dougherty, had agreed to personally take on my previous Princeton Book, *Exceptional People,* and was delighted when he encouraged me to write *The Butterfly Defect.* Peter has proved to be an exemplary publisher, providing much-needed guidance and working beyond the call of duty, including during his holiday, to help me frame and hone my arguments and enhance the manuscript. Together with his colleagues Al Bertrand, the European publisher for PUP, and Hannah Paul, as well as Peter Strupp and his colleagues at Princeton Editorial Associates, Peter Dougherty has expertly shepherded this book down the path to publication. Anonymous PUP referees provided most helpful feedback that we have taken on board to reshape the manuscript and improve our arguments. David Clark has once again proved to be the most extraordinarily effective editor, able to work calmly under the pressures of time and on a subject that is not his own. David has worked tirelessly to iron out a range of both substantive and editorial questions and graciously set aside his many other pressing commitments in order to devote himself to preparing our manuscript for publication.

As is evident from the above, Mike and I owe a great deal to the guidance and support of others. None of the individuals or institutions cited has any responsibility for the final text, and Mike and I alone are accountable for any errors or omissions.

My immediate family have suffered the consequences of my being absorbed in yet another book project. Nights and weekends spent reading or writing have been won at the cost of my being with them. It is to Tessa, Olivia, and Alex that this book is dedicated.

Ian Goldin, Oxford, UK

This book was written during my time at the Institute for New Economic Thinking at the Oxford Martin School. Ian offered me the opportunity to devote time to thinking beyond the technicalities of financial regulation, and—just out of my Ph.D. program—I gladly took it. It was a privilege to spend an intense year learning from his vast experience and trying to see the world from a different angle. I am grateful to him for trusting me with important parts of the project, for challenging and guiding me, and for the many discussions we were able to have.

In addition to everyone that Ian has already acknowledged, I am particularly thankful to my Ph.D. advisers, Ramon Marimon and Árpád Ábrahám, for supporting my detour into writing, and deeply indebted to my wife for sharing her knowledge as a political scientist with me. She challenged me on style, methodology, and—most fiercely—content and was vital in helping me through the frustrations that come with a project like this. Last, but most certainly not least, I am grateful to my parents for teaching me the importance of keeping an open mind, and to my brothers for continuing to keep me on my toes.

Mike Mariathasan, Vienna, Austria

THE BUTTERFLY DEFECT

Introduction

This book examines the consequences of living in a more connected, complex, and uncertain world.[1] The central theme is that globalization must be managed more effectively, which, as we show in the concluding chapter, includes investing in institutions and policies to build resilience at all levels. Globalization permeates every element of our daily lives. By *globalization* we mean the movement of people, goods, services, and ideas across a widening set of countries. The process of globalization is not confined to multinational corporations and their global supply chains or to banking conglomerates and their international investment portfolios. It affects even the most unsuspecting among us. Globalization has shaped our lives and options for the future.

Globalization informs not only our choices but the composition of almost all the goods and services we consume. We are more tightly linked than ever before, and the connections are more complex, more frequent, and more central to our lives and our economies. They shape the ways in which countries and societies are developing. Politics may be driven by local concerns, but, as this book shows, the key opportunities and risks facing societies are increasingly determined beyond national borders. At the same time, what happens in any one community can quickly cascade into a global event. Small places and single individuals can become globally significant, just as what happens globally can have dramatic consequences for the most remote locality or community.

To politicians, local concerns may often appear more important than global developments. Foreigners do not share a common history, background, or nationality, and laws, borders, and other restrictions separate global citizens. But whether we live in Manhattan, Moscow, or Mumbai, we are connected by an increasingly dense and complex web of over-lapping and intertwined links. These are both physical and virtual and have allowed us to take the principle of comparative advantage to levels that David Ricardo could not have imagined when he was writing his path-breaking insights on global development in 1817.[2] Although many are critical of globalization, few would deny the gains from integration and exchange. In this book we focus on neglected aspects of accelerated integration, notably the systemic risks that arise from globalization.

Following earlier waves of globalization (from about 1820 to 1914 and 1960 to 1980, respectively), the period since around 1990 has been associated with innovative leaps in information and transport technologies—alongside a fundamental reshaping of international politics and the global economy.[3] The haphazard development of a range of integrated global relationships and systems—such as those associated with infra-structure, finance, transport, information, economics, and business—means that the context of individual and other choices is constantly widening and becoming more complex. It is now impossible to account for all the consequences of any individual's choices. As we show, this shortcoming pervades the global system for the exchange of goods and services, skills, information, and people. Because the ramifications of in-dividual or collective decisions are increasingly unclear, defining respon-sibility, rewards, and punishments is more challenging.

As complexity increases, the task becomes harder. Our actions, as individuals and through our local and national governments, are bound to have systemic consequences that we are unable to foresee in advance and often fail to understand afterward. In a complex system, resilience becomes a separate goal and has to be considered separately from other goals.[4]

Two interrelated problems arise. The first is that although each of our individual actions may be rational, collectively they may lead to fail-ure. Economists and social scientists have studied the "tragedy of the commons" for centuries. The problem is compounded as the population grows and as incomes rise and individuals become freer to choose what they want to consume. Bluefin tuna fishing was once sustainable, but in January 2013 one such tuna sold for $1.7 million.[5] As in the case of rhinoceros horn, it is simply a question of time until the market mech-anisms lead to extinction. Similar problems arise with biodiversity, climate change, antibiotic resistance, and other management failures of the global commons. The more people there are on earth and the higher our incomes, the more each individual's activities have spillover effects.

The second challenge is that as complexity and integration grow, attribution becomes more difficult and the unintended or unknown consequences of actions increase. Failure to understand or even acknowledge the nonlinear and highly complex nature of global linkages on every level of governance leads to growing weaknesses and can paralyze decision making. The world has become like a living organism, with the physical connections equivalent to blood pumping through veins and the virtual connections comparable to our nervous system. Understanding the system dynamics and interdependencies has become vital to sustainable global growth and development.

Each element of the global system—finance, supply chains, health, energy, the Internet, the environment, and others—needs to be maintained in good health. The biggest systemic risk, however, is not the collapse of any one of these individual systems but rather our lack of capacity to manage the growing complexities and interdependencies between them. Politics and economics have demonstrated a singular failure to proactively address collective action failures or to resolve problems with international cooperation.[6] One way of addressing collective failure is through learning from past experiences. Often the lessons are learned relatively late in the day and are quickly forgotten. In cases in which genuine change ensues, it is not always sufficient for the intended purpose.

Historically, advances have arisen following terrible tragedies. Our current system of global management arose from the ashes of the Second World War. Our hope is that increased information and education and closer physical and virtual connections are giving rise to a more informed global citizenry that is capable of producing more effective governance. We are able to learn faster because there are more educated people with more information at their fingertips. There has also been a release of individual genius as billions more people have become educated and engaged globally, so, simply based on the random distribution of exceptionally talented individuals engaging in global activities and problem solving, humanity should be able to identify more solutions. Collective genius is an even more powerful source of innovation.

Many more minds can now be connected and contribute fragments of knowledge and information, leading to a more rapid evolution of ideas. Connectivity and complexity are not only curses. New networks and combinations of old and new ideas can yield powerful insights and new politics. These are urgently required to ensure that we are able to comprehend the power that has been unleashed and make sure that it is managed inclusively and in a sustainable manner. The failure to harvest this potential will mean that globalization will be perceived to be more of a threat than an opportunity. It will be in danger of being associated with increasing systemic risk and cascading crises. The consequences are likely to be rising xenophobia, protectionism, and nationalism as individuals around the world seek to reduce their exposure to exogenous shocks. Such actions would be counterproductive and would compound global mismanagement. The challenge is to get ahead of the curve and harvest the benefits of globalization while building resilience and mitigating against the inevitable interdependency and vulnerability arising from increased connectivity and complexity.

This book examines the consequences of living in a more connected, complex, and uncertain world. It aims to help us manage the risks associated with globalization. It is interdisciplinary in its approach, seeking to draw insights from the different dimensions of potential systemic risk. We focus on systemic risk in domains ranging from ecology to economics as well as industry and infrastructure. Although we highlight the systemic nature of risk within a number of apparently distinct areas, we also emphasize the common insights and linkages between them and explore the resulting risks for governance and for societies more generally.

We necessarily are not providing an exhaustive or specialist view of any one domain. Because we are economists, our analysis of finance is the foundation of our understanding of the key relationships between globalization and systemic risk. Outside economics, in health, infrastructure and other areas, we provide perspectives that are informed by our understanding of the key drivers and fragilities but that clearly require disciplinary expertise for further analysis. Drawing on lessons from scholars in other disciplines allows us to deduce general principles and to identify best practices. By bringing together for the first time evidence on the nature of systemic risk in each of these different sectors, we are able to identify the importance of the interdependencies generated by global-ization and the need to consolidate research and action.

The book is organized in eight chapters. Chapter 1 explains our concerns regarding systemic risk in the hyperconnected world of the twenty-first century. It identifies why we believe that there has been a fundamental change in the nature of global relations in recent decades, providing a historical perspective on global integration. We show why we care about globalization, as a source of unprecedented opportunity. We then show why we worry that this is not sustainable and that the systemic risks generated by globalization threaten to be its undoing. The chapter lays out the key concepts and provides the intellectual founda-tion for the chapters that follow.

Chapter 2 draws on our knowledge as economists, presenting evidence that the financial crisis of 2007/2008 was the first of the systemic crises of the twenty-first century. Finance has been at the cutting edge of glo-balization in recent decades. We show how a combination of technological and other advances in a climate of political and ideological failures created a recipe for the unsustainable integration and expansion of the system. We draw on the illustrative case study of Iceland to highlight the extent of incomprehension and mismanagement and show how the failures in Iceland are mirrored in the United States, Europe, and elsewhere. In chap-ter 2 we call for two pillars of systemic risk governance: (1) to improve efforts toward understanding, measuring, and predicting the evolution of the complex system and (2) to devise institutions and procedures that are globally coordinated yet locally flexible and responsive and are, in them-selves, based on simple rules that will allow us to manage complexity and change. We emphasize the need for simple rules and caution that rising complexity cannot be matched by ever more complex regulations.

Chapter 3 examines systemic risk in business and trade. It pays par-ticular attention to the risks associated with global supply chains and the globalization of management education. As is the case in finance, we see these resulting primarily from behavioral risks. The threat originates in the otherwise healthy desire of individual firms to maximize profits and to reap the benefits of streamlined risk-sharing strategies or produc-tion processes. Individual people similarly consider their own individual, family, and community interests rather than wider collective interests. The more that individuals and communities live according to the rules of free markets, the greater this individual expression of choice. Although this has been a key driver of global development and wealth creation, it simultaneously leads to an increasing failure to account for the spillover or systemic consequences of our individual atomized actions. The more that each individual or firm believes that system stability and sustainability are not their responsibility, the more the system as a whole may become unstable and subject to systemic risk. We show that this also reflects governance failures as governments have shied away from national or multilateral responsibility for the management of the rising externalities and collective risk arising from the rapid economic and population growth associated with the current phase of accelerated globalization.

In chapter 4 we focus on the physical infrastructure that has created the arteries through which the lifeblood of globalization flows. Without these, global integration would be impossible and our societies would become dysfunctional. Our focus is on the vulnerabilities of trade and travel networks, energy supply networks, and the global information technology architecture. We document the degree of integration in these areas and consider the risks of these networks' failure. We learn from past incidents about the propagation of hazards and the interaction between physical failure and crisis management. Our aim in the chapter is to identify the key characteristics of physical networks and establish how infrastructure may become more robust and resilient to systemic shocks so it is a source of stability rather than an amplifier of cascading shocks.

Chapter 5 examines ecological risks and the relationship between globalization and the environment. Globalization affects and is affected by the environment. We consider the dual causality by which the ecosystem is shaped and by which it influences the process of global integration. We show that although globalization has accelerated economic growth, it has been a cause of increased fossil fuel use, thereby increasing carbon emissions. It also has resulted in a sharp reduction in ecological diversity. The accumulation of greenhouse gases and declining biodiversity have the potential to engender catastrophic outcomes. The acceleration of human development associated with globalization threatens the stability of the ecosystem in a manner that is fundamentally different from that of the historical degradation of the past. This is because of its accelerated impact and potential systemic consequences. Globalization threatens the stability of the global ecosystem, but the environment is itself a source of growing hazard. Floods, droughts, and other extreme weather events, together with the consequences of accelerated degradation of land, water, and other natural resources, pose systemic risks that threaten to undermine many of the benefits of globalization and to compound its risks. This systemic risk has particularly negative consequences for poor people, not the least for those who live on marginal and vulnerable land.

Chapter 6 presents evidence on what is perhaps the oldest form of systemic risk, which is that arising from viruses and pandemics. The factors that characterize globalization increase these risks. These factors include the movement of people and goods at increasing speeds and over greater distances, with many passing through a small number of key airports and other hubs. Rising population density and urbanization and the increasing use of and proximity to animals as food and pets foster the development and rapid dispersion of pandemics. The development of antibiotics has brought some respite, but increasing antibiotic resistance is a major concern. Technological developments have the potential to be misused, and the exponential decline in the cost of DNA sequencing not only provides extraordinary new health care opportunities but also carries new risks due to the potential for contagious diseases to be constructed synthetically in laboratories. The current phase of globalization is adding new dimensions of complexity to the management of pandemics. The interplay of globalization and disease is not new, but, as we show in chapter 6, it has entered a dangerous new phase of systemic risk.

Chapter 7 is concerned with social risks. We focus on questions of economic inequality and social cohesion. Globalization has been associated with emerging markets' catching up with earlier developers, but this convergence masks the fact that dozens of countries are falling further behind. Globalization also has been associated with rising inequality in virtually all countries. We consider the causes and implications of growing inequality and the extent to which individuals and societies are disconnected or even disadvantaged by globalization. The uneven nature of globalization and the increasing restrictions on migration are part of the explanation, as is the failure of policies at the national and global levels to promote a more inclusive system. Of particular concern is the evidence that poor people and poor countries are the most vulnerable to systemic risk, which accentuates inequality. We see weakening social cohesion and the widening institutional failures as interrelated, with politicians receiving neither the mandate nor the support to focus on longer-term and strategic concerns. The attribution issues identified in chapter 1 also are seen to contribute to the weakness of leadership and to the growth of extreme parties. The drift to more local politics and rising support for extremist parties, as well as nationalism, protectionism, and xenophobic behavior, are seen to be responses to this as citizens seek to exercise greater control over their immediate environment and to wrest control from distant and apparently unaccountable institutions to which they feel little connection. When *foreign* is synonymous with *threat*, the case for collective action is made more difficult. Yet, as we show, it is only through collective action that we can build resilience and mitigate the gravest systemic threats. Social cohesion is seen to be a necessary condition for more effective management of systemic threats. We argue that a more inclusive globalization is a prerequisite for the continued success of global integration and globalization.

The concluding chapter 8 examines the interdependent nature of global systemic risk. We highlight the need for international coordination and interdisciplinary efforts and conclude that risk in our hyperconnected environment can no longer be treated as something that is confined to particular sectors or domains. The risks arising from the behavior of individuals and firms and those associated with physical infrastructure and the natural environment all influence each other. The environment is both affected by globalization and a serious threat to its continued services. The causalities in the relationship between economic integration and social cohesion run both ways as well.

A primary goal of this book is to alert government, business, and civil society leaders and policy makers as well as students and citizens to the relationship between globalization and systemic risk. To this end, we conclude the chapter by suggesting general principles and offering concrete recommendations for managing and sustaining globalization. We emphasize the need for a more thoughtful understanding and management of globalization and for striking a balance between economic integration and sustainable outcomes at the national and global levels.

1

⚭

Globalization and Risk in the Twenty-First Century

In recent decades we have entered a new era of connectivity and integration. Globalization not only affects multinational corporations and their global supply chains or banking conglomerates and their international investment portfolios. It also shapes the life of virtually every individual alive, every day. Transnational interactions have become the norm, and social networks are global. The connections between people around the world have grown at an astounding pace. "Right now a Masai warrior with a cell phone has access to better mobile phone capabilities than the President of the United States did twenty-five years ago. And if he's on a smart phone with access to Google, then he has better access to information than the President did just fifteen years ago."[1]

This interconnectedness manifests itself in every aspect of our lives, even when we do not consciously choose it. We are so accustomed to globalization that we take for granted the products and services we consume from around the world.

In the twenty-first century, trade is no longer primarily physical. Electricity, media, money, and ideas cross borders at speeds that make traditional trade, such as that in meat from Argentina or bananas from the Caribbean, appear almost anachronistic. We all depend on technologies, as well as on products and services from across our borders. For example, our information technology (IT) services may run on Israeli software provided from Mumbai as we consume entertainment from Los Angeles filmed in South Africa on computers manufactured in China or Taiwan assembled from parts from more than 20 countries. A German loan bails out the Cypriot government as the EU shapes the fiscal policy of the Greek exchequer. The fiber cables that enable the World Wide Web form a web across our oceans' floors, with the servers providing the necessary computing power located around the world and as likely to be in advanced economies as in what was once termed the "third world."

The traditional boundaries between the "developed" and "developing" worlds are fading. Although laws, borders, and restrictions separate countries, virtually all our activities and ideas have cross-border dimensions. Individual and local choices have global impacts and vice versa: what happens outside our borders has direct daily consequences for each of us, every day. These connections are complex, frequently opaque, and often beyond our control. Yet together they are shaping how the world develops. As we will see, there is a growing likelihood that events in one place will have cascading effects in other areas, jumping across national borders and sectors as well as the traditional divisions of different types of risk.

In this chapter we establish a framework for understanding this complex web. The defining characteristic of our age is increasing connectivity. We start by seeking to better understand the driving forces of growing connectivity. We then link this growth in connectivity to the concept of complexity and show how this link inherently implies instability. We also build on work in risk analysis to link this instability with uncertainty and systemic issues on the one hand and with the loss of individual and institutional responsibility on the other. Finally, we argue for reforms to promote a more *transparent* and a more *resilient globalization*.

GLOBALIZATION AND INTEGRATION

Globalization can generally be understood as the process driven by and resulting in increased cross-border flows of goods, services, money, people, information, technology, and culture.[2] These flows are multidimensional, and the number of connections between them is unprecedentedly large and growing exponentially. It is becoming deeper in that these connections penetrate a growing range of human activities. Increasingly not only people but also things are being connected—cars, phones, merchandise, and a rapidly widening range of inanimate objects and sensors.

The current period of integration is revolutionary in that a larger set of changes have occurred with a pervasively wider influence than over any comparably short time in previous phases of globalization.[3] We consider, in turn, two additional examples of global connectivity that we feel are unique and have significantly lowered the transaction costs of economic integration. The first is innovation and technological progress, particularly with respect to computing power and information technologies. In the late 1960s Douglas Engelbart, a computer scientist at the Stanford Research Institute, gave a demonstration of the new technological opportunities emerging with the advent of personal computing. His ideas on the user experience constituted a milestone in personal computer usage and inspired many of the breakthroughs that have gone on to transform the world. Today personal computing and Internet usage have entered a new paradigm. When Intel cofounder Gordon Moore first suggested in 1965 that the number of transistors on a chip would continue to double every year, he could not have anticipated the implications of his prediction.[4] Today "technology has . . . permeated through our normal daily routines, changing the way we cook and eat, the way we travel from A to B and the way we work and interact with one another."[5] Almost 50 years later, "Moore's Law" is still firmly in place, and it will underpin changes in the coming decades that will be at least as radical as those of the past two decades. Affordable IT and telecommunication devices have allowed us to create a virtual world that transcends national borders as well as traditional industry boundaries. They have enabled unprecedented degrees of global integration, and—by providing a platform for the exchange of information and skills—they continue to generate potential conduits for further globalization. Communication also allows the world to take advantage of its most valuable resource: the growing numbers of human beings who are increasingly educated and literate.[6]

The second example of global connectivity relates to the political and ideological changes that have both defined and facilitated the latest wave of globalization. The political revolutions that tore down the Berlin Wall and ended the Cold War were fundamental. In the same decade that the Berlin Wall fell and the Soviet Union splintered, the West normalized relations with China's 1.3-billion-person economy. Authoritarian regimes collapsed in more than 65 countries in Latin America, Asia, Africa, and Eastern Europe and were replaced with democratic systems that were more open to global trade, finance, and ideas.[7] In many but clearly not all countries, along with open borders came democratic institutions, intellectual property rights, and an economic paradigm shift toward market capitalism and more open economies.[8] The Uruguay Round of trade negotiations and reforms of macroeconomic policy brought more countries and people than had any previous wave of globalization into the global exchange of goods, services, and ideas. Cross-border capital flows have increased dramatically since the 1990s (from $1.5 trillion in 1995 to $6 trillion in 2007) and have recovered strongly in the wake of the financial crisis of 2007/2008 (reaching $4.4 trillion in 2010 following two years of volatility and decline).[9] Since the turn of this century, China (2001), Taiwan (2002), Saudi Arabia (2005), Vietnam (2007), Ukraine (2008), and Russia (2012) have joined the World Trade Organization (WTO). There are now 154 member states, and all major global economies have bound themselves to the WTO's rules.[10]

The liberalization of world capital and trade flows has not generally been accompanied by the removal of restrictions on the movement of labor and people across national or regional borders.[11] Despite these restrictions, the extent and scope of globalization across labor markets are remarkable. Since 1980 the number of migrants has doubled to well over 200 million globally.[12] The pattern of migration has also changed. The period 1840–1914 was mainly one of trans-Atlantic migration, whereas the movements that followed the aftermath of the Second World War and accelerated during the 1980s have spanned the entire globe.[13]

The global movement of goods and people has been facilitated by the expansion and development of an increasingly complex system of roads, railways, shipping routes, and air traffic.[14] In 2008 world container port traffic surpassed the threshold of 500 million TEUs (twenty-foot equivalent units) for the first time and was seven times greater than in 1988.[15] World air travel has more than doubled since the mid-1990s (see figure 1.1). Over the same period, the real value of world trade has more than quadrupled as the demand for high-value traded goods has risen more rapidly than incomes, and production processes have fragmented geographically with the rise in global value chains, facilitated by more efficient logistics.[16]

What most distinctively separated recent decades from previous ones was the coincidence of dramatic political, economic, and technological

Billions of passengers per kilometer

Billions of tons per kilometer

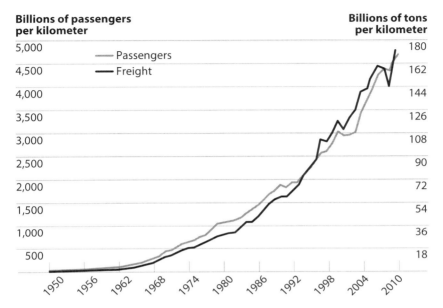

Figure 1.1. World air travel and world air freight carried, 1950–2011. Air Transport Association as reported in Jean-Paul Rodrigue, Claude Comtois, and Brian Slack, 2012, "World Air Travel and World Air Freight Carried, 1950–2011," in *The Geography of Transport Systems* (New York: Routledge), chap. 3, accessed 19 October 2012, http://people.hofstra.edu/geotrans/eng/ch3en/conc3en/evolairtransport.html. Figure by Jean-Paul Rodrigue. Used with permission.

change.[17] The end of the Soviet Union and the integration of China and many former autarkic regimes into the world community coincided with the technological revolution that brought us Amazon (in 1994), eBay (in 1995), Google (in 1998), and Facebook (in 2004). These political and communication upheavals significantly increased the tempo of globalization.

GLOBAL CONNECTIVITY AND COMPLEX SYSTEMS

In this section we illustrate what we mean by increased connectivity and show how the concept of complexity relates to the integrated systems created by globalization.

Connectivity

Accessing the Internet through mobile devices is an example of a relatively recent innovation. According to the Cisco Visual Networking Index, global *mobile data traffic* in 2010 was three times greater than *total global Internet traffic* in 2000.[18] In 2010 mobile traffic tripled for the third year in a row, and the average connection speed doubled between 2009 and 2010. Smart phone usage also doubled over this one-year period. By 2015 global mobile traffic is expected to increase 26-fold over 2010 levels, and it is expected that there will be nearly one mobile device per person—7.1 billion mobile connected devices for 7.2 billion individuals.[19] The transformative potential underlying these numbers is best understood when we realize that 48 million of these individuals will live with mobile Internet access *but without electricity*. In other words, there will be 48 million people with access to Google but not to artificial light. The Web will be more worldwide than light bulbs.[20]

Although the mobile Internet requires a significant physical infrastructure in terms of Internet exchange points, mobile phone masts, and backbone cables, individuals seeking to establish mobile connections have to make a far smaller investment than is required to access the Web through cabling and fixed connections to the physical Internet. In fact, provided that a suitable system is in place, consumers now simply require a capable mobile phone and a nearby outlet for charging the battery.[21] Not surprisingly, the growth of mobile Internet connections has been strongest in some of the world's poorest regions.[22] These developments enable those with relatively poor physical infrastructure to access information and education. Figure 1.2 provides a visual map of a sample of 10 million Facebook "friendships" in 2010. We see that, for the moment, the Middle East, China, and most of Africa remain relatively unconnected. This isolation is the result of missing physical connectivity as well as the development of alternative social networks spurred, in some countries, by political restrictions on Facebook's activities. The revolutionary potential of mobile Internet devices is that they can play an important role in information sharing and political mobilization. The "Arab Spring" is one manifestation of this potential; the global protests surrounding the treatment of dissidents in Russia and China are others.[23]

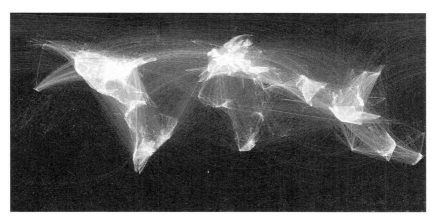

Figure 1.2. Facebook friendships, 2010. Paul Butler, 2010, "Visualising Friendships," *Facebook*, 13 December, accessed 27 January 2013, http://www.facebook.com/notes/facebook-engineering/visualizing-friendships/469716398919. Used with permission.

The relationship between the virtual and the physical can be further explored by comparing figure 1.2 with figure 1.3, which shows global civilian air traffic. One implication of this comparison is that virtual integration not only is a reasonable proxy for real-world interaction but also might act as an accelerator. Virtual connectivity allows users to learn about places and opportunities in other countries. Virtual friendships make long-distance journeys not only more desirable but also easier to organize. Virtual communication enables companies to maintain and develop contacts and manage employees and operations in far-flung parts of the world. Despite the many remaining barriers to international migration, the labor market is becoming globalized and the economy digitalized. Job vacancies are searchable from anywhere, and as work processes and cultures become more widely understood through improved communication, skills are becoming more transferable across continents. As a result of these developments, as shown in figure 1.1, there is a correlation between the travel patterns of people and the transport of goods. We see accelerated growth in both sectors since the 1950s, which reached totals of more than 4,500 billion passengers and upward of 170 billion tons transported per kilometer in 2011.

Figure 1.4 shows how domestic air travel in China and Europe increased between 1990 and 2010 in both volume and intricacy as more

10   25,000

Figure 1.3. Civil aviation traffic, 2004. The shades of gray reflect the number of passengers per day (see gray scale at the bottom of the figure) traveling between two airports. Lars Hufnagel, Dirk Brockmann, and Theo Geisel, 2004, "Forecast and Control of Epidemics in a Globalized World," *Proceedings of the National Academy of Sciences (PNAS)* 101 (42): 15124–15129, image on 15125. © 2004 The National Academy of Sciences, USA. Used with permission.

flights went to more destinations. Although the two regions started at comparable levels, growth in China has been most rapid, with a 1,745 percent increase in available seat-kilometers. The growth in airline activity has been part of a broader pattern of rising connectivity that has led to the emergence of China as a hub for global trade and to the development of a domestic trade web for goods sourced in China, as depicted in figure 1.5.

Finance, too, has seen a rapid expansion in connectivity and integration. An illustrative measure of volume is the interbank market activity conducted through the Federal Reserve System's Fedwire interbank payment network. Figure 1.6 represents this activity. On the left-hand side we see an extraordinary 70,000 links in just one day. The right-hand side depicts the core links at 75 percent of the day's activity.

A more global picture of integration in the financial sector emerges when we consider finance at the multinational level (figure 1.7). As well as

Global trends
China domestic frequencies

Domestic frequencies have increased more than 19-fold since 1990		1990	2010
	Total weekly ASKs*	388	7,158
	Weekly frequencies	2,088	43,708
1990	Total airport pairs	170	1,027
	Airplane size (seats)	156	156
2010	*Available seat-kilometers.		

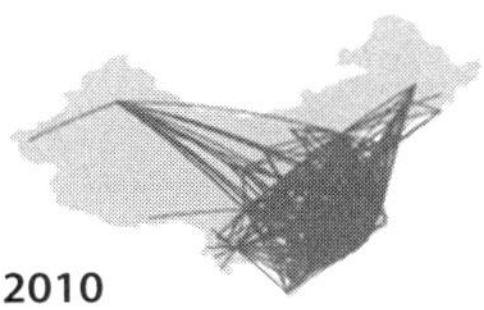

Global trends
Central Europe domestic frequencies

Liberalization stimulates air traffic		1990	2010
	Total weekly ASKs*	358	2,174
	Weekly frequencies	2,062	7,311
1990	Total airport pairs	294	1,045
	Airplane size (seats)	118	133
2010	*Available seat-kilometers.		

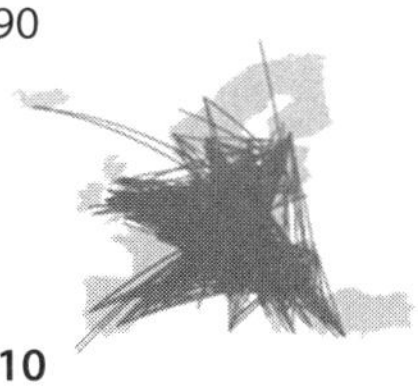

Figure 1.4. Domestic air traffic, Europe and China, 1990 and 2010. Boeing, 2011, *Current Market Outlook: 2011–2030* (Seattle: Boeing Airplanes Market Analysis), 12, accessed 4 February 2013, http://www.boeing.com/commercial/cmo/pdf/Boeing_Current_Market_Outlook_2011_to_2030.pdf. Used with permission.

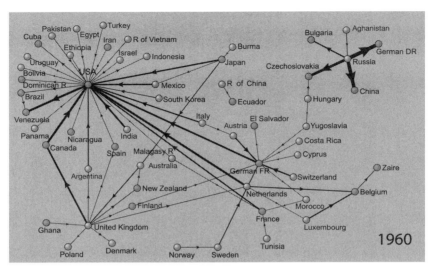

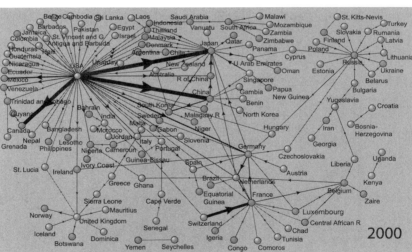

Figure 1.5. Dominant flows in global trade, 1960 and 2000. M. Ángeles Serrano, Marián Boguñá, and Alessandro Vespignani, 2007, "Patterns of Dominant Flows in the World Trade Web," *Journal of Economic Interaction and Coordination* 2 (2): 111–124, image on 119. Used with kind permission from Springer Science and Business Media.

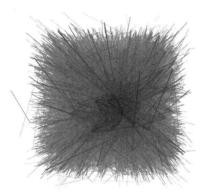 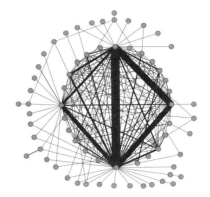

Figure 1.6. Fedwire interbank payment network, 2004. The graph on the left illustrates the interbank payment network on the first day of the sample. It includes 6,600 nodes and 70,000 links. The graph on the right illustrates the core of the network. The largest links represent up to 75 percent of the daily transferred value. Reprinted from Kimmo Soramäki et al., 2007, "The Topology of Interbank Payment Flows," *Physica A: Statistical Mechanics and Its Applications* 379 (1): 317–333, images on 319 and 320. Used with permission from Elsevier.

increased linkages within nations, in the figure we see the corresponding evolution of foreign direct and portfolio investments (figure 1.8). The picture that arises from these graphs is one of cross-border capital flows increasing from the late 1980s onward. This increase was particularly pronounced in industrial countries during the late 1980s and early 1990s, suggesting that a new wave of globalization occurred as former "less economically developed countries" started to take advantage of global integration.

Complexity

Global integration has been a key contributor to recent improvements in living and health standards, but these improvements have for a long time also concealed a mutual interdependence. More than simple *connectivity*, our increasing interdependence represents *complexity*.

Complexity describes "phenomena generated by interacting parts, all of whose causal connections are not easily discernible, [and] whose behaviour over time exhibits disorder and behaves unpredictably or chaotically."[24] We can further break down this broad definition into three levels:

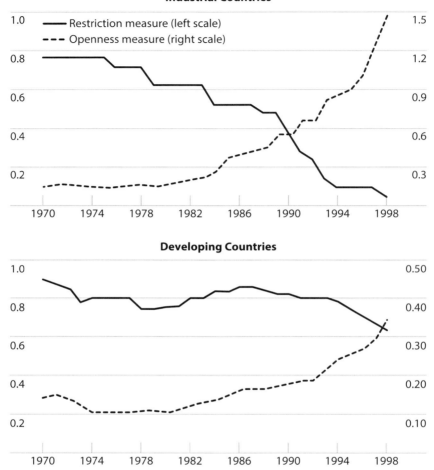

Figure 1.7. Financial integration in industrial and developing countries, 1970–98. Restriction measure—an unweighted cross-country average of a binary indicator that captures official restrictions on capital flows as reported to the International Monetary Fund. Openness measure—an unweighted cross-country average of financial integration based on gross stocks of foreign assets and liabilities as a share of GDP. Eswar S. Prasad et al., 2003, "Effects of Financial Globalization on Developing Countries: Some Empirical Evidence," IMF Occasional Paper 220, International Monetary Fund, Washington, DC. Used with permission.

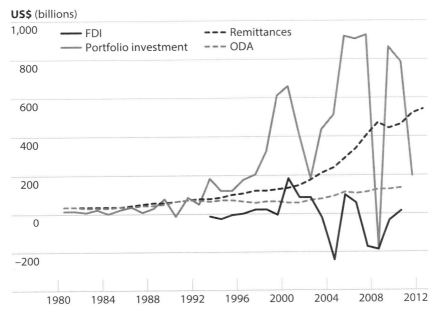

Figure 1.8. Comparing recent capital flows, 1980–2012. FDI, foreign direct investment; ODA, official development assistance. World Bank, 2013, *World Development Indicators*, World Databank, accessed 12 February. http://databank.worldbank.org/data/home.aspx.

"small-tent" complexity, "big-tent" complexity, and metacomplexity.[25] The first of these, small-tent complexity, is widely known as "Santa Fe complexity" and is the most commonly used in complexity research (see box 1.1 on the following page). This is the concept of complexity adopted in this book.

The second level of complexity, big-tent complexity, is broader and encompasses small-tent complexity as well as cybernetics, catastrophe, and chaos (with complexity as the first of these, the four Cs).[26] In other words, it is concerned with complex and unstable dynamics. The third level, metacomplexity, includes everything else and, in theory, can cover several distinct definitions.[27] Our discussion of global *connectivity* leads us to the conclusion that, as a result of globalization, the world today should be defined as a *complex* system.

Box 1.1. "Santa Fe Complexity"

This approach to complexity identifies six characteristics of a complex economy:

1. *Dispersed interaction:* What happens in the economy is determined by the interaction of many dispersed, possibly heterogeneous, agents acting in parallel. The action of any given agent depends on the anticipated actions of a limited number of other agents and on the aggregate state these agents co-create.

2. *No global controller:* No global entity controls interactions. Instead, controls are provided by mechanisms of competition and coordination between agents. Economic actions are mediated by legal institutions, assigned roles, and shifting associations. Nor is there a universal competitor—a single agent that can exploit all opportunities in the economy.

3. *Cross-cutting hierarchical organization:* The economy has many levels of organization and interaction. Units at any given level— behaviors, actions, strategies, products—typically serve as "building blocks" for constructing units at the next-higher level. The overall organization is more than hierarchical, with many sorts of tangling interactions (associations, channels of communication) across levels.

4. *Continual adaptation:* Behaviors, actions, strategies, and products are revised continually as the individual agents accumulate experience; the system constantly adapts.

5. *Perpetual novelty:* Niches are continually created by new markets, new technologies, new behaviors, and new institutions. The very act of filling a niche may provide new niches. The result is ongoing, perpetual novelty.

6. *Out-of-equilibrium dynamics:* Because new niches, new potentials, and new possibilities are continually created, the economy operates far from any optimum or global equilibrium. Improvements are always possible and indeed occur regularly.

W. Brian Arthur, Steven N. Durlauf, and David A. Lane, 1997, "Introduction," in *The Economy as an Evolving Complex System II,* ed. W. Brian Arthur, Steven N. Durlauf, and David A. Lane, Proceedings vol. 27, Santa Fe Institute Studies in the Science of Complexity (Reading, MA: Addison-Wesley), 1–14, material on 4–5. Used with permission.

Two consequences of these complex linkages stand out as particularly significant. The first may be characterized as positive feedback. It can be shown how real-life and virtual networks influence individual behavior as they interact, and exchange and debate their views.[28] Because more people and persons from different backgrounds and cultures are now able to interact, their behaviors, cultures, and risks will evolve.[29] Notice that "the positive aspects of the huge recent increase in knowledge about social and economic networks open up new possibilities for solving many long standing problems."[30] Designing the institutions that can govern these changes will remain a challenge throughout the coming decades.

The potential for mutual influence leads us to the second important consequence of complex linkages, an erosion of responsibility that occurs because our actions lead so indirectly to their effects. If a natural disaster disrupts a tightly linked global supply chain, who is to blame for the resulting shortage of cars, computers, or customized machinery? Is the owner responsible for not taking sufficient precautions? Is the manufacturer to be held accountable for operating in a risky location? Is the distributor at fault for using the supply chain without backups? Did the local government fail in its urban management duties by licensing an exposed area for industrial use? Is climate change the reason the disaster occurred in the first place? In this area, as in the case of financial crises, pandemics, and other highly complex cascading risks, it is increasingly difficult to identify the root cause of a hazard or even the channels of its transmission. Increasing global integration is making this task harder. Our actions are bound to have systemic consequences that we cannot foresee before they occur and often fail to understand afterward; this is true for us individually, but potentially even more so for policy makers and institutions seeking to provide guidance and management in this highly complex environment.[31]

GLOBALIZATION AND THE CHANGING NATURE OF RISK

Increasing *connectivity* means growing *complexity*. In this section we show how this complexity is leading to increasing systemic risk. We demonstrate the link between complex and unstable systems and show that complexity reduces our ability to make well-informed decisions and leads to a loss of responsibility globally.

Globalized Risk

To illustrate how connectivity and complexity can lead to risk, it is helpful to use a thought experiment from the field of epidemiolgy. Complex system researchers Dirk Brockmann, Lars Hufnagel, and Theo Geisel simulated the effects of a single individual infected with severe acute respiratory syndrome (SARS) placed anywhere in the world using data that accounted for 95 percent of the entire global civil aviation traffic and assuming virulence equivalent to that of SARS.[32] Whereas in previous centuries the insular nature of parochial communities would contain such an infection and give the authorities time to consider their options, now two plane journeys on average would require the vaccination of 75 percent of the world's population to avoid a global pandemic. After three flights, global vaccination would be required. This simulation illustrates an inevitable consequence of increased integration, but its message is not simply theoretical. SARS reached 30 countries and affected 8,400 people within only nine months of its detection in November 2002. Similarly, "bird flu" (H5N1), first detected in 2003, spread through the interconnected global agricultural network and had reached 38 countries by 2007.[33] We are fortunate that the wide and rapid spread of these pandemics had a relatively mild impact, as we show in our detailed analysis of pandemics in this book.

Analogous patterns of infectious risks spreading throughout the world can also be observed within the economic and infrastructural spheres. By 2009 the global financial crisis that began in 2007 had triggered losses of $4.1 trillion, with its effects felt in every world market.[34] Earlier events exhibited the same pattern of systemwide failure. The widespread implications of the 1929 Great Crash and the more recent 1987 stock market crash show how, already in the twentieth century, world systems were integrated and highly sensitive to distant shocks. More recently the turmoil of 1997–98 that began with the devaluation of the Thai baht led to the financial contagion associated with the Russian loan default, the collapse of the hedge fund Long-Term Capital Management, and crises across Asia.[35]

The common element in these crises was the intimate relationship of the nature and the depth of their potency to the characteristics of globalization. As in the example of pandemics, during the financial crisis of 2007/2008 the fiscal "pathogen" originated locally in the relatively small subprime market, but the disease spread quickly through intertwined balance sheets and risk-sharing vehicles that relied on one another in a complex web of interdependence.

According to international risk expert Ortwin Renn, the ability to act "in a strategic fashion by linking decisions with outcomes" is a fundamental requirement for "human agency" or, put differently, for making "well-informed choices."[36] An increasing degree of global interdependence reduces our ability to make well-informed decisions as the resulting complexity exceeds the ability of individual actors to predict the impact of their actions. By impairing the ability of individuals or institutions to act independently (impairing "agency"), globalization challenges us to design institutions that will allow us to reclaim control over our actions. In this book we take a first step toward outlining this design.

Risk Reevaluated

Risk typically refers to the possibility for negative phenomena to occur. In this section we clarify the concepts of risk and uncertainty to show how changes in the pace of innovation and globalization *inherently* create global fragilities. From the outset , it is useful to understand that risk and uncertainty are separate concepts. This distinction is usually traced back to the seminal work of Frank Knight and is clearly articulated by Larry Epstein and Tan Wang, who distinguish risk as a decision-making circumstance in which "probabilities are available to guide choice."[37] In contrast, they define *uncertainty* as a circumstance in which "information is too imprecise to be summarized by probabilities."[38] Although contested, Knight's distinction is the most widely accepted model and remains firmly embedded in decision theory.[39] As we show in box 1.2, the distinction can be characterized in simple terms: risk is *quantifiable* and *predictable*. Uncertainty, on the other hand, encompasses *unidentified* and/or *unexpected* threats. For our analysis, it is also useful to consider an additional concept. The United Nations (UN) emphasizes the potential of "hazards" to show the cost of erroneous risk management. These

Box 1.2. Risk

Hazard: A potentially damaging physical event or phenomenon that can harm people and their welfare. Hazards can be latent conditions that may represent future threats, as well as being natural or induced by human processes.

Vulnerability: A function of human actions and behavior that describes the degree to which a socioeconomic system is susceptible to the impact of hazards. Vulnerability relates to the physical characteristics of a community, structure, or geographical area that render it likely to be affected by or protected from the impact of a particular hazard on account of its nature, construction, or proximity to hazardous terrain or a disaster-prone area.

Risk: The probability of harmful consequences or the expected loss (of lives, people injured, property or environment damaged, or livelihoods or economic activity disrupted) resulting from interactions between natural or human hazards and vulnerable entities. Conventionally, risk is expressed by the equation

$$\text{Risk} = \text{Hazard} \times \text{Vulnerability}.$$

The resulting risk is sometimes corrected and divided by factors reflecting actual managerial and operational capability to reduce the extent of the hazard or the degree of vulnerability.

For the purpose of economic assessment, risk is quantifiable and is perceived in monetary terms. From an economic perspective, risk is specified as the annual cost to society from sudden accidental events and slow environmental degradation, determined from the product of the probability or frequency of occurrence and the vulnerability as social and economic losses in monetary terms:

$$\text{Risk (economic cost per year)} = \text{Probability (once in } n \text{ years)} \times \text{Vulnerability (economic cost / event).}$$

UN (United Nations), 2003, *Water for People, Water for Life—The United Nations World Water Development Report,* World Water Development Report 1 (Barcelona: United Nations Educational, Scientific and Cultural Organization and Berghahn Books), 279, box 11.2, accessed 11 January 2013, http://www.unesco.org/new/en/natural-sciences/environment/water/wwap/wwdr/wwdr1-2003/. Used with permission.

are "latent conditions that may represent future threats"[40] and thus are inherently linked to *uncertainty*.

From this perspective, managing risk requires that causal connections between actions and events *are* or *can be* known. This becomes necessary for the construction of decision-making scenarios in which the consequences of actions may be anticipated.[41] As our discussion of global complexity shows, the specification of contingencies becomes progressively more difficult as transport, communication, and financial and other world systems become increasingly integrated. This is because we start to lose sight of the effects of individual actions, introducing uncertainty and hazard. Given the pace of change, the traditional concepts of risk have become increasingly inappropriate as a basis of modern global governance.

This means that the notion of risk needs to be expanded to include nonstochastic elements that cannot be easily quantified or defined using traditional tools and formulas from probability theory and mathematics. The classical distinction between risk and uncertainty is beginning to unravel, in our view, due to rising complexity and the difficulty of classifying real-world phenomena as either of these two. Additional concepts are increasingly required to understand the "possibility" or risk of failure in an increasingly complex and connected world where assigning probabilities to risks is becoming more difficult.

We advocate the analysis of *systemic* risk drawing on the tools designed for *uncertain* environments. Systemic risk refers to the prospect of a *breakdown in the entire system* as opposed to the breakdown of individual parts. Implicit in this definition, which is given in box 1.3, is the understanding that risk and uncertainty become more virulent in systems as the number of linkages grows. A "systemic risk" is a risk of a "common shock which is not the result of direct causation but . . . [of] indirect impacts."[42] This distinction is crucial because it underlines the fact that it is increasingly difficult to identify direct causality for outcomes. This distinguishes our analysis and recommendations from traditional risk management.

As a consequence of this disjuncture between risk management and uncertain hazards, we see that globalization, as we have characterized it in the twenty-first century, naturally increases systemic risk.[43] This book discusses the policy lessons that can be derived from complexity research

Box 1.3. Systemic Risk

Systemic risk is "the risk or probability of breakdowns in an entire system, as opposed to breakdowns in individual parts and components, and is evidenced by co-movements (correlation) amongst most or all of the parts."[44] Although the precise meaning of the term *systemic risk* remains ambiguous, three of its main manifestations are as follows:

1. A large shock or "macroshock" triggered when relatively modest tipping points, breaking points, or regime shifts hit their thresholds and produce large, cascading failures in most or all of the system.

2. A shock propagated through a network via risk sharing (transferring) or contagion (transmission and amplification).[45] The latter involves a cascading failure, that is, the "cumulative losses [that] accrue from an event that sets in motion a series of successive losses along a chain of institutions or markets comprising a system."[46]

3. A "common shock," which is the result not of direct causation but of indirect effects. These indirect effects can be just as important as direct effects if not more so.[47] Systemic failure is also characterized by "hysteresis," whereby the effects are much less resilient to recovery and are in some cases irreversible.[48]

for a broad range of domains.[49] For the first time, the analysis not only covers finance but also encompasses and connects infrastructure, health ecology, the environment, supply chains, and social forms of systemic risk.

Geographical Risk

Another effect of the twenty-first century's increasing complexity is the transformation of how we use physical space. As societies and cultures connect, they reorganize not only how they interact but also the environment in which they operate. Elements that were previously isolated now merge or mutate, and the global infrastructure is remodeled by competitive pressures. Today it is primarily efficiency concerns rather than strategic political choices or logistical issues that determine the locations of production facilities, financial centers, and organizational hubs. These efficiency concerns have created a new class of *geographical* or *spatial risk*. We can divide this new type of risk into two categories: *vector risk* and *density risk*.[50]

The first of these, vector risk, relates to the coming together of agents. Globalization has led to improved opportunities for global movement and an increasing world population. These have resulted in widespread urbanization and heightened population density in cities. The risk that arises from these is illustrated best in the context of biological hazards and the transmission of viruses and diseases. One noteworthy study estimates that the breakdown of biogeographic barriers and the introduction of invasive species cost the world in excess of $120 billion annually.[51] This cost includes that of the rise of pathogens that directly affect the health of humans, livestock, and animals. The same study shows how the effects of globalization have enabled West Nile virus to flourish in regions that were previously immune due to their climates or remoteness. Yet it is essential to note that it is this same proximity that has led to the success of megacities like London, New York, Mumbai, and Shanghai. The challenge, which we explore in this book, is to ensure that proximity and connectivity can be sources of strength while we manage growing vulnerability due to the complexity and density of our connections.

The second geographical risk, density risk, relates to the growing concentration of activities in solitary or a small number of world epicenters. The global financial system is effectively rooted in New York and London, and global electrical manufacturing is concentrated in certain regions of China and Hong Kong, while Thailand produces 40 percent of the world's hard disk drives.[52] Silicon Valley continues to be the central hub for most IT engineering and innovation. The effects of this centralization are simple. We are at risk. When terrorists attacked the World Trade Center on 11 September 2001, the New York Stock Exchange was closed for nearly a week simply because of its physical proximity to the towers. The exchanges in London and Frankfurt were affected because such a high share of the listed corporations held offices on Wall Street. When the Nock-ten typhoon hit Thailand in 2011, it affected car and computer manufacturers all over the world because profit-driven outsourcing had led many firms to the same cost-efficient location. When the Icelandic Eyjafjallajökull volcano halted European air traffic for almost a week in April 2010, the loss of business and delays in parcel delivery caused an estimated US\$5 billion in losses to the world economy, with the effect felt as far away as Kenya and Zambia, which were unable to send flower and fresh fruit exports via air freight.[53] Similarly, the Japanese earthquake of 2011 and the subsequent tsunami that damaged the Fukushima nuclear power plant threatened to impair a major global bank's operations in Tokyo involving 1,500 employees and thereby to "disrupt sales and trading in Hong Kong, Seoul, and other capital centers."[54] What these instances had in common is that the source of the *economic* hazard in each case was entirely *geographical*. Had the financial system been less concentrated in lower Manhattan, the impact of the 9/11 attacks would have been felt, but the financial repercussions would have been lessened. Had the manufacturers relying on Thai hardware chosen to diversify their operations to India or the United States, the flood in Thailand would have had a smaller effect on world output. Had the Icelandic ash cloud not affected 3 of the world's 10 busiest airports, the cost of the eruption would have been significantly lower. The geographical choices we make when we globalize are, like so many other factors today, sources of *uncertainty*.

GLOBALIZATION: A DOUBLE-EDGED SWORD

Advocates of unfettered globalization point to the positive impacts of expanding flows of goods, services, money, people, information, and culture, which enables every one of us to benefit from exploiting our comparative advantage. Yet critics point to the shortcomings of globalization and the dangers associated with this simplistic view. In this book we recognize that globalization is a double-edged sword that can be a force for progress as well as a source of great harm.

There are numerous reasons to be concerned about globalization. Our focus is on the systemic risk that is embedded in the current wave of globalization and the complexity it engenders, which give rise to uncertainty and unintended consequences, including the erosion of the responsibilities of individuals and firms. These unintended outcomes are "externalities" because profit-maximizing agents do not incorporate these social costs in their cost–benefit analyses. Systemic risks may thus be considered a contemporary manifestation of the tragedy of the commons. Exploiting Ricardo's comparative advantage creates efficiency gains but simultaneously fosters interdependence.[55] Using the benefits of trade leads to output growth but also to inequality. The Internet has increased transparency and the flow of information but equally has the potential to facilitate the spread of rumors and panics as well as cybercrime and aggression. Low-budget flights nurture connectivity, but the corresponding carbon emissions fuel climate change. Container traffic accelerates the transport of goods but enables the proliferation of illegal trade in weapons and spreads viruses and diseases.

To deal with the asymmetric nature of progress as well as with its risk-creating properties, we believe there should be a greater focus on the idea of *resilient globalization* that fosters inclusivity and sustainable growth. Several noteworthy commentators have provided insights into the relationship between globalization and inequality.[56] Our contribution is to locate this issue in the context of systemic risk. Our overarching aim is the promotion of global processes that are more resilient to systemic shocks. This means that we need to find ways to close the yawning "governance gap" between accelerating globalization and the failure of national governments or global institutions to meet the rising need to address problems using collective action.[57]

Globalization and the closer integration of developing countries into the world economy have led to unparalleled leaps in both human and economic development. The past four decades alone have seen an increase in average life expectancy of over 20 years, a progression that had previously taken a millennium. In the same time frame, adult literacy increased from 50 to 75 percent and the number of people living on less than $1 a day fell by 300 million, despite the growth of the total global population by 2 billion.[58]

These and many other astonishing advances are associated with growing connectivity and the global spread of ideas and technologies, as well as the benefits of specialization and the development of more efficient and effective global infrastructure and management. Progress in information and communication technologies has been shown to enable social and economic development.[59] In business, the global exchange of ideas has promoted the comprehensive adoption of "lean" management and "just-in-time" production principles that have increased efficiency even though, as we show, it also has increased our vulnerabilities.[60] The spreading of new technologies and systems around the world has led to immense changes in how human beings interact and what they may achieve.[61] Poor people have benefited most; no era in human history has seen such a rapid reduction in the number of people in dire poverty, and the chances that an individual born in a poor family can escape poverty and live a long and healthy life are greater than at any point in history.[62]

Globalization, however, is by no means only a benign process. Globalization is also an uneven process of development that fragments just as it coordinates.[63] Strong policies at the international, national, and local levels are therefore required to ensure that integration's beneficial forces are maximized and that the negative consequences of globalization are understood and mitigated.

Although the benefits of free trade and the unchecked flow of capital are evident in theory, to simply rapidly and unilaterally open up borders would be the height of folly. Globalization introduces competitive pressures that profit those who are sufficiently skilled and advantages the educated. To give but one of many possible examples, the costs linked to lacking information are estimated to account for 11 percent of total production costs in Sri Lanka.[64] This is the corollary to the Ricardian advantage. A competitive *dis*advantage emerges for countries and organizations not sufficiently able to use modern technologies.

Imbalances at the national level are shaped by the interplay of domestic policy and global trade rules.[65] Aggregate indicators of world development often miss local disparities; although *global* life expectancy has been steadily increasing for decades, *regional* life expectancy has been rapidly decreasing in much of southern Africa and the former Soviet bloc. The positive trends in decreasing world poverty conceal the fact that the number of desperately poor people in Africa has increased by over 100 million in recent years.[66]

The underlying threat of globalization on a systemic level pertains to the formation of harmonized structures and a failure to ensure *resilient globalization*.[67] Here *resilience* is understood as "the capacity of a system to absorb disturbance and reorganize while undergoing change."[68]

In this chapter we have seen that the widening efficiency imperative associated with globalization has led to the creation of three main negative externalities: systemic risk resulting from uncertainty, geographical risk resulting from the concentration of people and processes, and asymmetric progress resulting from specialization. Although efficiency is a source of great progress, it also impedes resilience and can spur contagion. The growing standardization of world systems has curtailed the ability to improvise in response to unexpected events. Efficiency promotes "monocultures" of products and production and removes the fat that provides a cushion against shocks. Although in agriculture it has long been understood that monocultures are particularly susceptible to disease and extreme weather conditions, these simple insights have been neglected in other domains.[69] Harmonization not only increases vulnerability to external or exogenous "shocks" but also catalyzes risks within the system or endogenously.

THE WAY FORWARD

In summary, we have argued that the same technological advances that have precipitated global economic growth have also transformed the world, specifically the global economy, into what can be characterized as a *complex system*. We have shown that complexity is not a conscious choice. It is instead the unintended aggregate outcome, or externality, of many rational individual moves toward Ricardian efficiency. By integrating previously disconnected conventional risks we have created a systemic risk environment in which "the factors that determine the outcome and impacts . . . are frequently complex and poorly understood."[70] The crises precipitated by this system will not only be unpredictable but will also unfold in a seemingly chaotic manner. One reason for the failure to identify and contain the financial crisis of 2007/2008 in a timely manner was that the approach to governance was largely guided by thinking in linear and one-dimensional relationships. In a *complex* and highly nonlinear world, such thinking generates unintended consequences.

We have seen that systemic risk is a modern manifestation of the tragedy of the commons. This goes beyond the suggestions of Dani Rodrik, who prominently argues that systemic risk can be better managed by national governments.[71] The risks transcend national boundaries, they impact the global commons,[72] and they can be time delayed as a result of indirect causation.[73] To deal with the twenty-first century's new systemic risk, therefore, we see the need for greater responsibility coupled with fundamental reforms of global governance. The radical changes required include a renewal of mandates, shareholding, and skills to reflect current realities rather than the fossilized system that arose in response to the Second World War and previous crises.[74]

The remainder of this book provides examples of global systems and their associated risks across different domains. In combining these insights and by studying historic risk events and policy responses, we have two goals in mind. First, we aim to raise awareness of the dangers of systemic failure in the twenty-first century. Second, we want to identify best practices in different disciplines and discuss how they can be applied to improve risk governance more broadly. The key policy lessons are collected at the end of each thematic chapter.

To achieve these aims, we draw on insights from conceptual scholarly work in areas such as complexity and risk theory. We distill theoretical models to identify the practical implications for real-world policy making. We examine cases in which these techniques have been implemented successfully. At the Risk Center at the Swiss Eidgenössische Technische Hochschule Zürich (Federal Institute of Technology), Zurich, or in the Complex Agent-Based Dynamic Network at the University of Oxford, first steps toward a paradigm shift have been taken. We draw on the lessons from this research.

Following the collapse of Lehman Brothers, the world continues to struggle with the consequences of the first systemic crisis of the twenty-first century. Yet larger and potentially more harmful risks are lurking. These include climate change and pandemics. We see fragility in global supply chains and the interdependent physical infrastructure on which they rely. Latent systemic risks are prevalent in many domains, of which we have selected a few examples. Failure to understand these risks will lead to policy that draws on outdated maps of global threats. Systemic risk is not simply financial, environmental, or biological. Nor can it be confined to infrastructure or social risks. It extends across all these domains and must be dealt with in an integrative manner. John F. Kennedy noted in 1959 that *wēijī*, the Chinese word for crisis, encodes a fundamentally optimistic way of reacting to traumas: "When written in Chinese the word crisis is composed of two characters. One represents danger, and the other represents opportunity."[75]

The world experienced a financial crisis in 2007/2008 that continues to create havoc in our societies. This book identifies one possible opportunity that comes from enduring the financial crisis: we can avert even more cataclysmic systemic crises in the future by learning from the mistakes we made in the past.

2

⊙⅋⊚

The Financial Sector

With Co-Pierre Georg and Tiffany Vogel

In the previous chapter we argued that an immense change in the pace of innovation fundamentally altered the nature of globalization around the turn of the twenty-first century. This "hyperglobalization" is transforming the world into a complex system and creating instabilities linked to systemic risks. In this chapter we examine the financial sector and dissect how systemic risks materialized in 2008. We point to this as the archetypical example of how globalization has created a new form of risk. Further, we show how advances in information technologies led to revolution in the financial sector and how this complexity created underlying instability and systemic risk. We also discuss how complexity and the profit imperative led to a governance gap and illustrate why our current institutions are ill prepared to close this yawning regulatory divide. We identify the main regulatory and supervisory failures from before, during, and after the financial crisis. In closing, we consider how such deficiencies can be overcome to avoid future systemic failure in finance.

We have chosen to use the financial sector as our first case study for two main reasons. First, the global financial crisis that followed the failure of Lehman Brothers in 2008 constitutes the first truly global manifestation of systemic risk that we see as characterizing the twenty-first century. Although many blame the bursting of the real estate bubble for starting the crisis, few have examined how economic integration and financial innovation in a deregulated environment created a financial network that was inherently vulnerable to systemic risk.

Our second reason for choosing the financial sphere for our first analytical chapter is the stunning pace of innovation and technological advancement in this sector, which makes the financial system an incubator of globalization. This means that we can see how globalization has created new risks in just the past decade—even in a sector that seemingly featured one of the most sophisticated national and international regulatory regimes. Over the course of what was termed, without ironic foresight, the "Golden Decade" (1998–2007), systemic risks were born, matured, and eventually came to fruition in one of the most documented catastrophes in history.[1] We hope that by understanding this recent systemic risk life cycle we may better be able to anticipate future systemic risks before they result in collapse of the system.

THE FINANCIAL CRISIS OF 2007/2008

There are many ways to tell the story of the financial crisis that struck the world in 2008. One particularly revealing way is by telling the story of Iceland. With its 320,000 citizens and a fishery-driven economy, Iceland seldom appears in world news. In 2001 the government of Premier Davíð Oddsson passed a law that allowed banks to massively expand their foreign activities. By 2008 Icelandic banks had accumulated $75 billion in foreign debt—about $250,000 for every man, woman, and child in Iceland.[2]

It is no surprise that with all the excess liquidity, inflation was accelerating, reaching 14 percent prior to the crisis.[3] This trend was largely due to Icelandic banks' indexing mortgage loans to inflation, a practice almost unheard of in industrialized countries and one that many economists view as a recipe for higher inflation. In reaction, the Icelandic central bank adopted a high-interest-rate regime. The effect of this policy, however, was quite the opposite of that intended, for outside investors now deposited large amounts in Icelandic krónur, leading to an increase of more than 50 percent in the supply of money.[4] The situation was aggravated by Icelanders' increasingly taking out mortgages for 100 percent of their home value at relatively young ages or refinancing their existing homes on better terms to purchase cars and other consumer durables.[5]

The rise of Icelandic finance was fast; the meltdown, however, was even faster. The Icelandic króna dropped from 122 krónur to the euro in August 2008 to over 180 krónur to the euro by the following November.[6] Given the large amount of foreign debt, this devaluation made it impossible for Icelandic banks to sustain their solvency. During October 2008 all three major Icelandic banks collapsed, and on 19 November 2008 a US$4.6 billion bailout package from the International Monetary Fund (IMF) was agreed upon.[7] (In 2007 the GDP of Iceland was around US$11.9 billion.)[8] The effects of the crisis were devastating. A country with virtually no unemployment suddenly faced soaring unemployment that reached a record high of 9.3 percent in February and March of 2010.[9] Pension savings were crippled, because many of the savings funds were based on listed stock investments and the Icelandic stock market was completely destroyed during the crisis and eventually shut down. Icelanders have to repay U.K. depositors 4 percent of Iceland's GDP in sterling between 2017 and 2023. An additional 2 percent of GDP in euros will be repaid to the Netherlands over the same period.[10]

Iceland's history over the past 15 years shows that globalization punishes financial mismanagement severely. The more deregulated and integrated an economy, the weaker become the domestic policy levers that may be used to shield citizens and businesses from external events. Following extreme deregulation, the Icelandic financial system became interconnected with the global financial system in an unparalleled manner. The business conduct of a small group of elite "Viking Raiders" exploited the absence of regulation and extracted unprecedented profits from the system.[11] Banks became highly interconnected goliaths, taking on mushrooming systemic risks. Although Iceland is unique, we see its policy shifts toward deregulation and the growing leverage of its banking system, as well as its growing interdependency, as indicative of the developments in the United States, the United Kingdom, and elsewhere.

The Icelandic example is also indicative of a different problem resulting from global interconnectedness: the problem of accountability. What we mean by "the problem of accountability" becomes evident when we ask, Who should be held accountable for the crisis in Iceland? Should it be the politicians who enabled banks to become so large and interconnected that they could take down an entire country? Conservative prime minister Davíð Oddsson became the governor of the Central Bank of Iceland after he left office in 2005. The newly elected government of Jóhanna Sigurðardóttir had to change central bank law to force Oddsson to step down. Oddsson subsequently became an editor of the largest newspaper in Iceland, prompting the *Telegraph* in Britain to raise concerns about "the secrecy, interconnection and conflict of interest in public life."[12] Or should we hold ordinary citizens accountable if they purchase houses they cannot afford with 100 percent debts and in the context of floating interest rates? After all, purchasing a house without any down payment whatsoever and investing all their life savings in risky high-yield investment funds cannot work for society as a whole. But who would not be tempted by the prospect of acquiring a house without saving first and retiring as a millionaire just by "letting their money work for them"?

It is the role of governments to prevent excess. Unfortunately, as we will show, Iceland is just the tip of the proverbial iceberg. Global governance has failed to take complexity and systemic risk into account in the design of national and global financial systems. In the next section we describe the main drivers of financial globalization before turning to the resulting complexity and systemic risk.

FINANCIAL GLOBALIZATION IN THE TWENTY-FIRST CENTURY

The global financial system has become more interconnected than ever before over the past decade due to policy and regulatory changes that have opened markets combined with the massive surge in computer power described in chapter 1. The increase, however, comes at the expense of a much higher potential for cascading collapse, as was evident in the contagion of financial markets that we discuss in the next section. It also has been associated with a higher level of dependence on computer systems, which increases the vulnerability of markets to technical failures, human error, and cybercrime.

More computing power implies greater complexity in code, increasing the potential for breaches of cybersecurity and also the potential for bugs. One of the earliest operating systems for personal computers—Windows NT 3.1, developed in 1993—had around 4.5 million lines of source code. By 2001 the number of source code lines in Windows XP had expanded to 40 million.[13] The effects of growing complexity and reliance on computerization have been felt already. Knight Capital Group Inc. suffered a $440 million loss in 45 minutes after installing a new computer program with an unforeseen glitch to conduct trades on 1 August 2012.[14] When Knight introduced the new program, it had had 17 years of experience and had settled around $20 billion in daily trades on the New York Stock Exchange. Errors occur not only due to poor programming or interfacing problems but also as the result of human interaction with computers. The most notorious of these mistakes are so-called fat-finger trades, which occur when a trader mistakenly enters the wrong amount for a trade, for example, by keeping a finger on the "0" key on the keypad and adding an additional order of magnitude. On 18 September 2012 a fat-finger trade caused major market volatility when the shares of Rowan Cos., National Oilwell Varco Inc., and other oil drillers and equipment manufacturers jumped between 3 and 9 percent.[15] Relying heavily on computer systems carries the inherent risk of unanticipated errors and mistakes as well as increasing vulnerability to cyberfraud or cyberaggression.

In 1997 Lawrence J. White accurately anticipated that new information technologies would revolutionize the financial sector. He forecast "new instruments, such as financial options and futures" and "modifications to traditional instruments, such as securitized loans."[16] He foresaw that these revolutions would be organized around "new services, such as PC-based home banking," and "new exchanges for trading securities."[17] White was particularly attentive to how these technologies would create modern platforms for financial integration, and he noted the importance of these in digitized arenas such as the Cincinnati Exchange. He understood that accessible and affordable computing power, mobile telecommunication, and the Internet would enable better opportunities for the users of financial services to interact with one another.

As is often the case with predictions of globalization's transformative potential, actual events exceeded expectations and world markets experienced unimagined growth. By the end of the Golden Decade, the value of U.S. financial assets had gone from 101 percent of U.S. GDP in 1990 to more than four times this percentage at its peak in 2007. The financial market also experienced rapid growth at the international level. World debt and equity grew from 261 to 356 percent of global GDP between

1990 and 2010,[18] and world credit tripled in absolute terms after 2000, reaching $21 trillion in 2008.[19] As national financial markets have rapidly expanded, cross-border capital flows have grown along with them. This increase in transnational activity reflects the progressive integration of global finance.

Global financial concentration also increased. The share of the top three banks increased from 10 percent in 1990 to about 40 percent in 2008 in the United States and from about 50 percent in 1997 to almost 80 percent in 2008 in the United Kingdom.[20] Such significant increases in market concentration lead to implicit bailout guarantees by the state in the event of insolvency. These guarantees, as the 2007/2008 crisis shows, can quickly turn into explicit guarantees that erode market discipline and encourage the largest banks to take on excessive risks, safe in the knowledge that they will be rescued if something should go wrong. Moral hazard thus fuels systemic risk and, as we can see with hindsight, is a significant source of financial instability. Concentration as a source of systemic risk is not found just in the financial system, however. A number of studies show how concentration in commodity networks also enables firms to exert control over suppliers, "making them captives."[21]

The increasingly complex financial network expanded not only in terms of size but also in terms of sophistication. Drawing on increased processing power, financial traders have invented new ways to trade and to gain access to credit. Though marginal at the turn of the century, credit default swaps, collateralized debt obligations (see box 2.1 for a nontechnical explanation of these products), and the resale market for capital had all become ubiquitous operations by 2008. In less than a decade the over-the-counter derivative market expanded to 10 times global GDP, or roughly $600,000 billion. Put simply, "globally integrated markets and innovation . . . led to a transformation of the financial landscape."[22]

Growing Complexity

The rise of securitization and structured financial products was one of the most striking features of the Golden Decade. Figure 2.1 shows the issuance of corporate debt and asset-backed securities between 1990 and 2009. Until 2002, banks issued more corporate debt than asset-backed securities. In 2005, however, banks issued almost twice as much in

---

Box 2.1. Glossary of Securitization

Derivative: A financial product governed by a contract that specifies the conditions under which payments are made between the parties. Its price is based on expectations regarding the value of underlying assets.

Securitization: The practice of consolidating and repackaging different types of debt (such as mortgage, loan, or credit card obligations) for passing on to investors.

Hedging transaction: A business deal that attempts to limit investment risk by ensuring that the profits or losses from one trade are offset by another.

Special-purpose vehicle (SPV): A specially created company designed to have limited liability and insulate the ultimate beneficial owners from risks associated with investments and/or to obscure ownership of financial assets and liabilities. Sometimes known as a "special-purpose entity" or a "financial vehicle corporation" instead.

Collateralized debt obligation (CDO): An investment security composed of a wide range of assets that is passed on to different classes or tranches of owners who face varying degrees of risk.

Credit default swap (CDS): A financial swap agreement that transfers the credit link of a financial product between parties. It usually involves the seller compensating the buyer in return for a payoff in the event of a default.

Asset-backed security (ABS): A security collateralized or backed by combining pools of assets (such as car loans, credit card debt, or royalty payments).

---

complex asset-backed securities as in corporate debt. The same trend can be observed when looking at the global issuance of collateralized debt obligations, which increased by a factor of five between 2002 and 2006 (see figure 2.2).

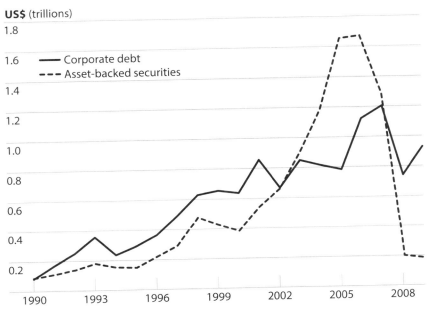

US$ (trillions)

Figure 2.1. Issuance of corporate debt and asset-backed securities (US$ trillions), 1990–2009. Excludes debt issued by federal government agencies and government-sponsored enterprises. Garry B. Gorton and Andrew Metrick, 2010a, "Regulating the Shadow Banking System," *Brookings Papers on Economic Activity* 41 (2): 260–312, 271, accessed 5 February 2013, http://www.brookings.edu/~/media/projects/bpea/fall%20 2010/2010b_bpea_gorton.pdf.

What triggered this development? One answer is that regulation did not allow institutional investors to directly invest in loans and mortgages because these assets were too risky. In order to transfer risks from the financial system to these large institutional investors, investment banks started to fabricate securitized assets. Securitization is the process in which banks repackage a number of risky assets (for example, mortgages, credit card receivables, and student loans) and sell claims to different parts of the return stream.[23] Although securitization in itself might not be destabilizing, excessive securitization has a number of detrimental effects, including excessive opacity and complexity. One important reason for the excessive transfer of risk through securitization was that this process was a convenient method to reduce the amount of capital

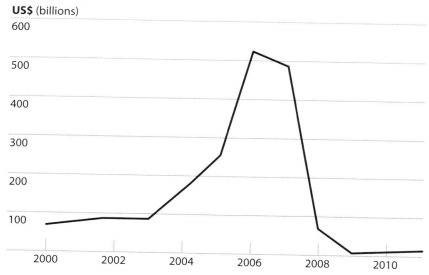

US$ (billions)

Figure 2.2. Total global CDO issuance (US$ billions), 2000–2010. CDO, collateralized debt obligation. Mahmoud Elamin and William Bednar, 2012, "How Is Structured Finance Doing?," Cleveland Federal Reserve Bank, 10 February, accessed 5 February 2013, http://www.clevelandfed.org/research/trends/2012/0312/01finmar .cfm. Used with the permission of SIFMA (the Securities Industry and Financial Markets Association).

required for a certain risk. The models on which regulatory capital requirements relied had a tendency to overlook tail risks.[24] This loophole was exploited by banks that took $100 worth of loans for which they had to hold $8 of capital to generate a $100 security for which they had to hold much less, if any, capital. This regulatory and ratings arbitrage made it increasingly attractive for banks to engage in securitized lending. It also implied that the banks' assets received favorable pricing. With the endorsement of rating agencies, banks were able to combine small, risky individual mortgages into one large apparently riskless security. Incentive schemes that focused on short-term profit rather than sustainable profit further fueled this development.[25]

A number of theoretical reasons have been advanced to explain why banks might issue excessive numbers of securities. For example, it has been argued that markets for securities might become fragile if investors were to demand safe assets but neglect certain tail risks.[26] Such a situation closely resembles that in the period between 2003 and 2007, when large numbers of new mortgage-backed securities were issued that investors perceived as safe. It has also been shown that heterogeneous expectations and adaptive behavior can lead to a situation in which more hedging instruments can destabilize markets.[27] A similar motive emerges with respect to financial innovation, which typically increases the part of portfolio variance that is due to speculation when traders do not share the same assumptions about the evolution of markets.[28] All of these findings rely on models that deviate from the traditional mantra of maintaining full rationality where all agents have perfect knowledge about the economy and each other. What this literature clearly shows is that even a slight deviation from perfect rationality can lead to financial instability when banks issue excessive numbers of securities. So why would banks want to issue securities in the first place, and, more important, why did regulators allow them to do so?

When banks started issuing securitized assets they engineered a way to increase the share of highly rated assets and subsequently reduced the amount of capital they had to hold. In combination with light-touch regulation, securitization allowed banks to leverage up to unprecedented levels (see figure 2.3). Through securitization, risks could also be transferred to legal entities called special-purpose vehicles (SPVs). These vehicles in certain respects were like a bank, with the crucial difference that they were not subject to regulation. Moving risks to these SPVs was possible due to loopholes in the existing regulatory framework. And even if regulators had wanted to go after such SPVs they could not have done so because these legal entities were set up in places like the Cayman Islands, Liechtenstein, and other regulatory and tax havens. Banks then issued guarantees to the SPVs, which in turn enabled them to issue short-term liabilities (so-called asset-backed commercial papers) to outside investors. These investors often were very large insurance companies or mutual funds that could not have invested in risky loans but were allowed to purchase these seemingly riskless securities. This apparently endless cycle resulted in a systemic maturity mismatch that ultimately led to a breakdown of markets once "the fuse was set on fire" and Lehman Brothers filed for insolvency.

Securitization allowed banks to transfer large risks off their balance sheets, making credit available to investors with a seemingly insatiable appetite for allegedly riskless assets. When banks started leveraging

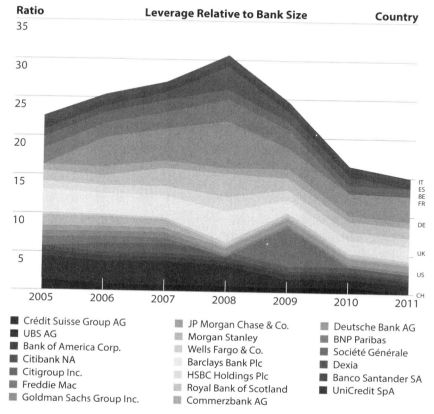

Figure 2.3. Leverage ratios of large commercial banks, 2005–11. Individual-country contributions are weighted with relative sizes of banks assets. ISO (International Organization for Standardization) country codes used are IT, Italy; ES, Spain; BE, Belgium; FR, France; DE, Germany; UK, United Kingdom; US, United States; CH, Switzerland. Bankscope, https://bankscope2.bvdep.com/.

instead of creating larger capital cushions, they were able to expand their balance sheets substantially. More and larger deals led to higher profits for the banks. Yet most of the profits from leveraging were not used to capitalize the banks but were paid out either as dividends (see figure 2.4) or as bonuses (see figure 2.5), typically based on short-term successes such as revenue increases in a given quarter.

A major contributor to instability was the fact that poorly designed remuneration schemes for senior executives and traders favored short-run profits and asset accumulation over prudence and stability. Bankers

US$ (billions)

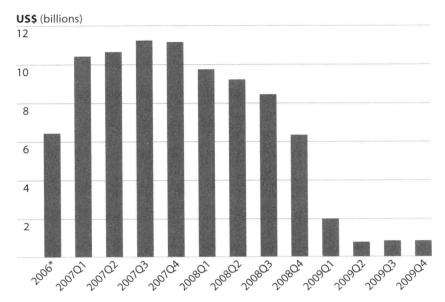

Figure 2.4. Dividend payments for U.S. banks (US$ billions), 2007 Q1–2009 Q4. *The bar for 2006 is an average for the four quarters. Viral V. Acharya, Irvind Gujral, Nirupama Kulkarni, and Hyun Song Shin, 2011, "Dividends and Bank Capital in the Financial Crisis of 2007–2009," NBER Working Paper 16896, New York University Stern School of Business, New York, National Bureau of Economic Research, Cambridge, 26, accessed 21 January 2013, http://www.nber.org/papers/w16896.

responded to these incentives, so it should not come as a surprise that they were primarily concerned with maximizing their returns (for example, through leverage) and minimizing each individual's risk exposure. With the rise of securitization, bonuses on Wall Street tripled within six years, reaching an all-time high of nearly US$35 billion in 2006. The trend did not stop there, though. Even when bonuses were declining, generous dividends were still paid. In 2008, when the crisis reached its pinnacle when the insolvency of the U.S. investment bank Lehman Brothers was declared on 15 September, bonuses and dividend payments totaled about US$130 billion.[29] Two weeks later, U.S. President George W. Bush enacted the Emergency Stabilization Act, which granted a US$160 billion bailout package to major U.S. investment banks.[30]

The Emergency Stabilization Act was the unfortunate logical conclusion to a series of legislative actions that, if they did not fuel it, at the

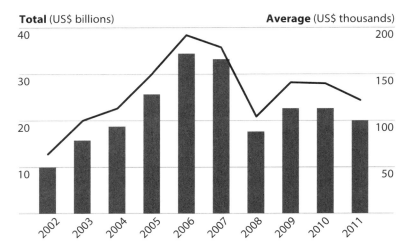

Total (US$ billions)   **Average** (US$ thousands)

Figure 2.5. Wall Street bonuses (total, US$ billions [bars], and average, US$ thousands [curve]), 2002–11. *Economist*, 2012d, "Wall Street Bonuses," 3 March, accessed 4 February 2013, http://www.economist.com/node/21548981. Used with permission.

very least did not do much to prevent the financial crisis of 2007/2008. Although new information technologies provided the tools for financial services to spread across the world, the rapid expansion of the sector was aided by a political culture that favored deregulation at the national level, along with resolute noncommittal to international regulation. Due to international competition among the various financial hubs around the globe, a race to the bottom led to the reduction in already weak regulatory standards. In the short term this provided more financial activity, higher revenues, more taxes, and more growth and explains why so many policy makers argued that their domestic financial system had to become "more competitive," which they took to mean bound by less regulation. Referring to the so-called Glass-Steagall Act of 1933 (which limited the possible interaction between commercial banking and securities firms), Senator Phil Gramm, chairman of the Senate Committee on Banking, promoted the Gramm-Leach-Bliley Act of 1999, stating: "We are here today to repeal Glass-Steagall because we have learned that government is not the answer. We have learned that freedom and competition are the answers. We have learned that we promote economic growth and we promote stability by having competition and freedom."[31]

Other countries like the United Kingdom followed the United States in the quest to reduce regulation. When asked about deregulation in the United Kingdom, then governor of the Bank of England, Sir Mervyn King, complained, "The power to regulate banks had been taken away from us. . . . Our power was limited to that of publishing reports and preaching sermons."[32]

The culture of deregulation became entrenched worldwide despite the efforts of groups such as the Basel Committee on Banking Supervision and warnings of a number of the world's foremost economists.[33] At the height of subprime lending in the United States, the attorneys general of all 50 states were seeking to investigate these risky practices but were "blocked by a coalition of major banks and the Bush administration," which used the archaic National Banking Act of 1863 to prevent state-level action.[34]

In the United States, the world's largest national financial market, legislation such as the Glass-Steagall Act had aimed to foster financial stability since the Great Depression. Commercial and investment banking activities were separated, reducing speculation and risk taking by stopping banks from "gambling" with savings. In the decades after Glass-Steagall's ratification, however, administrations convinced of the merits of uncontrolled capital flow began to undermine such efforts. The repeal of the Glass-Steagall Act by the Gramm-Leach-Bliley Act in 1999 constituted the final removal of the divide between commercial and investment banking. Although this had effectively been breached already, the repeal formally reintroduced the potential for dangerous conflicts of interest in the financial sector. Now nothing prevented multiple claims from being made against debtors or the implicit extension of deposit insurance.[35] It is noteworthy that Phil Gramm, who was one of the major proponents of deregulation and whom CNN calls the "#7 culprit of the collapse," joined the investment banking division of UBS immediately after his retirement from the Senate in 2002.[36]

The Spread of the Financial Crisis

In the integrated world of finance, risk should not be evaluated solely at the national level, and deregulation in the United States or other financial markets has global systemic effects. Even relatively small countries, as the example of Iceland at the beginning of this chapter demonstrates, can have wide-ranging consequences. Following the collapse of Icelandic banks, a number of local authorities and universities in the United Kingdom, together with many pensioners and other individuals, lost a significant share of their savings and investments.

In order to remain competitive with the U.S. financial market, the European economies felt compelled to create matching opportunities for investors and similarly succumbed to deregulatory pressures. Often lobbied by bankers, politicians sought to safeguard financial services in London, Frankfurt, Singapore, and other financial nexuses. This led to a commitment to light-touch regulation and the use of overly expansionary monetary policy.[37] Policy makers were taken by arguments that the future of their financial capitals and a significant share of their tax revenues required a reduction in regulatory burdens and red tape.[38] They argued that regulation would constrain the innovation needed to support further economic growth and stability.[39] Above all, politicians and regulators drew comfort from the economists' consensus of "the Great Moderation," which argued that the U.S. economy had exhibited low volatility since the 1990s and that there were no hidden risks building in the system as a result of their actions.[40]

The implications of national deregulation and an integrated market led to a global financial network that Andrew Haldane from the Bank of England has described as a "monoculture."[41] In the United Kingdom, the financial and insurance sector grew 108 percent between 2000 and 2011, vastly outpacing all other sectors.[42] By 2011 financial and insurance services contributed over £125 billion annually to the U.K. economy and were responsible for 9.4 percent of total value added.[43] As securitization of subprime mortgages increased, the government became increasingly beholden to what was becoming a homogeneous source of employment and tax revenue. Consequently, national intervention in financial institutions became increasingly difficult as banks grew more powerful and more influential.

At the same time that regulators were stumbling, the collapse of the U.S.-based hedge fund Long-Term Capital Management following the 1997–98 financial crisis signaled that banks deemed "too big to fail" could expect to be bailed out by national governments. Together with the widespread use of value-at-risk models (which underestimated tail risks), this

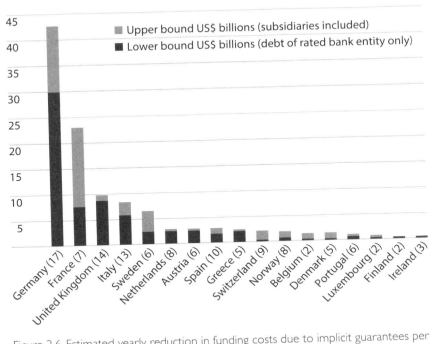

Figure 2.6. Estimated yearly reduction in funding costs due to implicit guarantees per country where banks are headquartered (US$ billions), March 2012. Number of banks in parentheses. Estimated implied yearly reduction in cost of outstanding debt in US$ billions, per country in which banks are headquartered (with the exception of Dexia; Dexia Credit Local is allocated to France and Dexia BIL to Luxembourg, even though the Dexia group is headquartered in Belgium). Note that these esti-mates do not necessarily imply equivalent local taxpayer burden. The total number of banks is 123. Sebastian Schich and Sofia Lindh, 2012, "Implicit Guarantees for Bank Debt: Where Do We Stand?," *OECD Journal: Financial Market Trends* 2012 (1): 10, accessed 22 January 2013, http://www .oecd.org/finance/financialmarkets/Implicit-Guarantees-for-bank-debt.pdf. Used with permission.

expectation obscured risk managers' incentives and effectively eliminated the downside risk for those large financial institutions that were systemi-cally the most relevant. Implicit government guarantees had a substantial impact on banks' funding costs. One estimate puts the yearly reduction in funding costs due to implicit guarantees at between US$70 billion and US$120 billion between 2002 and 2011 (figure 2.6).[44] Implicit guarantees are effectively a transfer of wealth from taxpayers to the financial system.

As a consequence of securitization, fueled by deregulation and aided by implicit guarantees, gross exposures escalated in a manner that bore no resemblance to the net exposures of the banks. The total outstanding debt of the domestic financial sector in the United States increased from just over US$250 billion in the first quarter of 1975 to a peak value of over US$17 trillion during 2008.[45] Like the national policy makers tasked to regulate them, banks had no concern for the global risks they helped to manufacture. In fact, it appears that regulatory regimes were effectively encouraging regulatory arbitrage. Financial institutions in the United States, for example, could essentially choose whether they wanted to be supervised by the Office of the Comptroller (designed for banks) or the weaker Office of Thrift Supervision (designed for savings and loans).[46] Abetted by permissive legislation and regulation, the financial system became systemically risky.

Many authors now agree that deregulation was a major cause of the international financial crisis. In box 2.2 we briefly consider some of the possible counterarguments before moving on to a discussion of complexity and systemic risk.

Box 2.2. Did Deregulation Cause the Financial Crisis?

We briefly consider five arguments intended to show that the repeal of the 1930s Glass-Steagall regulation contributed—at least partly—to the financial crisis.

First, it has been suggested that the repeal of Glass-Steagall did not contribute to the crisis because the banks that failed (such as Bear Stearns and Lehman Brothers) had not combined with commercial banks. This argument appears to overlook the fact that these banks transmitted shocks from a small sector of the U.S. economy (the mortgage sector) to the entire financial system. In the absence of commercial banks engaging in risk lending, it would have been possible to contain the worst of the financial crisis. Another reason the crisis became so costly is that the government was effectively forced to bail out banks deemed systemically important. Such banks were typically hit by losses from investment activity but provided vital credit to the real economy.

Box 2.2. (*continued*)

Second, it has been argued that the Dodd-Frank Act will shift business into the unregulated shadow banking sector. Acknowledging this point does not imply that we should avoid regulation. Instead it seems to imply that we should extend regulation to the shadow banking sector.

Third, it has been argued that investment banks were not actually deregulated by the U.S. Securities Exchange Commission in 2004 because sizable regulation did not exist prior to that time. It is difficult to see how the existence of a (largely) unregulated system can be taken as a starting point for an argument supporting deregulation. As we have seen, it was the largely unregulated—or inadequately regulated—banking sector that caused the crisis.

Fourth, it has been suggested that the growth of CDS markets did not constitute systemic risk but rather improved the information available for investors. This argument conflicts with the weight of the evidence summarized in this chapter. As we have seen, the exponential growth of CDSs and their increased complexity and interconnectedness did contribute to systemic risk. In fact, prior to the crisis many regulators and banking supervisors created special working groups to address systemic risks emerging from over-the-counter derivatives.

Finally, it has been suggested that the surge of mortgage markets was fueled by regulation rather than deregulation—specifically by the American Dream Downpayment Assistance Act of 2003, which aimed to ensure that every U.S. citizen can purchase his or her own home. This act and the underlying political agenda, however, were driven by a *social* rather than a financial goal. It was the way the goal of increasing the availability of cheap mortgage finance for the purchase of real estate (mainly housing) was facilitated, by loosening the financial market, that was the cause of subsequent financial turmoil. It is inappropriate to compare two totally different forms of government policy as if they were equivalent.

The discussion here represents the authors' partial response to arguments advanced by David Barker, 2012, "Is Deregulation to Blame for the Financial Crisis?," *Bank & Lender Liability* (a Westlaw Journal), 18 June.

COMPLEXITY AND SYSTEMIC RISK

In the buildup to the crisis, the global financial network could be likened to "the dynamics of ecological food webs" or "networks within which infectious diseases spread."[47] Within these networks an increasing number of nodes and links, along with the corresponding opportunities to trade and share risks, created the illusion of enhanced financial stability.[48]

Figure 2.7 shows connectivity in the financial sector just prior to the crash. The figure's right-hand side, focusing on the linkages among transnational corporations in the financial sector, displays the hallmarks of a complex system. The interplay between complexity and uncertainty also emerges in a noteworthy "model of fire sales and market breakdowns."[49] In this model banks face an inherently uncertain environment when assessing counterparty risk. In a network of interbank lending the default risk of a bank depends on the default risk of all the banks' counterparties. This, in turn, depends on the default risk of the counterparties of counterparties, and so on. It follows that complexity can make healthy banks reluctant to buy, which can lead to the evaporation of liquidity and the breakdown of markets. The relationship between complexity and uncertainty is also emphasized by Andrew Haldane in a 2012 speech given at the annual Jackson Hole symposium, the central gathering of the world's leading central bankers.[50] Haldane points out that regulation itself has become increasingly complex.[51] Whereas Basel I, the predecessor of the current Basel III agreement, had a total length of 30 pages in 1988, the revised Basel II accord ran to 347 pages in 2004. Basel III almost doubled the regulatory text to 616 pages in 2010. The same trend holds for the national implementation of transnational agreements. The implementation of Basel I took 18 pages in the United States and 13 pages in the United Kingdom. Haldane estimates that by the time Basel III is fully implemented in the United States it will take up to 30,000 pages.

Extreme integration means that if one node of a network collapses (for example, Lehman Brothers), the others will be affected. Extreme *complexity* indicates that the effects are indeterminate and the corresponding hazards are unknown. Failing to account for these externalities in the period before the financial crisis rendered the risk management strategies of firms virtually ineffectual. In light of the above arguments,

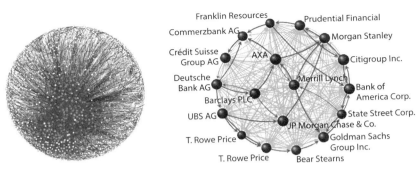

Figure 2.7. Networks of global corporate control. The graph on the left depicts corporate interlinkages of strongly connected transnational corporations (TNCs). The graph on the right focuses on linkages among TNCs in the financial sector. Stefania Vitali, James B. Glattfelder, and Stefano Battiston, 2011, "The Network of Global Corporate Control," *PLoS ONE* 6 (10), accessed 4 February 2013, http://www.plosone.org/article/info%3Adoi%2F10.1371%2Fjournal.pone.0025995. Used with permission.

one has to ask whether (stochastic) *risk* management is even appropriate in the face of complexity or whether banks should aim to manage *uncertainty*. Looking back on the factors leading to the financial crisis, it is evident that regulatory and supervisory institutions failed to detect or contain the systemic risks that accompanied the transformation of the financial sector. Market participants and regulators alike were not necessarily aware of the extent to which complexity and homogeneity intrinsically introduce fragility to networks. Despite all the data and resources at their command, even the most seasoned of bankers may well have been taken by surprise, as they have stated, when the connectivity that had enabled rapid growth suddenly turned to amplifying and spreading systemic risks. Had the regulators been aware of what was happening, a separate question is whether they would have been able to do anything about it given their lack of power, particularly over the largest countries (such as the United States) and the largest banks.

Systemic risk itself is a broadly defined term, and it has been used to describe a widening set of phenomena in the course of the recent financial crisis. Until then, systemic risk was predominantly understood as the probability of contagion effects that cause cascades of defaults. The crisis, however, revealed that systemic risk might also emerge from two other sources: (1) a common shock leading to a simultaneous default of several financial institutions at once and (2) information spillovers whereby, for example, bad news about one bank increases the refinancing costs of all other banks.

It is therefore possible to distinguish between a broad and a narrow notion of systemic risk. Contagion effects on interbank markets pose a systemic risk in the narrow sense, whereas systemic risk in the broad sense is characterized as a common shock to many institutions or markets.[52] This distinction is also followed by the Basel-based Financial Stability Board, which defines systemic risk as "a risk of disruption to financial services that is (i) caused by an impairment of all or parts of the financial system and (ii) has the potential to have serious negative consequences for the real economy."[53] The European Central Bank suggests that systemic risk can be described as the risk of experiencing a strong systemic event that adversely affects a number of systemically important intermediaries or markets.[54] The trigger of the event could be a shock either from outside or from within the financial system. The systemic event is strong when the intermediaries concerned fail or when the markets concerned become dysfunctional. Because all these different dimensions of a systemic event interact with each other, it is clear that systemic risk is a highly complex phenomenon.

The Sources of Systemic Risk

Contagion occurs due to direct linkages between financial institutions. Probably the most prominent example of these linkages is contagion via interbank markets. An interbank market can be described as a financial network consisting of a set of nodes—that is, banks or other financial institutions like hedge funds or insurance companies—and a set of links that form the connection between these institutions.[55] The interconnection in the interbank market can lead to an enhanced liquidity allocation and increased risk sharing among banks.[56] At the same time, however, increased connectivity can also amplify contagion effects.

Analyzing linkages in the form of overlapping claims suggests that contagion is more likely to occur if the network structure is incomplete because, in comparison with complete networks, uneven networks are more vulnerable to smaller idiosyncratic shocks. Although greater connectivity in the financial system reduces the probability of contagion, when it does occur the outcome may be more severe[57] as the likelihood that institutions or nodes might repeatedly be affected increases. Haldane argues that connectivity is a knife-edge property. Up to a certain point, financial networks and interbank linkages serve as a form of mutual insurance of the financial system and thus contribute to systemic stability. Beyond this point, the same interconnections might serve as shock amplifiers and thus increase systemic fragility.[58]

The stabilizing function of an interbank market might furthermore be affected by the structure of financial markets. In some cases the contagion probability is lower where the interacting institutions are homogeneous in terms of size or investment opportunities, because then no institution becomes significant for either borrowing or lending.[59] In other cases, however, there is no significant evidence to suggest that the heterogeneity of the financial system has a negative impact on financial stability.[60] Haldane describes the financial system in the buildup to the recent crisis as being characterized by complexity and homogeneity and argues that these two ingredients lead to fragility by referring to literature on complex systems and ecology.[61] The analysis of additional structural factors suggests that higher capitalization levels, lower interbank liabilities, and a less concentrated interbank market reduce the likelihood of direct contagion in the interbank market.[62]

Another source of systemic risk emerges from indirect linkages between banks in the form of common shocks. If a number of banks hold identical or similar assets, this correlation between their portfolios can give rise to a fire sale that is typically associated with significant losses for a large number of banks. Banks are incentivized to increase the correlation between their investments (and thus risk a common endogenous shock) in order to prevent costs arising from potential information spillovers.[63] The banks' returns of the most recent period are signals according to which risk-averse depositors update their prior assumptions about future returns. Compared with the situation in which two banks' signals are positive, depositors expect lower returns in the future if one bank's signal is negative and hence demand higher deposit rates in order to compensate for potential failures. Accordingly, a bank with a positive signal faces higher borrowing costs if the other bank sends a negative signal. This sets an incentive for both banks to increase the correlation between their investments to increase the probability of joint success (and joint failure).

Banks are also incentivized to induce an endogenous common shock in order to avoid negative externalities arising from a bank failure. The driving factor behind this behavior is that a default imposes both positive and negative effects on the surviving competitor. Negative effects arise because not all depositors are able or willing to lend their money to a bank, so the surviving bank faces higher refinancing costs.[64] However, the failure also leads to a reduction of monitoring and information costs when the surviving bank takes over staff and technology of the failed bank. Depending on which effect prevails, the payoffs of the surviving bank's shareholders either increase or decrease in comparison to the situation in which there is no bank failure. Accordingly, if the failure generates negative externalities, banks are incentivized to increase the correlation of their portfolios ex ante and thus increase the probability of a joint failure.

Analyzing the impact of central bank activity in a network model with interbank markets shows that common shocks constitute a larger threat to financial stability than does contagion.[65] Empirical studies confirm an increase in correlation between large and complex financial organizations during the 1990s,[66] indicating that this development was more severe for North American than for European banks.[67]

Research indicates that information spillovers are another form of systemic risk that has to be taken into account.[68] This effect is sometimes called informational contagion, but that name is misleading because it poses a systemic risk in the broad sense.[69] The main idea behind information spillovers is that the insolvency of a bank can increase the refinancing costs of the surviving banks—especially in times of crises, when financial markets exhibit herding behavior. Acharya and Yorulmazer develop a model of bank herding behavior based on a bank's incentives to minimize the information spillover from bad news about other banks. In their model, the returns on a bank's loans consist of a systematic component (such as the business cycle) and an idiosyncratic component.[70] If there is bad news about a bank, this news reveals information about an underlying common factor and thus affects all banks. The authors show that even the possibility of information contagion can induce banks to herd with other banks. Herding behavior in this model is a simultaneous ex ante decision of banks to undertake correlated investments and thus gives rise to correlations among the banks' portfolios.[71]

The different forms of systemic risk are not independent of each other, and a bank default does not happen instantaneously. During the buildup to the default, the bank will start deleveraging and selling assets. This may cause fire sales in certain asset classes and exacerbates the problems of the bank. At the same time, rumors about the bank and similar banks will spread in the markets, causing market participants to tighten their liquidity provision. Because the first bank already is struggling, this tightened liquidity can lead to default of this bank. This default then triggers contagion effects and possible further defaults of banks that have issued interbank loans to the first bank. As the recent financial crisis has shown, financial markets show herding behavior as described in Acharya and Yorulmazer and are aware of it, too.[72] In a situation of high uncertainty about the fundamental and idiosyncratic risks in the financial system, liquidity provision will dry up and market volatility will increase. Although one can distinguish the various forms of systemic risk by their manifestation, it is impossible to separate them in reality. Contagion effects and common shocks will inevitably trigger informational contagion and vice versa. Therefore, information contagion is a clear indication of systemic risk and has to be taken into account in macroprudential regulation to enhance financial stability.

Attribution

In order to derive meaningful policy measures for regulating systemic risk, it is necessary for regulatory authorities to measure and operationalize systemic risks. It has been argued that the distinction between the time and cross-sectional dimensions of aggregate risk is critical.[73] In the time dimension, leading indicators of financial distress are needed, whereas in the cross-sectional dimension a robust quantification of the contribution of each institution to systemic risk is necessary.

In the literature there are various approaches to achieving these goals. The European Central Bank differentiates among four types of indicators to measure systemic risk: (1) coincident indicators of financial stability, which measure the current state of instability in the system; (2) early warning signal models, which detect the buildup of systemic crises; (3) macro stress tests, which can assess the resilience of the financial system to aggregate macroshocks; and (4) contagion and spillover models, which are used to analyze the impact of a crisis on the stability of the financial system.[74] Using a set of such indicators, central banks and regulatory authorities try to assess the different dimensions of systemic risk. A precondition for a useful measure of systemic risk is that it needs to take all dimensions of systemic risks into account, and this involves combining at least some systemic risk indicators. A major problem to date is that there is no reliable indicator of informational contagion following a default. This leads to a significant element of uncertainty when assessing systemic risks.

The discussion of systemic risk shows that it is a complex phenomenon. It is thus very difficult and maybe even impossible to establish clear causality. This raises the question of how we attribute responsibility in situations in which causality is not clearly established. Can we hold actors accountable for undertaking actions when they cannot foresee the consequences? Although this is first and foremost a legal question, it also is a political and ethical one. The financial crisis of 2007/2008 spurred political protest in many countries. In Reykjavik, Iceland, around 6,000—out of a population of only 320,000—protested against the government's lack of responsibility.[75] Such public outrage, however, is usually short lived. The greater danger for any democratic society comes from a subtler and quieter trend toward disaffection, growing inequality, and other social consequences of crises. This danger is discussed in chapter 7.

Can financial reform and global governance account for the drastic increase in complexity and the radical change from risk toward *systemic* risk? We address this vital question in the next section.

GLOBAL FINANCIAL GOVERNANCE

The deregulation at the *national* level that we detailed above was possible due to a lack of global governance on the *international* stage. When sovereign nations are competing for *less* regulatory burden on their banks, international coordination is the only way to prevent an equilibrium that will leave the financial system under-regulated. At the time of the 2007/2008 financial crisis, three major supranational institutions existed to take responsibility for global financial stability: the IMF, the Bank for International Settlements (BIS), and the Financial Stability Forum (from 1997 onward). Not one of these agencies was able to confront the rapid increase in financial complexity with an appropriate set of rules or a system of interventions. None was successful in promoting international codification, transparency, or accountability in a way that could have mitigated the impact of the crisis. None was endowed with the necessary means to reinstall global financial stability even once the scope of the global problem became known.[76]

One major attempt had previously been made at regulating the global financial system. The Basel Committee on Banking Supervision's regulatory recommendations (the Basel standards, or Basel I) were first introduced in 1988 and were intended to create international standards for financial regulation. As one would expect from a global set of rules, they were subject to criticism from their inception and were substantially revised at the turn of the century. The revisions reflected the growing influence of global banks, hedge funds, and other financial institutions and effectively rendered many of the initial rules hollow. The Basel II regulations, codified in 2004, relied heavily on the use of internal risk models for the calculation of risk weights. This provided the banks themselves with some leeway in determining the riskiness of their balance sheets and therefore in the regulatory capital they were required to hold.[77] Furthermore, the BIS capital requirement focused on the individual risk management of each bank instead of the interactions of banks holding asset portfolios with a high correlation of returns.[78]

A failure by regulators to properly monitor bank activities was mirrored by a failure to anticipate the development of new means for banks to transfer liabilities through new derivative instruments. By giving banks the potential to offset their risks with counterparties, regulators failed to envisage a situation in which such risks would be sold hundreds, if not thousands, of times. The revisions of Basel I thus left rules skewed in favor of the banks and reflected extensive regulatory capture. In fact, national politicians egged on by lobbyists turned the original Basel standards on their head by providing regulators with significant room for discretion at the *national* level, a feature that the first set of rules had been devised to eliminate.[79]

Despite being widely discussed, deregulation, disregard for externalities, and misguided incentives were not the only factors that contributed to the crisis. Both national and supranational institutions were simply unable to comprehend the array of new hazards that evolved as a result of changes to the financial sector brought on by technological innovation. As a consequence, many regulatory responsibilities were simply left undetermined. In the case of finance, a lack of oversight allowed banks to accumulate undetected cross-border risks and to exploit supervisory ineptitude around the globe.

The indeterminate nature of regulatory responsibilities was particularly damaging during the crisis, because a lack of understanding led to a vacuum of responsibility, creating a "governance gap." Not only did this gap force governments into arduous negotiations that slowed down institutional responses during the crisis; it also destabilized financial markets, because reactive measures often turned out to be fragile compromises. This failure to coordinate and inability to display commitment often turned policy responses into impediments rather than remedies for financial instability. This could be seen in the Eurozone, where the disintegration of financial regulation and the promotion of national interests in negotiations were at odds with the single market and shared currency. Similar tensions between local and collective interests can be observed in the United States and other parts of the world. National institutions are not well suited to dealing with international (systemic) risks. Shortcomings of a national approach to regulation are abundantly evident in the recent financial crisis and its aftermath and include the failure to coordinate on a rescue plan for Fortis Bank and the default of Iceland.[80] They are also seen in the ongoing debate about how to proceed with floundering peripheral states in Europe and the continuing lack of unity in guidance from national regulators over "living wills" to ensure an orderly exit from the market of a major bank that collapses in the future. To fill the "governance gap" and to overcome partisan interests, the world needs an international approach to financial regulation and, as this book shows, to global risk management in general.

Having identified the main driving forces of the global financial crisis, in the final section of the chapter we use our findings to draw distinct governance lessons from it. But first we identify key points for the financial sector to take account of as global networks start to rebuild.

Generalizing from there, we show that all forms of resilient globalization must rely on two "pillars" and note these pillars' value for systemic thinking.

Relevant Factors for the Financial Sector

Recent research emphasizes the role of resource constraints for financial regulators and highlights the value of simplicity in regulation. One recommendation, from Dewatripont and Rochet, is this: "If public authorities are unwilling to increase spending on supervision then, other things being equal, the regulatory regime should be simplified."[81] This is a diversion from the mainstream "conventional wisdom" that more intricate rules are "nuanced" and encourage growth.

Andrew Haldane impressively quantifies the increased complexity of financial regulation itself, concluding that regulation should focus on simple instead of elaborate and complex rules.[82] White identified this prescription long before the crisis.[83] That the lesson ex post so closely resembles White's ex ante warnings highlights a main weakness of the current institutions. We see clearly that existing academic concerns were not translated into political action. Although a number of experts saw that new technology would transform the financial industry, leaving existing supervisory structures behind, they failed to capture the attention of the critical institutional decision makers at either the national or the global level. But that picture is slowly changing. Haldane, at the Bank of England, has been doing groundbreaking work on complexity; the New York Fed has been undertaking novel network analysis; and within Europe there is a growing focus on interbank networks from the European Central Bank and a number of the national central banks.

Although a growing chorus of economists cautioned against unchecked deregulation, the mainstream of the profession saw the lowering of transaction costs as economically sensible. These economists provided cover for those in government and business who were unwilling to curtail the flow of cheap credit that was driving consumers' confidence and sense of good fortune. It is never easy to turn off the music or take away the punch bowl while a party is in full swing. Politicians who profited from the bubble in credit and expectations, along with bankers who were intoxicated by bonuses, not surprisingly resisted attempts to enforce tighter standards. Profit overtook reason and common sense. It was not simply the case that institutional procedures were too sluggish to respond to policy directives, or even that politicians and regulators simply ignored expert warnings. There were also plenty of experts, some funded by lobby groups, who supported the arguments for deregulation, confusing politicians and electorates and allowing choices to be made on the basis of political bias and personal and institutional gains.

The financial crisis demonstrates that we must do better. Now is the time for economists to do some soul-searching and for the profession to address with renewed commitment the critical challenges of our time. The financial crisis has shown that economists need to develop a better understanding of collective action failures, behavioral biases, and the capture of governance by narrow interests.

LESSONS FOR THE FINANCIAL SECTOR

Our analysis in this chapter has shown two basic flaws in how the financial system was managed. The first pertains to the time *before* the crisis, when fragilities were not detected, risky behavior was not curtailed, and resilient globalization, far from being promoted, was becoming more fragile and prone to systemic risk. The second relates to what global institutions were able to do once the crisis was precipitated, when a lack of both knowledge and authority hampered policy responses. To overcome these flaws, we see two fundamentals that should form the "pillars" of resilient globalization:

1. *Mechanisms for understanding complex systems* and detecting and monitoring systemic vulnerabilities.

2. *Legitimate and authoritative institutions* at both the national and the international level that are able *to devise and implement policy* quickly in the face of changing circumstances.

Both these pillars are intimately linked to the problem of complexity that we discussed in the previous chapter. In complex environments the relationships between cause and effect become blurred, calling for more sophisticated mechanisms for detecting them (pillar 1). At the same time it becomes increasingly likely that some risks will remain undetected, and that interventions must be decided upon ex post, that is, after risk events have materialized (pillar 2).

Although this book is aimed primarily at understanding the nature of systemic risk today and at deriving general principles for its management, it is worth noting that our two pillars for resilient globalization can also be applied to different sectors. To draw specific policy implications, we suggest four lessons for managing systemic risk in the financial sector:[84]

Lesson 1: The current global financial regulation framework is inadequate
The international regulatory framework for global finance was the most sophisticated of the global governance regimes.[85] The crisis of 2007/2008 highlights the inefficacy of even the most effectively resourced, data-rich, and powerful global regulation network. Profound shortcomings in the governance system stemmed from a lack of understanding of systemic risk in the twenty-first century. It was a lack of imagination and conceptual failure, not a lack of data, skilled personnel, or resources, that led to the inability to identify and arrest the escalating threats. The crisis also was the result of a critical power imbalance. The institutions responsible for stability—most notably the IMF at the international level and the Federal Reserve and Treasury in the United States and their equivalents, such as the Bank of England and Treasury in the United Kingdom and elsewhere—were unable to stand up to the dominant politicians. In the case of the IMF, a shareholding structure that gives the United States a veto and, together with Europe, undue influence meant that it was unable to exercise sufficient authority over politicians intoxicated by the credit boom. The problem was even more acute at the national level, with domestic institutions and regulators weakened by deregulation and unable to exercise effective restraint. The failure to prevent the crisis has highlighted the scale and urgency of the need to address the challenge of global governance. A key lesson is that urgent reform of the governance structures, authority, personnel, and processes of the international financial system is required. Existing reform efforts, such as the transformation of the Financial Stability Forum into the Financial Stability Board and the establishment of the Basel III recommendations, do not go far enough and are unlikely to stop the next financial crisis.

A major problem with the world's response to the crisis was an inability to effectively agree on a single program. Ad hoc interventions, particularly during the second phase of the collapse (the European sovereign debt crisis) often simply aggravated the problem; they were either too slow or deemed not to display true commitment. The idea that financial governance must be legitimate and decisive thus brings financial reform into line with our second pillar. Independent and yet accountable national and supranational agencies are required—and these must have the necessary authority and ability to oversee and promote the stable evolution of the global financial system.

Lesson 2: The financial system is complex, and thus must be analyzed systemically

Our first lesson tells us that the existing regulation is inadequate; the second provides advice on how to begin rebuilding existing institutions. The financial crisis emphasized the need to adapt our fundamental understanding of economic networks to include the systemic complexities of the twenty-first century. Because we did not adequately understand the systemic vulnerabilities caused by increasing complexity, regulatory arbitrage grew outside the control of regulators. We now know that nodes of the financial network cannot be analyzed in an additive or linear manner. They cannot be isolated from their interactions with other links in the broader network. Systemic analysis must examine nodes, pathways, and the relationships between them, because "catastrophic changes in the overall state of a system can ultimately derive from how it is organized—from feedback mechanisms within it, and from linkages that are latent and often unrecognised."[86] All banks should be required to map their interdependencies in terms of the volume and frequency of their trade, and their net and gross exposures to their counterparties, not least in trading, should be fully understood by their audit and risk committees. Similarly, national and global regulators need to be able to map the evolving financial landscape to ensure that no one particular trading house or institution—or, over time, one geographic location—is systemically becoming too big to fail. They also need to use a combination of the soft power of persuasion and the hard power of regulation and competition policy to ensure the stability of the system. Reforms like these necessarily imply a major renewal of the mandate, resources, skills, and executive capabilities of the regulators at the national and the international levels.

Lesson 3: Financial reform demands greater accountability

In the following chapter we show that prior to the financial crisis, supply chain managers came to value resilience in a way that financial traders did not. We believe that the reason lies in accountability. A final goods producer is likely to be held responsible for a failure to deliver products and, as a consequence, has an incentive to monitor the quality and reliability of his supply chain. In finance, however, it is often difficult for a consumer to distinguish careless monitoring from exogenous risks outside the trader's control, leading to a dilution or avoidance of accountability. This is because, to a certain extent, the risk of failure is an implicit feature of any financial dealing that is paying interest above the "risk-free" rate. Lenders accept the risk that borrowers might not be able to repay their loans and thus demand interest payments in return. In a complex world, however, it is increasingly hard to determine whether a failure to repay occurs as a result of exogenous variables or because of reckless behavior on the part of the borrower. In this sense, the concept of responsibility is even more blurred in finance than in global production. As a result, financial managers are left with much weaker incentives than other managers to monitor product quality carefully. Through regulators, society should hold financial managers responsible for their products and for their advisory and other services. In part this can be achieved through remuneration and positive incentives, but penalties are also required. In this regard, the pursuit for accountability of bankers who have mis-sold products and who have traded against their clients' interests is a welcome development and reduces systemic risk.

Lesson 4: Simplicity, not complexity, will allow global institutions to manage local issues

Complexity impairs market discipline in finance because it blinds regulators, bank supervisors, and others to the underlying causal relations. In addition, target values are easily manipulated. Instead of complex rankings, we should rely on the principle of simplicity. This might result in a proposal to use an array of crude indicators for financial stability rather than one sophisticated benchmark, such as risk-weighted capital requirements.[87] In this way, the Basel III proposals to incorporate simple leverage ratios in regulatory recommendations are a significant step in the right direction; they are obscured, however, by an excessive regulatory framework that may well open more loopholes than it closes. Simple rules should be developed based on precautionary principles that draw on historical precedents.

Simplicity will help ease the tension between international and subnational levels of financial governance. It has been observed that "in many ways, the subprime crisis occurred because the 'global' ignored the complexities of the 'local.'"[88] Poor coordination between local and global groups tasked with financial surveillance resulted in informational asymmetry. Traders developed models that calculated risk in a complex, poorly understood way that confused regulators by eschewing "local knowledge in favour of formula-based risk management on a global scale."[89] The failure of local and global institutions to coordinate was largely ignored because the system seemed profitable. Therefore, when the bubble burst, no one had prepared. Actors in the financial system at all levels must work together to coordinate and collaborate because no level of governance is sufficient as an island of regulatory control. The high degree of integration and interconnectedness across the financial system calls not only for vertical regulation but also for horizontal regulation across all silos of governance.

The good news is that financial regulators are beginning to acknowledge the value of simplicity in regulation. Drawing on behavioral economics work, Andrew Haldane made the issue of complexity a central one in global financial regulation in his 2012 speech at the annual Jackson Hole Symposium.[90] This constitutes an important step in the right direction.

In our view, it is not only regulators that need to become aware that growing complexity cannot be fought with ever more complex rules but also managers and others, who should allow themselves to rely more on basic ethics and intuition. For example, when bonuses spiral beyond all historical precedents, remuneration committees should not need to be forced to show restraint. Similarly, when low-paid or even unemployed individuals are buying second homes on credit and housing markets bubble, it should be obvious even outside the banking sector that there is an unsustainable boom. Acting on intuition becomes even more important when there are increasing risks of being paralyzed by analysis using ever more complex data.

3

❦

Supply Chain Risks

We have argued that globalization has contributed to economic integration, efficiency gains, and growth but also to the hidden systemic risks that materialized in the 2007/2008 financial crisis. In this chapter we show that global integration has transformed the nature of the real economy in terms of the actual production of goods and services. Globalization has facilitated the widespread creation of extensive supply chains, defined as systems of organizations, people, technology, activities, information, and resources involved in moving a product or service from supplier to customer.[1]

With global supply networks, even small, localized events can have ramifications on an international scale. When a fire broke out in a Philips-owned semiconductor plant in New Mexico in March 2000, for example, the supply networks of a Nordic telecommunications company and a European competitor were hit by a supply shock. Both relied on chips manufactured in the burned-down plant to power their mobile phones. The Nordic firm was more resilient to this shock and quickly patched together a work-around, allowing it to continue its operations. The competitor firm was less resilient to this shock; its stock lost about 3 percent of its value, and the firm was ultimately forced to withdraw from key markets.[2]

Another telling example of the centrality of network approaches to supply chain management is the recent discussion about so-called rare earth elements. These scarce metals are vital ingredients for many twenty-first-century technologies, including cell phones, iPads, laptops,

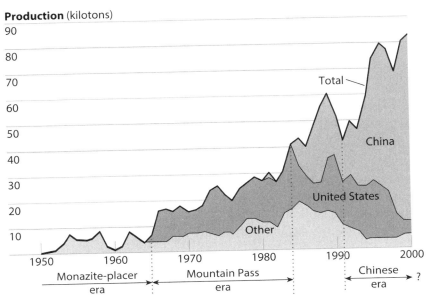

Figure 3.1. Global production of rare earth elements (kilotons) and geographical decomposition, 1950–2000. Gordon B. Haxel, James B. Hedrick, and Greta J. Orris, 2002, "Rare Earth Elements—Critical Resources for High Technology," Fact Sheet 087-02, U.S. Geological Survey, accessed 4 February 2013, http://pubs.usgs.gov/fs/2002/fs087-02/.

hybrid cars (both the NiMH, or nickel–metal hydride, batteries and the engines depend on rare earth elements), and solar cells. Starting in the mid-1980s, China substantially increased its production of rare earth elements, strategically subsidizing its producers.[3] By the turn of the millennium China had dominated the market, establishing a de facto monopoly on the production of rare earth elements (figure 3.1). China used the power of its economic dominance in the production of this key commodity during a maritime conflict with Japan and blocked the exports of rare earth elements. This episode shows how supply chain dependencies can be exploited to achieve strategic geopolitical goals.[4]

In 2006 a special report in the *Economist* attempted to appraise the scale of supply chains worldwide. The editorial, appropriately titled "The Physical Internet," likened these networks of transportation, communication, and negotiation to the World Wide Web. The *Economist* also noted the intrinsic link between globalization and supply chains: "Globalisation requires greatly increased co-ordination of transport by road, rail, sea, air and now also by an entirely new route to market: the internet. This makes logistics vastly more complex. The job of ensuring that all these things work together is known as supply-chain management."[5]

Globalization and supply chains have a symbiotic relationship. Although this section focuses on how the rise of international trade created longer and deeper supply networks, it is important to remember that these networks, in turn, fuel globalization. In this chapter we diagnose the risks of supply chain management and of global business management more generally. As in the case of the financial sector, we show that the efficiency benefits of globalization have associated risks and that profit-maximizing behavior can create negative externalities. We start by noting the rise of international trade in the twenty-first century. We examine how political changes and technological innovation gave rise to global supply chains. An analysis of "best practices" in supply chain management shows how these supply networks are vulnerable to systemic risk. We then seek to identify ways to make supply networks more resilient. This chapter's conclusion draws lessons for systemic thinking from supply chain management and considers how the resilience and robustness of the system may be improved.

GLOBAL SUPPLY CHAINS

We begin by considering the rise of global supply chains in the late twentieth and early twenty-first centuries. We show how political and technological changes shaped global trade and international relations and how supply chain management adapted to suit this new transnational environment.

The Rise of International Trade

The end of the Cold War and the fall of communism brought down more than an iron curtain and united more than two halves of a divided Berlin. After more than 50 years of strained relations between East and West, political animosity and the threat of armed conflict no longer stood in the way of business. Entrepreneurs across hemispheres were now able to cooperate and compete. The "new political climate" brought closer economic ties and multilateral trade arrangements.[6] The Uruguay Round of the GATT (General Agreement on Tariffs and Trade) negotiations concluded in 1993 and established the World Trade Organization (WTO) as a permanent body in 1995. The North American Free Trade Agreement and the European Economic Area both went into effect on 1 January 1994. In addition to these "big-name" treaties, numerous smaller agreements, such as the Free Trade Area of the Association of Southeast Asian Nations (28 January 1992) and the Central American Integration System (1 February 1993) were also born into this new, more open world. Although the individual effects of each agreement vary greatly, together they are indicative of increasing international cooperation. Nations reduced their politically motivated protectionism and engaged in more open, but by no means unfettered, global trade. The increased application of the market system allowed significant efficiency gains as multilateral negotiations reduced average tariff rates. In high-income countries the average tariff on manufactured goods is now just 1.8 percent, whereas it stands at 5.5 percent in middle-income countries and 14.2 percent in low-income countries.[7] The participation of a growing number of countries and the fragmentation of production globally meant that trade growth leapt ahead of other indexes of economic activity. The creation of bilateral trade agreements alongside multilateral agreements has further increased the complexity of global linkages.

Between 1951 and 2004, the average annual growth rate of world trade was 5.7 percent.[8] Figure 3.2 graphically depicts the rapid growth in world trade that started in the late 1980s and early 1990s as political, economic, and technological change drew a growing number of countries into the international division of labor. Declines in the cost of shipping and air transport now make it both possible and profitable for supply chains to operate across a wider range of countries. Companies today function transnationally, outsourcing everything from manufacturing to engineering as raw and processed materials flow from one continent to another.

Figure 3.2 reveals more than an increased volume of world trade; it also hints at the new role of China in global manufacturing and industry. There was an extraordinary eightfold increase in that country's

US$ (billions)

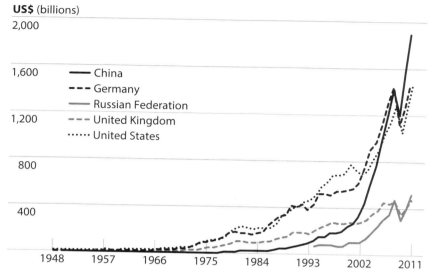

Figure 3.2. Total merchandise trade of selected areas—exports (US$ billions, current prices), 1948–2011. Prior to 1990, the former German Democratic Republic is excluded from the series of Germany; beginning in 2010, the series of the Russian Federation includes an adjustment for bilateral trade with Kazakhstan that is no longer recorded by customs following implementation of a bilateral customs union. WTO, 2013b, *Statistics Database*, World Trade Organization, accessed 4 February, http://stat .wto.org/Home/WSDBHome.aspx?Language=E. Used with permission.

exports between 1999 and 2008, more than double those of other high-performing export economies, such as Germany. Three decades ago, as the flat line prior to 1980 in the figure shows, China was isolated from world markets.

The transition to a trade-based economy is the direct result of political liberalization achieved by the late twentieth-century reforms of Deng Xiaoping, then leader of the Chinese Communist Party. In 1978 he launched a "second revolution" heralding the emergence of China's closed economy into the global economy.[9] The first stage of reform took place during the 1980s and aimed to facilitate growth and competition. It involved the decollectivization of agriculture, the creation of small businesses, and the reduction of tariffs to encourage investment. The second stage of reform occurred later, in the early 1990s, and centered on privatization and the contracting out of state-owned industries. These policies entailed a lifting of price controls, a dismantling of protectionism, and a wave of deregulation. The policies were remarkably successful, and by 2005 the private sector accounted for almost 70 percent of China's GDP.

The integration of China into the world market was extraordinarily rapid but nevertheless was symptomatic of a more widespread change and integration of emerging markets into international trade. The growth of the real economy has been spurred not only by liberalization and technological advances but also by the development of world air and freight traffic, as well as containerization. One noteworthy study reports that between 1975 and 2004, the air tonnage of non–bulk traded goods grew at 7.4 percent per annum.[10] It also recounts how "improvements in the quality of transportation services—like greater speed and reliability—allow corresponding reorganizations of global networks of production and new ways of coping with uncertainty in foreign markets."[11]

The emergence of China into world markets went hand in hand with a shift toward high-tech products. Figure 3.3 shows the exports of integrated electronic circuits in 1995 and 2010. The global market for electronics exports has expanded over the past decade, with China emerging as the dominant player.[12] This reflects the deeper economic transformation of China and her corresponding integration into the global economic system.[13]

What triggered the integration of China into the world economy? And, more generally, what triggered the emergence of global supply networks? In the interaction of politics and economics, new transport technologies played an important part. The most significant innovation, however, came not from new planes or cargo devices but from the Internet. As the standardization of container size and freight technology made international transport easier by substantially reducing transaction costs, the virtual world experienced a parallel standardization with the invention of the Internet Protocol Suite, which significantly simplified communication between disparate networks and across borders.

World container traffic was almost seven times as high in 2008 as in 1988; in the intervening period, the Internet fundamentally transformed our commercial habits. These two trends were not unrelated.[14] Consider the following simple example of the link between the Internet

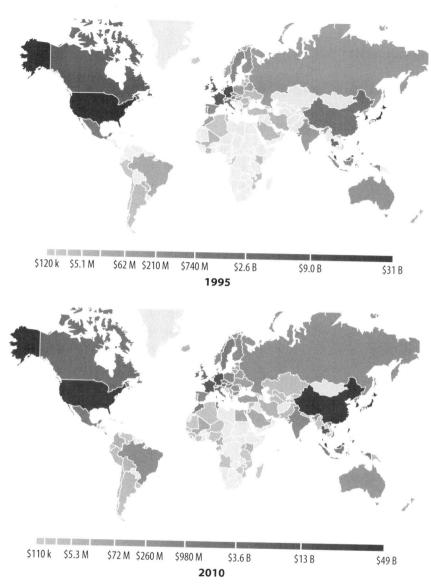

Figure 3.3. Exports of integrated electronic circuits (US$ billions), 1995 and 2010. Atlas, 2013, "Who Exports Electronic Integrated Circuits?," *The Observatory of Economic Complexity* (Map App), accessed 7 February, http://atlas.media.mit.edu/.

and commerce: "Each person who shops at home on the Internet, or uses a handheld Internet device to gather information about the transportation system before embarking on a trip, might only change his or her overall pattern of travel behaviour just a little. But there are millions of people worldwide who will be doing similar things on any one day. The small effects scale up to be significant."[15] The very nature of commercial exchanges in the twenty-first century has changed as a result of recent innovations. Books, toys, and electronics are now bought on Amazon, not at stores, and even groceries can be purchased via the Internet, bypassing the physical market. The Internet and modern communication have helped to overcome geographical borders and drastically reduced the barriers to entry.

Mercurial supply chains arose to service this new wave of international business and trade. When a company can have its headquarters in the low-tax Swiss enclave of Zug, its production plants in China, and its retail stores in New York, the supply chain and logistics are key determinants of profitability. Surprisingly little attention has been paid to the systemic risks that simultaneously are being created.

Supply Chain Management

There is an extensive business literature on different paradigms of production practices.[16] Moving from the craft production of nineteenth-century Europe, management theory began to endorse mass production during the early twentieth century. "Fordism," as it became known, drew on the innovative strategies of Henry Ford, who pioneered the American automobile industry. Ford's ideas focused on standardized and centralized production factories that were able to produce identical goods in vast quantities. The standardization of output, use of assembly lines, and division of work into small, uncomplicated tasks came to dominate manufacturing until after the Second World War.

In the latter half of the twentieth century, however, management thinking began to change again. Businessmen in Japan, led chiefly by innovators such as Taiichi Ohno, began to develop new practices focused on efficiency and the elimination of economic waste, which is known as *muda*.[17] Toyota was one of the first companies to implement these practices, and it correspondingly achieved rapid success. It more than doubled its production, from just over 4 million cars in 1990 to nearly 10 million in 2009, eventually overtaking General Motors as the world's largest car manufacturer. Toyota's profits grew accordingly, from around US$1 billion in 1990 to over US$17 billion in 2008.[18]

The ideas that enabled this growth were famously embodied in the Toyota production system, whose main objectives were to eliminate three unwanted inefficiencies: *muri* (overburden), *mura* (inconsistency), and *muda* (waste).[19] The system became known as "lean management" as an excoriation of these three Ms stripped down supply chains ever further. Toyota relied on efficient transportation platforms and data exchange networks to deliver parts when they were needed but not before. This "just-in-time" manufacturing helped to cut muda and was essential to the "Toyota Way." Toyota also pioneered the practice of supply chain fragmentation, outsourcing the manufacture of various components to subsidiaries around the world. It was the first company to recognize that by leaving the production of individual parts to specialized suppliers it could optimize efficiency and operate more cost-effectively. This quest for efficiency moved Toyota to open multiple manufacturing facilities in over a dozen countries worldwide. The firm overcame geographic, linguistic, and cultural barriers to search out the most cost-efficient locations, balancing production costs, speed to market, and access to labor. What was regarded in the 1980s as Toyota's exceptionalism has become the ubiquitous driving principle of globalized production.

Following Toyota's example, the prevailing logic of supply chain management today is that the production of goods, where possible, should be outsourced to the most cost-efficient provider. In a world where information is readily available and the movement of goods no longer constitutes a significant constraint, producers now draw their required components from a wide range of sources. Supply chains and production processes have become increasingly fragmented as companies scout the world looking for the most cost-efficient locations. Emulating Toyota's dictum of lean management, firms now schedule deliveries just in time, seeking to avoid tying up working capital in supply chains as well as holdings of stock. In short, Toyotism has come to define globalization and dominates management thinking.

SUPPLY CHAIN RISK

The *Economist's* discussion of the development of supply chain networks recognized that the latest innovations in management thinking increased risks and cut resilience as well as costs. It noted:

> Supply chains harbour dangers too, and managing risk is becoming a pressing issue. . . . Most firms have been organising their logistics to make themselves leaner. Many now carry little or no inventory to save money. Indeed, sometimes their entire inventory consists of what is moving from the factory directly to the consumer in the back of a truck or an aeroplane. If something goes wrong—and it often does—business will quickly grind to a halt.[20]

The search for efficiency gains can lead to unwanted negative externalities. Through the transformation of supply chains, globalization has made production more efficient but simultaneously left the world trade network susceptible to systemic failures.

The 2011 Thailand Floods and Supply Chains

Our first example examines the 2011 Thailand floods and the systemic consequences for global supply chains. Following a 30 percent increase in rainfall and four violent tropical storms, almost every industry operating in Thailand was affected by the waters—from agriculture to manufacturing and computing.[21] As tides submerged paddy fields in one of the world's largest rice producers, annual rice production slumped by 20 percent. Meanwhile, the inundation of factories led to a 28 percent drop in the production of hard disk drives (HDDs) worldwide.[22] A concomitant effect due to demand and substitution inflated the market price of solid-state drives and dynamic random access memory drives (DRAMs). Disruptions stalled the production of notebooks, digital imaging systems, and digital video recorders. The waters devastated the production plants of car manufacturers like Honda, Nissan, and Toyota and halted the operations of computing firms such as Toshiba and Western Digital. The World Economic Forum (WEF) concluded in 2012 that these widespread consequences had occurred because of an "efficient . . . supply chain which did not leave much room for catastrophic events."[23] The proverb that lends its name to the butterfly effect says that the fluttering of a butterfly's wings in Brazil can cause a storm in the United States. In this case a storm in Thailand caused the fluttering of shareholders' balance sheets in California as Intel saw profits fall by over $1 billion in the last quarter of 2011 alone.[24]

It is worth noting that the systemic effects of the 2011 Thailand floods are by no means unique or unprecedented. The WEF *Global Risks 2012* report cites a number of examples. Having investigated the systemic effects on supply chains of the 2011 Japanese tsunami and the resulting meltdown of the Fukushima nuclear power station, the report goes on to warn, "The danger of such disruptions can be quickly forgotten as companies revert to the principles of lean business models, which imply that building redundancy and excess inventory into supply chains are [sic] a waste of resources."[25]

The reason that the Thailand floods had such a devastating impact on manufacturing potential worldwide was that prevailing management thinking had created a supply network at risk of systemic failure. It is common for management strategies to be guided by best practices and to emulate those of successful firms. On the industry level, however, such behavior reduces resilience and generates systemic instabilities in the same way that it drove the financial system into a state of homogeneity (with banks trading in similar assets using similar business models and making the same underlying assumptions) and complexity (with markets becoming increasingly opaque due to the high volume of complex securities traded).

To see one manifestation of the risk ensuing from best practices, consider the case of a car manufacturer that profitably outsources the production of one of its key components, for instance, the steering system. We saw earlier how this practice formed a key part of the revolutionary Toyota production system. If only the industry leader delegates its production, there does not seem to be a sizable systemic risk. A failure at the production plant will affect the supply chain of the outsourcer but will leave the chains of its competitors intact. The industries dependent on the manufacturer (for example, logistics firms), as well as consumers, will have the opportunity to substitute the missing goods for competing products, leaving the market largely unaffected. Because infrastructure in competitive locations, particularly in developing countries, tends to be fragile (see chapter 4), such failures are not rare; they can arise from transport problems, natural disasters, and local governmental mismanagement (among other things). If the entire industry adopts the outsourcing strategy of the most successful firm (as the industrywide race to adopt best practices advises), the consequences will be more profound—particularly if all the companies in question rely on supplies from the same locations.

In practice, firms do subcontract production to shared producers, or at least to the same cost-efficient areas, where they benefit from the increasing returns of agglomeration. In Thailand, the world's two largest producers of HDDs and Japan's biggest car manufacturer, among other industries, outsourced their manufacturing to a single area. By the same token, Korea's two leading semiconductor manufacturers accounted for almost 50 percent of the global market for flash memory drives and DRAMs in 2010.[26] Many other examples of the global concentration of electrical components (and other products) can be found. The result is that a local event can affect entire sectors. Because supply chain hiccups now have systemwide effects, consumers will be constrained in their ability to substitute. The Toyota system's emphasis on fragmentation means that supply chains are now multilayered, creating many more opportunities for efficiency but also for systemic risk. This cascades up or down production chains. The steering system producer is likely to depend on his own network of suppliers, and failure by any of them affects world auto production.

A real-world example of such risks can be seen in table 3.1, which shows sourcing for the manufacture of Apple products worldwide. The company assembles parts delivered from producers around the globe. Under normal circumstances, these parts arrive just in time, resulting in profit-maximizing efficiency for the final producer, here Apple. Under adverse circumstances, however, the fragmentation of supply chains leaves firms exposed to risks beyond their control. In the case of Apple, quality problems and a strike at the Foxconn production plant in Zhengzhou, Taiwan, for example, caused delays in the delivery of the iPhone 5 during October 2012.[27]

TABLE 3.1
APPLE SUPPLIERS, 2011

AAC Technologies Holdings Inc.
AcBel Polytech Inc.
Acument Global Technologies
Advanced Micro Devices Inc.
Amperex Technology Ltd.
Amphenol Corporation
Analog Devices Inc.
Anjie Insulating Material Co. Ltd.
Asahi Kasei Corporation
AU Optronics Corporation
Austria Technologie and
    Systemtechnik AG
austriamicrosystems
Avago Technologies Ltd.
Brady Corporation
Brilliant International Group Ltd.
Broadcom Corporation
Broadway Industrial Group Ltd.
BYD Company Ltd.
Career Technology (MFG.) Co. Ltd.
Catcher Technology Co. Ltd.
Cheng Loong Corporation
Cheng Uei Precision Industry Co. Ltd.
    (Foxlink)
Chimei Innolux Corporation
Coilcraft Inc.
Compeq Manufacturing Co. Ltd.
Cosmosupplylab Ltd.
CymMetrik (Shenzhen) Printing Co.
Cyntec Co. Ltd.
Cypress Semiconductor Corporation
Daishinku Corporation (KDS)
Darfon Electronics Corporation
Delta Electronics Inc.
Diodes Inc.
Dynapack International Technology
Elpida Memory Inc.
Emerson Electric Co.
ES Power Co. Ltd.
Fairchild Semiconductor International
Fastening Technology Pte Ltd.
FLEXium Interconnect Inc.
Flextronics International Ltd.

Fortune Grand Enterprise Co. Ltd.
Foster Electric Co. Ltd.
Fuji Crystal Manufactory Ltd.
Fujikura Ltd.
Grand Upright Technology Ltd.
Gruppo Dani S.p.A.
Gruppo Peretti
Hama Naka Shoukin Industry Co. Ltd.
Hanson Metal Factory Ltd.
Heptagon Advanced Micro-Optics Pte Ltd.
Hi-P International Ltd.
Hitachi-LG Data Storage
Hon Hai Precision Industry Co. Ltd.
    (Foxconn)
Hynix Semiconductor Inc.
Ibiden Co. Ltd.
Infineon Technologies AG
Intel Corporation
Interflex Co. Ltd.
International Rectifier Corporation
Intersil Corporation
Inventec Appliances Corporation
Jabil Circuit Inc.
Japan Aviation Electronics Industry Ltd.
Jin Li Mould Manufacturing Pte Ltd.
Kaily Packaging Pte Ltd.
Kenseisha Sdn. Bhd.
Knowles Electronics
Kunshan Changyun Electronic Industry
Laird Technologies
Lateral Solutions Pte Ltd.
Lens One Technology (Shenzhen) Co. Ltd.
Lg Chem Ltd.
Lg Display Co. Ltd.
Lg Innotek Co. Ltd.
Linear Technology Corporation
Lite-On Technology Corporation
Longwell Company
LSI Corporation
Luen Fung Commercial Holdings Ltd.
Macronix International Co. Ltd.
Marian Inc.
Marvell Technology Group Ltd.

TABLE 3.1
(*continued*)

Maxim Integrated Products Inc.	Seiko Epson Corporation
Meiko Electronics Co. Ltd.	Seiko Group
Microchip Technology Inc.	Sharp Corporation
Micron Technology Inc.	Shimano Inc.
Mitsumi Electric Co. Ltd.	Shin Zu Shing Co. Ltd.
Molex Inc.	Silego Technology Inc.
Multek Corporation	Simplo Technology Co. Ltd.
Multi-Fineline Electronix Inc.	Skyworks Solutions Inc.
Murata Manufacturing Co. Ltd.	Sony Corporation
Nan Ya Printed Circuit Board	Standard Microsystems Corporation
Corporation	STMicroelectronics
NEC Corporation	Sumida Corporation
Nippon Mektron Ltd.	Sumitomo Electric Industries Ltd.
Nishoku Technology Inc.	Sunrex Technology Corporation
NVIDIA Corporation	Suzhou Panel Electronic Co. Ltd.
NXP Semiconductor N.V.	Taiyi Precision Tech Corporation
ON Semiconductor Corporation	Taiyo Yuden Co. Ltd.
Optrex Corporation	TDK Corporation
Oriental Printed Circuits Ltd.	Texas Instruments Inc.
Panasonic Corporation	Tianjin Lishen Battery Joint-Stock Co. Ltd.
PCH International	Toshiba Corporation
Pegatron Corporation	Toshiba Mobile Display Co. Ltd.
Pioneer Material Precision Tech	Toyo Rikagaku Kenkyusho Co. Ltd.
Prent Corporation	TPK Holding Co. Ltd.
Primax Electronics Ltd.	Tripod Technology Corporation
Qualcomm Incorporated	TriQuint Semiconductor
Quanta Computer Inc.	Triumph Lead Electronic Tech Co.
Renesas Electronics Corporation	TXC Corporation
Ri-Teng Computer Accessory Co. Ltd.	Unimicron Corporation
ROHM Co. Ltd.	Unisteel Technology Ltd.
Rubycon Corporation	Universal Scientific Industrial Co. Ltd.
Samsung Electro-Mechanics Co. Ltd.	Vishay Intertechnology
Samsung Electronics Co. Ltd.	Volex plc
SanDisk Corporation	Western Digital Corporation
SANYO Electric Co. Ltd.	Wintek Corporation
SDI Corporation	Yageo Corporation
Seagate Technologies	Zeniya Aluminum Engineering Ltd.

Note: The table covers 97 percent of procurement expenditure for materials, manufacturing, and assembly of Apple's products worldwide in 2011.

Source: Apple, 2011, "Apple Suppliers 2011," accessed 16 October 2012, http://images.apple.com/supplierresponsibility/pdf/Apple_Supplier_List_2011.pdf.

The strategy of fragmenting supply chains into outsourced locations has proved so profitable that it is now a management standard in many manufacturing industries. The example of flooding in Thailand illustrates what can happen when centers for outsourcing experience problems or, as the *Economist* puts it, "when the chain breaks."[28] The reason that so many different industries were so severely affected by the floods was that cost-minimizing locations such as Thailand tend to be seen to address a range of efficiency concerns. Low taxes, low wages, liberal regulation, and other incentives make specific locations attractive across industries. Although one generally thinks of globalization as a process involving a multiplicity of locations, and thus a geographical diversification of risk, in practice it has also resulted in a concentration of risk and instability. By allowing these nexuses to arise, the world is literally putting all its eggs in one basket and leaving itself vulnerable to highly disruptive hazards.

"Lean Management" and "Just-in-Time" Production

Although one best practice is the outsourcing of production, another crucial operation is that of lean management. We saw that the Toyota production system aimed at reducing muri (overburden), mura (inconsistency), and muda (waste). According to Toyota engineer and visionary Taiichi Ohno, muda can be broken down into six subcategories:

1. Waste of time on hand (waiting)

2. Waste of transportation

3. Waste of processing itself

4. Waste of stock at hand

5. Waste of movement

6. Waste of making defective products[29]

An investigation of these apparent wastages, however, shows that management just might be too lean. What the Toyota production system labels "waste of stock at hand" might also be thought of as buffer stock. What Ohno called "waste of overproduction" might ensure that supply chains do not experience gaps if one element in the supply chain fails or delivery is delayed. The reduction in surplus and an increasing reliance on just-in-time production and deliveries makes the chain taut. A shock or slippage at one link of the chain cascades rapidly through the system. The effect of failure is amplified as other businesses dependent on the chain are unable to fulfill their obligations.

Just as the financial crisis served as a case study for systemic risk in global finance and the Thailand floods demonstrated the risk of outsourcing and fragmentation, Toyota itself serves to illustrate the risks of the Toyota system.[30] Starting in 2009, the seemingly flawless Japanese company began to experience problems. The first sign of trouble came in October 2009, when a poorly fitted floor mat caused mass recalls. Toyota, the paragon of efficiency, was operating with a per-mat cost of less than US$10, with no buffer stock at hand.

In January 2010, Toyota issued a further recall for 2.3 million cars to fix "sticky accelerators." These had caused unintended acceleration, making cars speed up even when the driver applied no pressure. Capacity constraints at CTS (the supplier of the faulty pedal), however, meant that deliveries of replacement parts would take months to complete. Until it could secure the necessary parts from this one small factory, Toyota's entire global supply chain was forced to shut down. By late January, the company had announced an indefinite global moratorium on sales and a cessation of manufacture for affected models. The company that had pioneered the art of cost minimizing lost between US$5 and US$15 million in revenue *per day*. We believe that this was a predictable consequence of lean management. Materials were arriving just in time from small plants to which they had been outsourced, and buffer stocks were viewed as a waste. Management choices thus contributed to the creation of systemic instabilities.

Although it is difficult to obtain explicit data on the number of firms that have adopted the risk-making best practices of firms like Toyota, the usage of the expression "lean management" in the literature provides a reasonable proxy for their significance. Figure 3.4 confirms that discussion of lean management principles increased sharply during the 1990s, which correlates with a rise in their popularity. Furthermore, we see that the principles experienced a second boom during the early twenty-first century.

Per one hundred million

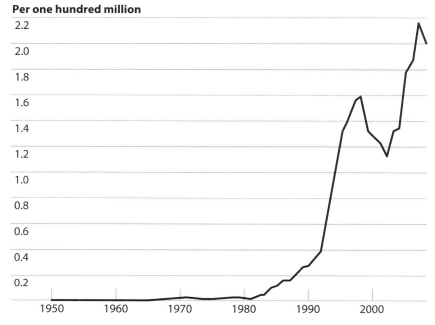

Figure 3.4. Use of the expression "lean management" in books (per one hundred million), 1950–2008. Reflects usage in the corpus of English books, with a smoothing parameter equal to two. The pattern is repeated if the usage in the corpus is reset to "American English" with the same smoothing parameter. Google Ngram, 2012, "Google Books Ngram Viewer," accessed 2012, http://books.google.com/ngrams.

Management Education

Our third case study of specific risks in supply chain management comes from the homogenization of management education. We have seen how the emulation of outsourcing and the replication of "best practices" for profitable strategies can amplify risk. Perhaps more worrying, however, is an increasing reliance on standardized management education rather than experience. Not only does a proliferation of management pedagogy cement the spread of practices such as lean management and outsourcing; it also leads to an over-reliance on a homogenized box-checking approach to risk management. This is no substitute for judgement, intuition, and experience or for the challenge that comes from having a diverse set of individuals who see risk as their concern rather than relying on a separate "risk manager" who applies rigid rules.

The upward trend in figure 3.4 is analogous to a volumetric increase in the management literature.[31] This increase in scholarship on management science is a symptom of the growing role of management education and has its origins in the "emergence of scientific management" that accompanied the Industrial Revolution.[32] Much of the standardization of management science has to do with the dissemination of the master's in business administration (MBA) degree, which has become the "standard credential for managerial ability" and has contributed to a "convergence of management thought."[33] It should be recognized that this convergence is not a phenomenon exclusive to the United States and that the creation of joint degrees by leading universities worldwide contributes further to the global adoption of common best practices.[34] This is now so commonplace that it occurs across continents; the University of Hong Kong offers a joint MBA with Hautes Études Commerciales (Higher Commercial Studies) Paris, while the Anderson School of Management of the University of California, Los Angeles, runs a program with the National University of Singapore. When universities institute these programs, students in these emerging Eastern universities learn the techniques of their older, Westernized counterparts and vice versa, facilitating the spread of current best practices. Figure 3.5 demonstrates the growth in the overall number of applicants for MBA programs over the past decade (with the exception of two brief dips following recessions) and the growing popularity of management education. From figure 3.6 and table 3.2, however, we see that the impact of the MBA is particularly strong in those regions that have only just begun to compete globally.

The first MBA program to be introduced in China had just 86 students in its inaugural year of 1990.[35] In 1991 there were only six MBA programs in China compared to 236 programs only 20 years later, in 2011. Total enrollment over the same period had grown to an astounding 36,000 students.[36] This growth has not been limited to China, however. The MBA is a highly sought prize in India, too. In 2009 more than nine hundred programs were offered, and admission is reported to be "fiercely competitive" as applicants vie for the opportunity to get their "management credential."[37] In fact, the number of applicants from the Asia–Pacific region to MBA programs abroad is larger than the number

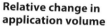

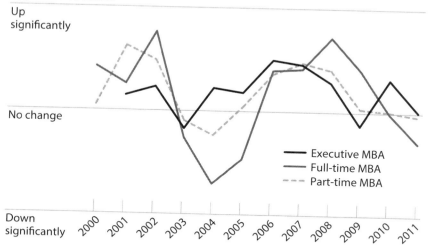

Figure 3.5. Relative change in MBA application volume, 2000–2011. GMAC (Graduate Management Admission Council), 2011, *Application Trends Survey* (Reston, VA: Graduate Management Admission Council), 4, accessed 4 February 2013, http://www.gmac.com/~/media/Files/gmac/Research/admissions-and-application-trends/applicationtrends2011_sr.pdf. Reproduced with the permission of the Graduate Management Admission Council®.

of MBA applicants from Europe, the United States, and the rest of the world combined (see figure 3.6 and table 3.2).

This wave of new managers is being taught to apply the practices that led to the devastating losses at Toyota and Intel, not to mention the enormous systemic consequences of the Thailand floods. Management students are willing to pay high fees for a degree from a prestigious business school, with global rankings providing guidance to prospective students regarding the success of past cohorts. The comparisons invariably use standard criteria for their rankings, and the universities use remarkably similar case studies and curricula.

It can be highly beneficial for an individual student or firm to learn from techniques and procedures that have proven to be successful in the past (the use of best practices). The standardization of management education, however, impairs the ability of graduates to draw from their diverse backgrounds and to react to unexpected circumstances. Uniform

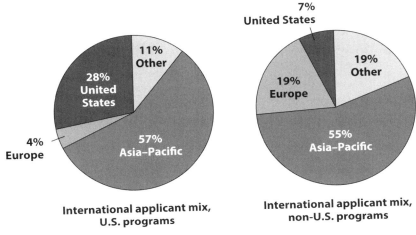

Figure 3.6. Percentage of two-year full-time international MBA applicants by world region: U.S. versus non-U.S. programs, 2011. GMAC (Graduate Management Admission Council), 2011, *Application Trends Survey* (Reston, VA: Graduate Management Admission Council), 11, accessed 4 February 2013, http://www.gmac.com/~/media/Files/gmac/Research/admissions-and-application-trends/applicationtrends2011_sr.pdf. Reproduced with the permission of the Graduate Management Admission Council®.

TABLE 3.2

DISTRIBUTION OF FOREIGN APPLICANTS TO ONE-YEAR FULL-TIME MBA PROGRAMS
BY GEOGRAPHIC REGION (PERCENT), 2011

World region of applicant	United States	Asia-Pacific	Europe	Other
Africa or Middle East	11	8	16	25
Asia-Pacific	40	64	37	38
Canada	1	1	3	15
Europe	6	12	23	4
Latin America	5	1	10	13
United States	36	14	11	6
Total[a]	100	100	100	100

[a]Total may not equal 100 percent due to rounding.

Source: GMAC (Graduate Management Admission Council), 2011, *Application Trends Survey* (Reston, VA: Graduate Management Admission Council), 13, accessed 4 February 2013, http://www.gmac.com/~/media/Files/gmac/Research/admissions-and-application-trends/applicationtrends2011_sr.pdf. Reproduced with the permission of the Graduate Management Admission Council®.

teaching of textbook techniques ensures efficiency during standard periods and thus responds well to standard tests. These techniques, however, are unprepared to respond to unexpected circumstances or to react to rare events. With the proliferation of management education, there is standardization and shared models of how to deal with risk. This means that when an event occurs that is not predicted by textbook analysis (and we know from our discussion of global complexity that this is increasingly likely), all managers will be similarly unprepared and will respond in a similar fashion. Systemic risk is, by its nature, surprising. In the face of unusual challenges, there is no manual or textbook response. Ingenuity and the pooling of different perspectives are required. Responding to systemic risk requires managers who can think originally and draw on a heterogeneous set of perspectives to come up with novel solutions to often uniquely testing circumstances.

FROM MANAGEMENT OF RISK TO RISK MANAGEMENT

Learning to contain the risks we have discussed is particularly important because supply chains do not function in isolation. In addition to the intrinsic risks for manufacturers, we also see potential danger in the link between firms' production activities and their investments. The real economy is not distinct from its virtual counterpart (as we discuss in the following chapters), and what we have discussed in this chapter affects the world of finance we previously analyzed. Researchers at the WTO, for instance, have shown that there is a "resonance effect" between supply chains and monetary circuits.[38] They provide evidence of cross-sectorial systemic risk and identify international supply chains as potential conduits for the spread of financial shocks. Recent studies have also explored how globalized supply chains contributed to the collapse of global trade during the 2007/2008 financial crisis.[39] Their findings support the view that the magnitude of financial shocks depends on the structure of the "physical Internet." Although we can learn much from studying individual risk sectors, these different sectors can no longer be compartmentalized. When systemic shocks arise, they jump over sector boundaries and the different dimensions of potential risk affect each other. To deal with these concomitant effects, interdisciplinary perspectives and coordinated regulatory efforts are required.

Current Responses

The U.K. Manufacturers' Organisation (EEF) conducted a survey of 150 companies that showed that 40 percent had experienced a significant supplier failure.[40] The survey also found that a similar share had brought their production back in-house, while a quarter of companies had increased their use of local suppliers. Although some companies have started to retreat from supply chain fragmentation and are attempting to build resilience into their systems by bringing more of their production in-house, others have attempted to move beyond lean management. The computer manufacturer Dell, for example, has started employing modular design to insulate its supply chains from risk. These modular supply chain architectures are "flexible in structure, with highly standardized interoperability and standard connections for subsystems."[41] They use standardized modules but retain flexibility in structure to allow different modules to be combined and reduce reliance on any one source of supply.

It is not just the private sector, however, that has attempted to deal with systemic risk in this field, and the National Strategy for Global Supply Chain Security issued by the White House in January 2012 marks an important step toward containing supply chain risks. The report acknowledges that "advances in communications technology, along with reductions in trade barriers and production costs, have opened new markets and created new jobs and opportunity for workers."[42] At the same time, however, it also raises awareness of the threat of an "adverse impact" on "global economic growth and productivity" that would result from natural disasters such as earthquakes, tsunamis, and volcanic eruptions, as well as from criminal and terrorist networks "seeking to exploit the system or use it as a means of attack."[43]

The interest of the White House is illustrative of how the events in the financial sector have enhanced political awareness of how globalization is linked to systemic risk. The brevity and abstract nature of the report mentioned above, however, also signal that political efforts remain in their preliminary stages. Great change is required to fortify global supply chains and to protect the economy from a repeat of the 2007/2008 systemic failure.

The Problem of Complexity

As in the financial sector, it appears that highly interconnected firms lack the resources to appraise all of their risk factors. This is in part because such risks extend to their trading partners, subcontractors, suppliers, and others, and the resulting complexity is of the kind examined in chapters 1 and 2.[44] Here complexity not only interferes with the ability of companies to manage risks; it also, as in finance, affects the capacity of regulators to monitor instability. This creates opportunities for deliberately irresponsible behavior—for example, in the circumvention of ecological or ethical restrictions. The crux of the problem is that "international fragmentation blurs the concept of country of origin" and makes it increasingly difficult to hold firms accountable or to assign regulatory responsibilities.[45]

The effects of outsourcing and subcontracting in global supply chains are in many ways comparable to the effects of securitization and secondary market trading in the financial sector. All of these innovations can diversify risk and may be profitable for individual firms, yet they also fail to account for their negative externalities and the creation of systemic risk. The result in both cases is that profit-driven firms inject unsustainable fragility into the global economy.

Supply networks and financial networks are not independent of each other. Whenever a commodity is sold from a supplier to a retailer, the supplier faces the risk that the retailer will file for insolvency after obtaining the good but before making the appropriate payment.[46] A model that captures this behavior within a general macroeconomic framework and is capable of reproducing many of the stylized facts of industrial demography has been developed by Stefano Battiston and associates.[47]

Battiston et al. also distinguish a number of different propagation mechanisms for contagion. Downward and upward propagation is shown in panels A and B of figure 3.7; horizontal default propagation occurs when each level transmits shocks both downward and upward. This shows how supply chain shocks can be transmitted not only across different layers of the supply network but also across competitors within the

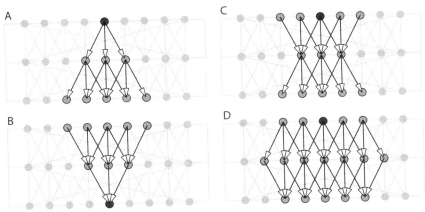

Figure 3.7. The propagation of default cascades in a production network. The direction of production is from top to bottom. Edges through which failure propagates are in darker gray. The firm triggering the avalanche is represented in black. Reprinted from Stefano Battiston et al., 2007, "Credit Chains and Bankruptcy Propagation in Production Networks," *Journal of Economic Dynamics and Control* 31 (6): 2061–2084, diagrams on 2073. Used with permission from Elsevier.

same layer. If the insolvency of a major supplier triggers the insolvency of a large retailer (because the retailer does not receive the appropriate supply in time, as was evident in the example of the Nordic versus the European telecommunications company), this can, in turn, affect other suppliers that are not being repaid by the retailer. The Battiston et al. model highlights the risks associated with integrated supply chains and makes a strong case for the analysis of systemic resilience in global supply networks.

Learning from Supply Chains

Many supply chain managers are aware of the risks we have discussed. In a recent survey of international supply chain managers, McKinsey and Company found that product complexity and financial volatility were among the most important determinants of supply chain strategies.[48] Their survey also documents that these professionals perceived supply chain risk as being greater in 2008 than in 2006. The risks that executives reported were linked to the difficulty of obtaining accurate information on the state of global supply chains, something that has become more difficult as globalization has made the world more complex. The executives emphasized that substantial resources are required for the management of global supply chains. These findings are consistent with the results from a separate, more extensive survey conducted among three hundred global manufacturing companies by the Massachusetts-based consultancy PRTM.[49] The company's research found that some managers today actually believe that outsourcing is an impediment to competitiveness under certain circumstances as a result of its negative impact on resilience, going against the core of lean management philosophy. This transforms the risks identified earlier from negative externalities to active factors in companies' cost–benefit analyses. The researchers report that "60% of the study participants say the lack of supply chain flexibility is a major barrier to sustainable globalization."[50] There is also some evidence to suggest that supply chain managers were ahead of financial managers in that they already considered a resilient market structure a valuable asset prior to the financial crisis.[51]

The question remains as to whether this insight prevails in situations in which short-run profits would have to be sacrificed for resilience. The role that competitive pressures can play in contributing to the fragility of global supply chains is reflected in a definition of supply chain risk from the U.S.-based insurance broker Marsh and McLennan. According to them, twenty-first-century supply chain risk can be characterized as follows:

> Supply chain risks include everything from natural hazards, terrorism, pandemics, and data security to demand variability and supply fluctuations. Fierce competition and tight margins can further magnify the impact of a supply chain failure on a business. . . . Economic pressures exacerbate supply chain–related risks particularly in relation to supplier viability given tightening credit markets, downward pressure on costs, and shrinking consumer markets.[52]

We do have reason to be optimistic, however, because it appears that managers are beginning to value resilience as profit maximizing in the long term. This is because a final-good producer is likely to be held responsible for failure to deliver products and therefore has an incentive to hold his supply chain accountable.

LESSONS FOR SUPPLY CHAIN MANAGEMENT

In evolutionary biology, particularly in the field of marine research, there is a distinction between robust and resilient structures. Coral reefs are an example of the robust, relying on underlying strength to withstand unfavorable conditions. Plankton bodies, however, are classed as resilient; although resilient structures can also survive in harsh environments, they succeed by their ability to adjust and adapt.[53] Transferring this distinction to the domain of supply chains, we see by analogy that there are two ways to limit exposure to systemic risks. The robust approach is to accumulate sufficient buffer stocks and to create self-contained units with limited exposure to external dangers. This method resembles how coral reefs withstand hazards. A problem with robust structures, however, is that they are costly in terms of opportunity costs; after all, this is the reason Toyota began to reduce what seemed like unprofitable waste (muda). These costs make the robust approach particularly hard to sustain for firms that may run into liquidity or solvency problems in the short run, not least in the face of increasing global competition. The costs associated with robust structures are also one of the prime reasons that such structures are often robust only to known, or at least expected, risks. Politically and economically, robustness can typically be afforded only if the risk can be specified sufficiently or if the corresponding hazard is sufficiently threatening (as in the case of a nuclear reactor).

The resilience approach, on the other hand, is designed to facilitate responses to unknown risks. An example might be modular design, which can be viewed as a creative managerial implementation of the resilience exhibited by plankton bodies. These organisms do not withstand adverse conditions but rather have the ability to adapt. The equivalent in supply chain management would be the creation of diverse structures and an acceptance of heterogeneity in risk management. This appears to be the less costly and more practicable of our two approaches. Unfortunately, for the time being it is precisely the spread of best practices emulation and the proliferation of standardized management education that have hampered resilience.

Below are some lessons for systemic thinking that can be derived from supply chain management.

Lesson 1: Network resilience should be promoted

Economic reform should promote resilience not only through the diversification of supply chain risk but also—often more importantly—through the available strategies for risk management.[54] As our analysis has shown, the globalization of management education and the ability to homogenize knowledge worldwide are currently promoting the exact opposite: fragility through homogeneity. Although adopting best practices and learning from few teachers and books are perfectly rational from the perspective of individual entrepreneurs, they are less optimal from a global governance perspective. Educators and policy makers should both promote (and maintain) diversity in the personal characteristics of their students and managers and actively promote the potential for use of different business models. Just as homogeneity in education is problematic, geographical homogeneity—or concentration—is also a source of risk. The concentration of U.S. automobile manufacturing in the Detroit area or of microchip and semiconductor production in flood-prone regions of Thailand or Taiwan may serve these industries well during normal times but ensure that the repercussions of any local hiccup or catastrophe are especially harsh when things go wrong. A systemic approach recommends diversification, but local authorities have strong incentives to attract specialized businesses. The "diversification of strategy" is thus an important imperative for the global governance of supply chains, and one that equally applies for reforming financial regulation.

Lesson 2: Negative externalities such as counterparty risk need to be recognized and addressed

We have argued that the financial system is characterized by a number of externalities that prevent socially optimal outcomes and inevitably trigger financial crises. Many of those externalities can be found in the study of global supply networks as well. Counterparty risk, in particular, is a clear concern of suppliers. Although the financial sphere has accepted the existence of such externalities and reacted by proposing so-called macroprudential regulatory responses, a similar reaction is nowhere to be seen in global supply networks. Banks are now obliged to hold substantially more capital in order to sustain large funding and market shocks. In a similar fashion, firms relying on global supply networks should not adapt the practice of lean management but should instead allow for loss absorption buffers. When we put all our eggs in one basket, be it in the form of holding similar assets or producing certain goods in only one geographic region or by only one manufacturer, the least we should ensure is that the basket is well cushioned and that we have a few spare eggs.

Lesson 3: Regulation is needed to promote emergency planning for systemic shocks

Other measures introduced in the financial system incorporate a liquidity ratio that requires banks to hold a certain fraction of their assets in a highly liquid form (either as cash or as highly liquid government and corporate bonds). The idea is that banks can easily "unload" those assets from their balance sheets without incurring losses. Translating this idea to global supply networks, firms have to make emergency plans for quickly changing from one supplier to another. Some firms already have such emergency plans in place, but others choose to acquire and vertically integrate with their suppliers. Helping large global corporations to prepare for systemic disasters can also include making detailed plans on how to shut down their operations without affecting substantial parts of the global economy. For example, a major pandemic could severely disrupt financial markets or a major earthquake in China could destroy a significant part of global rare earth element production, negatively affecting the production of many high-tech products.

Lesson 4: Underused capital, stock, and people can be assets as well as liabilities, and regulation is required to ensure adequate buffers in strategic sectors

The audit profession and management schools' implementation of mark-to-market accounting and quarterly, if not daily, reporting based on current valuations has become part of the problem. Working capital and stocks are priced as liabilities and, just as in the financial sector capital not leveraged or used is regarded as unproductive, in the manufacturing sector stocks in warehouses or staff not fully employed are seen as liabilities. The reduction in spare capacity is a management imperative imposed in order to survive the regular scrutiny of analysts and auditors. Increasingly this applies to the public sector and utilities, too. For instance, the stocks of oxygen bottles, bandages, spare beds, and spare nursing capacity are being run down as hospitals come under pressure to reduce their tied-up working capital and become "lean and mean." The corporatization of public assets and utilities has seen staffing and resources treated as commercial considerations. The result is that spare capacity and stocks, rather than being valued as assets, are valued as liabilities. The implication is that increasingly all parts of the system are less able to withstand shocks or respond to unexpected demand or failures in the supply chain. A pandemic that required more hospital beds would quickly overwhelm capacity and the supply of drugs in most societies. In finance, inadequate supplies of capital revealed in the financial crisis are being addressed through regulations that require minimum levels of capital, liquid assets, and stable funding. The enforcement of regulations regarding buffers in vital services is similarly required.

The financial crisis has translated into austerity packages across Europe and the United States, which have translated into budget cuts in vital services. Almost invariably this has led to even less spare capacity and tolerance for shocks in countries suffering from austerity, making their societies particularly vulnerable to the next systemic shocks. In such circumstances, there is an even greater role for regulation in ensuring that industrial production as well as vital public services and systems are maintained.

Lesson 5: Competition policy needs to address the geographical risks that emanate from the concentration of industry in specific localities

Competition policy can play a key role in improving certain dimensions of system stability. In particular, such policy can seek to guard against the risk that any one firm or supplier will be too big to fail in terms of the consequences for society. In competition policy, more attention needs to be paid to geography. For example, competition policy that allowed many firms to co-locate in one place that was prone to flooding or might be overwhelmed by a pandemic or terror attack would not provide comfort. Ensuring that production facilities, as well as vital backups such as data centers or key personnel, are not all in the same geographical location is as vital as ensuring that one or two firms do not account for all production. Indeed, it may be better from a risk management perspective to have international firms with backup and operational capacity that is globally dispersed than to have the majority of firms or suppliers concentrated in one location.

Regulation to ensure the stability of networks is hard to reconcile with the idea of a free market and free enterprise. It can harm short-term profits and outrage firms' shareholders. However, the benefits of governments and society ensuring system stability and accordingly sustainable and more predictable economic development in the face of systemic risks far outweigh the costs that may arise from systemic catastrophes.

4

❦

Infrastructure Risks

So far we have examined the risks associated with globalization emanating from cross-border flows of finance and physical goods. We have shown that connectivity in both the financial sector and the real economy has increased dramatically in the twenty-first century and that global governance has failed to match the speed of global integration. The resulting governance gap has led to systemic risk in the financial sector and to instability in the global supply chain network.

Global supply chains and financial systems operate on the foundation of increasingly sophisticated infrastructure networks. Infrastructure includes the freight and travel networks touched on in chapter 3 but also the world's energy grid and the information superhighway that has given us the World Wide Web. Infrastructure underlies and provides the framework for the networks we have already examined and thus facilitates the creation and growth of these networks. Yet infrastructure can itself become a vector of systemic instabilities and in its design and operation can become a source of systemic risk.

The focus of this chapter is on considering infrastructural risk from three perspectives. First, because infrastructure underlies all other sectors, shortcomings in infrastructure spread to other domains with particular virulence—an electrical glitch can lead to a financial collapse, an airport closure can disrupt a global supply chain, and an Internet crash can destroy communications arrays, with infrastructure collapses quickly cascading across sector boundaries. Second, the growing complexity of infrastructure systems and the significance of a small number of increasingly connected nodes mean that particular pinch points in the system are sources of instability. Britain's Heathrow and a handful of other airports serve as Europe's gateway. A few oil refining and transshipment centers account for most U.S. fuel. Power, communication, financial, and other systems are increasingly geographically concentrated, with little real option to relocate. Third, the pace of population and economic growth and the rapid rise in connectivity and technological change mean that in much of the world the supply of infrastructure has lagged further and further behind demand. Many of the networks on which existing transport, water, and sanitation systems rely in the advanced economies are more than 50 years old and in some cases more than a century old and are operating well beyond their design capacity. With the economic crisis reducing the capital allocated to investment in new building and maintenance, a growing number of societies are suffering from increased aging of infrastructure. In this chapter we look at the risks in three infrastructural sectors: transport, energy, and the Internet, then draw lessons for global infrastructure and more broadly for the management of systemic risk.

TRANSPORTATION

There are two dimensions of systemic risk in transport infrastructure today. The first dimension has to do with *complexity* and *efficiency*. Today transport networks are operating at close to capacity, and chokepoints such as airports (for instance, Chicago's O'Hare) or junctures (for example, the Suez Canal) process significant shares of regional and even global traffic with wafer-thin margins of flexibility. Through economies of scale, key ports can process far more traffic than smaller competitors and can claim ever-larger regional shares. Similarly, cargo lines using larger and larger ships and planes to transport goods efficiently in bulk have managed to push smaller players out of the market. An over-reliance on critical nodes and lines means that natural disasters and human error are more likely to be amplified and become systemic failures.

The second dimension of systemic risk in infrastructure is that, as well as creating a risk of cascading failures, globalization has increased the *vulnerability* of these critical nodes. As many infrastructure systems become outdated and are undermonitored, they become more vulnerable. High-volume traffic means that there is little time for maintenance. Meanwhile, the international nature of these nodes makes national regulation incomplete and less effective. These two risks can be illustrated simply: *complexity* means that a failure at one node (for example, an airport) is likely to have systemic consequences that could easily affect multiple sectors of the economy, multiple countries, and millions of only indirectly connected global citizens. *Vulnerability* means that this one node is more likely to fail.

Spatial Risks

In recent years there have been numerous examples of hazards striking the transport network and hence being turned into systemic events. The largest-scale example is the impact of Icelandic volcano Eyjafjallajökull's eruption on 14 April 2010. The resulting ash cloud was carried across Europe and had effects worldwide. The particles of volcanic ash consisted of "small jagged pieces of rock, mineral and natural glass" that ranged in size from as small as 0.001 millimeters ($\frac{1}{25,000}$ inch) to 2 millimeters ($\frac{1}{12}$ inch).[1] The cloud forced many countries to halt air traffic for six consecutive days amid fears that particles would disrupt plane engines and flight paths. The United Nations Environment Programme reports that the delays affected hundreds of thousands of travelers worldwide, resulting in US$2.2 billion in lost revenue for commercial airlines.[2] A study by the British consultancy Oxford Economics found that losses from the wasted productivity of stranded workers amounted to US$490 million and furthermore that missed visitor spending, for instance in hotels and restaurants, amounted to losses of US$1.6 billion for destination economies.[3] The forgone tourism, refunded payments for plane tickets, and marooned workers directly created wide-ranging costs, but the indirect effects felt through the impact on supply chains and production systems exceeded the direct impact, reflecting the nature of interdependencies in the contemporary world.

The world economy is highly dependent on the movement of goods by air, and many industries were directly affected by an inability to transport stock due to the eruption. Drug companies and agricultural producers suffered losses on "perishable goods," and even organ transplants had to be

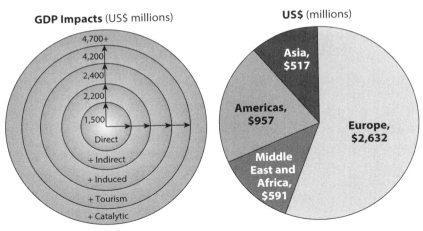

GDP Impacts (US$ millions)

US$ (millions)

Figure 4.1. The global impact of the Eyjafjallajökull eruption. Oxford Economics implies that these costs relate to the immediate disruption of air traffic in the weeks following the eruption. Oxford Economics, 2010, *The Economic Impacts of Air Travel Restrictions Due to Volcanic Ash*, report prepared for Airbus (Oxford, UK: Oxford Economics), 5. Used with permission.

canceled as Europe's skies were suddenly emptied.[4] The aggregate impact of the eruption was estimated to be a loss of about $5 billion in global GDP, with the negative impact not restricted to Europe (figure 4.1).

Although Eyjafjallajökull's eruption was a particularly large-scale event, disruptions of transport infrastructure from natural disasters are not rare. In February 2012, worsening weather conditions caused the closure of all of Italy's main motorways.[5] Because the Autostrade were so heavily used and backup routes were underdeveloped, leading global logistics company Compass Worldwide Logistics anticipated that "collections and deliveries of freight [would be] severely affected and delays ... inevitable."[6] Similarly, snowfall and cold during the winter of 2010 led to the suspension of numerous flights and train services in London and to the temporary closure of production plants.[7] Here also, the concentration of transport meant that one failure interrupted the efficient functioning of many global supply chains.

Vulnerability is not limited to concentration and over-reliance on a single node or network link, such as an airport or highway. More fragmented transport systems could be equally vulnerable to the disruptions described above. More airports or road networks would not have curbed the impact of the volcanic ash, snowfall, or floods. Geographical concentration in terms of over-reliance on regional nodes and linkages plays a role, too. If regional connections between nodes are knocked out (for example, during a widespread flood), the possibility of rapidly switching to a different transport network within the affected area or falling back on external transport networks such as airlifts is limited.

The emergence of transport hubs and geographical concentration has implications for other forms of systemic risk, including those arising from pandemics and the concentration of finance in certain geographical localities. These themes are discussed elsewhere (in chapters 1, 6, and 7).

Vulnerability

Disruptions of transport networks are not limited to natural disasters or attacks, and human error can equally cause the failure of crucial nodes. The capacity for oversight of personnel is lagging well behind the growth of the networks in usage and complexity. In April 2011, some 6,000 tons of excess cargo accumulated at India's Chennai Airport due to administrative failures by the Airport Authority of India and a shortage of manpower from the subcontracted agency Bhadra International.[8] Similarly, in 2010 a lack of space at Guarulhos Airport in Brazil led to more than eight thousand occurrences of missing cargo.[9] It is also worth noting that such disruptions are not always accidental. In February 2012, for example, strikes of the union of air traffic controllers at Frankfurt Airport led to the cancellation of 22 percent of daily flights.[10] That even a *planned* upset, as opposed to an unpredictable hazard, could have such a dramatic affect on airport operation shows how underdeveloped existing safeguards are. Virtually all Europeans have experienced the cascading impact of a strike, and Londoners have become familiar with the frustrations arising from cancellations of public transport.

Lean management practices compound the vulnerabilities. Snowfall of under 2 inches (5 centimeters) at London's Heathrow airport in 2013 led to extensive delays and cancellations arising from inadequate investment in snow-clearing or de-icing equipment. Even when the airport was reopened, small perturbations to the deployment of personnel, equipment, or flights resulted in cascading consequences because the airport operates at 98 percent capacity.[11]

Rapid Globalization and Challenges for Governance

The rising risk and the associated cost of disruptions to increasingly complex networks make dealing with these vulnerabilities an essential but difficult and hence often neglected task for leaders. Transport is a particularly troublesome issue for politicians. The decisions they make tend to be big and bulky and to have high short-term financial, environmental, and other costs and significant political fallout, whereas the benefits are longer-term, diffuse, and often manifested beyond the life of the government. The political dances around building vitally needed additional airport capacity in South East England or in Frankfurt am Main, Germany, are indicative of the political challenge.

Major infrastructure investments are slow to be implemented and hard to undo, so mistakes have long-term negative consequences. Given the long lead and lag times between design and ultimate use, typically 10 to 20 years by the time projects are completed, they rarely have remained fit for their original purpose. Indeed, what initially seemed to be optimal civil engineering sometimes turns out to be detrimental. A historical example is the 1909 Burnham Plan for the city of Chicago, which has led to modern-day inefficiency and delays due to the failure to anticipate both the volume of modern freight traffic and the relevance of access to the city's waterfront (among other things).[12]

Examples such as this abound and are of particular concern in the current epoch, when society is undergoing rapid transformation as infrastructure investments lag further and further behind. Those societies, such as China, that are able to devote the necessary attention, funding, and political capital to investments in infrastructure are unusual and, as a result, are significantly improving their competitiveness, whereas most other countries are slipping behind due to their lagging pace of investment.

ENERGY

In February 2011, the *New York Times* reported that the uprising in Egypt at the time raised concerns about a potential blocking of the Suez Canal, which would lead to risk for the transport of oil.[13] This is another example of vulnerability arising from a concentrated transport hub, and it reflects the importance of fuel and energy in the world today, not least for transport systems.[14] In the United States, for example, the transportation of goods by truck and freight consumed 42 billion gallons of fuel in 2007.[15] In France, such transport of goods generates 14 percent of national greenhouse gas emissions, having grown at 26 percent per annum from 1990 to 2006.[16] Failure at the energy level of infrastructure can create problems in many other systems and may thus be conceived of as a systemic risk.

Connectivity

Just as extreme connectivity in the transport network could act to spread disease, with flights carrying infections around the world (more on this in chapter 6), the energy network can become a conduit for system overload and the diffusion of risks. A well-known example is the blackout that struck the U.S. Northeast on 14 August 2003. The blackout was a systemic failure that started with a problem in the Ohio Eastlake generating plant.[17] The innocuous event of a tree falling in the U.S. Midwest led to the tripping of multiple East coast power generators as a result of grid failures.[18] It cast 9,300 square miles into darkness and left 50 million people without electricity for, in some cases, more than 30 hours.[19] The overall cost of that tree's falling is estimated to have ranged from US$6 to US$10 billion.[20] Here connectivity meant that although efficiency could be achieved through the rapid and unhindered transmission of power, risk was being spread along with electricity. Figure 4.2 gives the sequence of the blackout's unfolding and shows how, from Ohio to Michigan and then eventually to the densely populated East coast, power surges spread through the energy infrastructure.

Vulnerability

Although exceptional in size, the Northeast blackout was not exceptional in nature, and such failures will increase in number if globalization continues to outpace precautions for resilience. This is because globalization, as well as enabling the spread of failure through power grids, has also left these aging networks particularly vulnerable. In July 2006, a nine-day

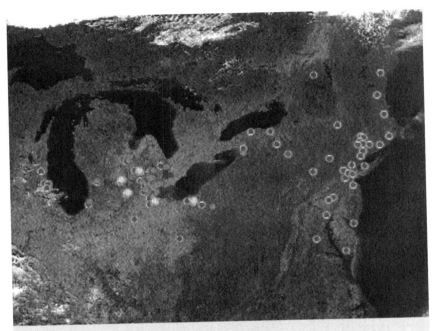

BLACKOUT SEQUENCE OF EVENTS, AUGUST 14, 2003

1:58 p.m. The Eastlake, Ohio, generating plant shuts down. The plant is owned by First Energy, a company that had experienced extensive recent maintenance problems, including a major nuclear-plant incident.

3:06 p.m. A First Energy 345-kV transmission line fails south of Cleveland, Ohio.

3:17 p.m. Voltage dips temporarily on the Ohio portion of the grid. Controllers take no action, but power shifted by the first failure onto another power line causes it to sag into a tree at 3:32 p.m., bringing it offline as well. While Mid West ISO and First Energy controllers try to understand the failures, they fail to inform system controllers in nearby states.

3:41 and 3:46 p.m. Two breakers connecting First Energy's grid with American Electric Power are tripped.

4:05 p.m. A sustained power surge on some Ohio lines signals more trouble building.

4:09:02 p.m. Voltage sags deeply as Ohio draws 2 GW of power from Michigan.

4:10:34 p.m. Many transmission lines trip out, first in Michigan and then in Ohio, blocking the eastward flow of power. Generators go down, creating a huge power deficit. In seconds, power surges out of the East, tripping East coast generators to protect them, and the blackout is on.

Figure 4.2. The Northeast blackout of 14 August 2003. ISO, Independent System Operator. OrbView-2 satellite image courtesy of GeoEye, from Eric Lerner, 2003, "What's Wrong with the Electric Grid?," *Industrial Physicist* 9: 8–13, image on 13. Used with permission.

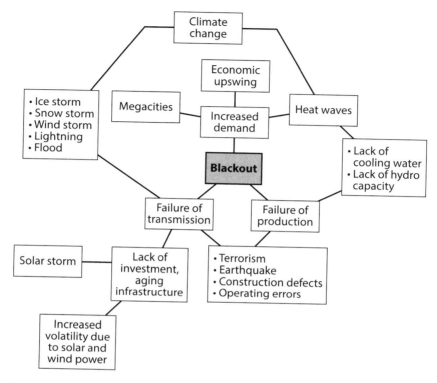

Figure 4.3. Potential causes of power blackouts. Cro Forum, 2011, "Power Blackout Risks: Risk Management Options," Emerging Risk Initiative Position Paper, November, 9, accessed 25 January 2013, http://www.agcs.allianz.com/assets/PDFs/Special%20and%20stand-alone%20articles/Power_Blackout_Risks.pdf. Used with permission.

power outage in Queens, New York, left 100,000 people without electricity. The cause of the disruption was deterioration of the 30- to 60-year-old cables that serviced the area.[21] As the Cro Forum, a professional risk management group, noted in a survey of global power blackout risks in 2011, "Typically power blackouts are not caused by a single event but by a combination of several deficiencies. There is no outage known where a faultless grid collapsed completely due to a single cause" (figure 4.3 provides an overview of potential threats).[22]

The two distinct but at times interrelated problems of failures due to complexity and the over-reliance on outdated systems are by no means limited to advanced economies such as the United States or Europe. Such risk precipitated the systemic power failure of March 1999 in Brazilian cities such as São Paulo and Rio de Janeiro.[23] The late 1990s saw Brazil experiencing an investment crisis, so the power grid was improperly maintained and underprotected. This meant that when lightning struck a power station in Bauru, São Paulo, most of the plant's 440-kilovolt circuits tripped.[24] Because of underinvestment, the system was fragile, and the loss of Bauru created a gap in the grid, which in turn caused other stations to shut down. At the time, the Itapúa hydroelectric plant on the Brazil–Paraguay border was the world's largest power station, and the dam there was forced to supply the electricity missing from the 440-kilovolt grid. Unfortunately, the corresponding surge in usage along the 750-kilovolt AC and 600-kilovolt DC lines that connected Itapúa tripped as they were pushed far beyond their safe capacity. This led to a power cut that left 60 million people in the dark and whose effects reached far beyond darkened light bulbs. Military police in Rio were enlisted to stem riots amid widespread fears of looting. More than 60,000 people were stuck in the São Paulo subway. Lifeless traffic lights caused havoc on the roads.[25] In short, the Bauru lightning strike led to cascading failure, highlighting the systemic risks inherent in a stretched power system.

The problem in South Brazil was twofold: the energy network suffered from inadequate maintenance and investment but was also not designed with sufficient resilience to enable alternative grid and power generation capability. Over-reliance on single or stretched networks and overloaded nodes increases the potential for cascading failure.

Another example comes from July 2006, the same month as the New York blackouts, when a violent thunderstorm in St. Louis took out an oil refinery, leaving 700,000 people without electricity.[26] An over-reliance on the ConocoPhillips plant, the United States' third-largest oil refinery, meant that the area did not have a backup to its electrical hub.[27] It was therefore inevitable that when a natural disaster struck (and we discuss in chapter 5 how globalization and climate change are making such hazards more frequent), the energy network and all systems reliant on it came crashing down.

The networks for gas and oil supply are similarly complex and vulnerable. The U.S. gas pipeline network is as exposed to failure as the fragile electrical system that faltered during the 2003 Northeast blackout

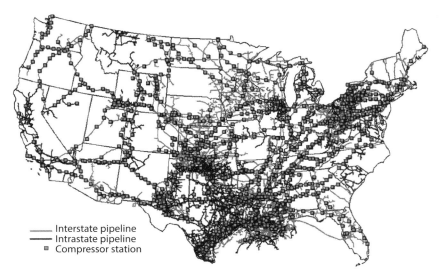

Figure 4.4. U.S. national gas pipeline map, 2008. EIA (Energy Information Administration), 2008, "U.S. Natural Gas Pipeline Compressor Stations Illustration," Energy Information Administration, accessed 4 February 2013, http://www.eia.gov/pub/oil_gas/natural_gas/analysis_publications/ngpipeline/compressorMap.html.

(figure 4.4). The high density of nodes in the Southeast, as well as the extreme connectivity displayed, increases the risk of cascading breakdowns. Furthermore, oil and gas face additional risks in that they rely not only on internal networks for distribution but also on imports. This was starkly illustrated in 2012 in the impact of Hurricane Sandy on New York, which had dramatic effects on energy and fuel supplies in New York and beyond.

In Europe, gas is supplied through pipelines from the north (Norway) and the east (Russia) as well as being shipped from the Middle East and Africa (Qatar, Egypt, Libya, Algeria, and Nigeria).[28] The complexity and length of these networks as well as the significance of critical nodes, as in the case of oil, are worldwide sources of vulnerability (figures 4.5 and 4.6). The task of monitoring and safeguarding these systems cannot be confined to national approaches. These networks, in essence, have become arteries for globalization and can be thought of as global public goods that require a greater degree of collective management. The management of systemic risk in the energy sector is both a national and an international imperative.

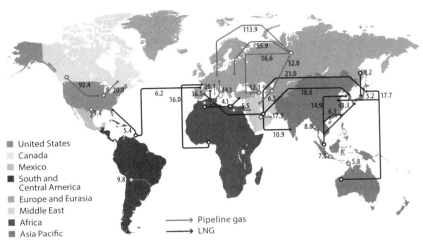

Figure 4.5. Major trade movements: Gas (billions of cubic meters), 2010. BP (British Petroleum), 2011, *BP Statistical Review of World Energy, June 2011* (London: British Petroleum), 29, accessed 4 February 2013, http://www.bp.com/assets/bp_internet/globalbp/globalbp_uk_english/reports_and_publications/statistical_energy_review_2011/STAGING/local_assets/pdf/statistical_review_of_world_energy_full_report_2011.pdf. Used with permission.

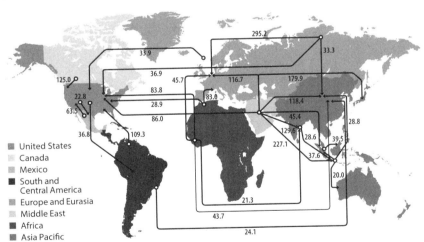

Figure 4.6. Major trade movements: Oil (millions of tons), 2010. BP (British Petroleum), 2011, *BP Statistical Review of World Energy, June 2011* (London: British Petroleum), 19, accessed 4 February 2013, http://www.bp.com/assets/bp_internet/globalbp/globalbp_uk_english/reports_and_publications/statistical_energy_review_2011/STAGING/local_assets/pdf/statistical_review_of_world_energy_full_report_2011.pdf. Used with permission.

THE INTERNET

Whereas transport and energy systems have evolved over hundreds of years, the Internet is a relatively recent phenomenon. In many respects it has defined the twenty-first century, with virtual connectivity using the vector of a physical infrastructure to allow communication and information flows that have become the nervous system of our global economy and society.

The Internet has grown at an astounding pace (figures 4.7 and 4.8). Although there were 428,269,181 Internet users in 2000, this number grew to 2,301,333,683 in 2011,[29] a more than fivefold increase. In 2011 the number of networked devices equaled the world population. This growth will continue, and by 2015 the number of networked devices is anticipated to be double the number of global inhabitants. In the same year, the number of wireless devices is expected to surpass the number of wired ones. In 2013 total Internet data traffic exceeded 1 exabyte per *day*, or 1 million (10^{18}) terabytes. This colossal amount of information was the same as *annual* data traffic only 10 years before.[30] The historical context of cyber growth can be seen in figures 4.7 and 4.8. These diagrams illustrate both the increase in volume and a change in the *nature* of connectivity: it was only in 2003, for example, that the Internet became primarily a consumer platform. The figures show the growth of opportunities for businesses using the Internet and the rise of e-commerce.

Cyber Risk

Parallel to financial and physical connectivity, the Internet carries its own risks. These risks can be physical as well as virtual—they can relate to the network structures and hardware in addition to computer codes and the transmission of reliable data. Both the physical and the virtual networks that underpin the Internet matter and are essential for the integrity of the system. However, most analyses of cyber risk tend to focus on the vulnerability of the virtual network and the issue of cybersecurity.[31]

As the number of institutions and individuals active on the Internet has increased, so have the gains to exploitation. This is partly because

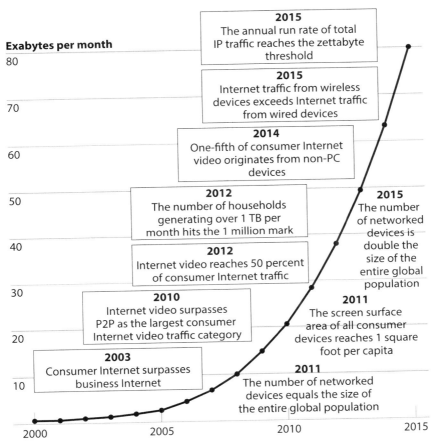

Exabytes per month

2015
The annual run rate of total IP traffic reaches the zettabyte threshold

2015
Internet traffic from wireless devices exceeds Internet traffic from wired devices

2014
One-fifth of consumer Internet video originates from non-PC devices

2012
The number of households generating over 1 TB per month hits the 1 million mark

2015
The number of networked devices is double the size of the entire global population

2012
Internet video reaches 50 percent of consumer Internet traffic

2010
Internet video surpasses P2P as the largest consumer Internet video traffic category

2011
The screen surface area of all consumer devices reaches 1 square foot per capita

2003
Consumer Internet surpasses business Internet

2011
The number of networked devices equals the size of the entire global population

Figure 4.7. Milestones of connectivity, 2000–2015. IP, Internet protocol; P2P, peer to peer; TB, terabyte. Cisco, 2011b, "Entering the Zettabyte Era," article no longer available from http://www.cisco.com; however, this figure is reproduced by Daily Wireless, 2011, "Cisco's Traffic Forecast," 1 June, accessed 7 February 2013, http://www.dailywireless .org/2011/06/01/ciscos-traffic-forecast/.

of an increased reliance on the efficiency gains offered by digitalization. Networked computers are used to provide public and private services that now permeate all aspects of our lives. Attacks have the potential to bring commerce and social engagement as well as crucial public services, such as e-government, water, power, and communication, to a halt.

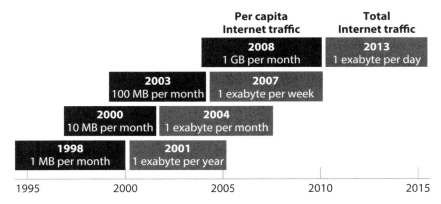

Figure 4.8. Connectivity in historical context, 1995–2015. Cisco, 2012, "The Zettabyte Era," white paper, May, 5, accessed 4 February 2013, http://www.cisco.com/en/US/solutions/collateral/ns341/ns525/ns537/ns705/ns827/VNI_Hyperconnectivity_WP.html.

The dangers of over-reliance on networked computers became evident following a series of attacks on Estonia in 2007. During a dispute with Russia over the removal of a Soviet statue, the country suffered three successive waves of *blanket cyberaggression.* Hackers used hundreds of thousands of captured "zombie" computers to flood Estonia with Internet traffic. Dozens of websites were compromised, including those of the Estonian president, most of the government ministries, and two of the country's largest banks. It is unclear how deep the damage went or to what extent networks were compromised. There is no reliable estimate of the financial cost. However, Estonia is unusually dependent on e-commerce—for instance, 90 percent of its bank transactions are conducted online.[32] The damage is therefore likely to have been substantial.

Another risk stems from *targeted cyberaggression* intended to strike specific government or industrial control systems. National e-government services as well as the national infrastructure, including power plants, electricity grids, and oil pipelines, use networked control systems to decrease their operational costs. The concentration of information and power in these digital systems creates points of vulnerability that are open to attack by malevolent forces. One example of such an attack is the deployment of the Stuxnet virus, discovered in 2010, which is widely thought to have caused damage to a uranium enrichment plant in Iran. The virus is believed to have been developed for this purpose by experts with detailed knowledge of Iranian systems and with the involvement of at least one government.

Another threat to the virtual integrity of the Internet is *cybercrime.* The notion of cybercrime is used to denote security threats motivated by financial gain (although in many countries acts of cyberaggression are illegal, too). Cybercrime differs from conventional crime in terms of automation and scale. Sending thousands of e-mail messages is essentially costless, and only one person must be gullible enough to open an attachment granting the hacker access to the Internet system via a "back door" to make the scam a success. A well-known example of a cybercrime is the unleashing of the waledac botnet, a computer worm that spread rapidly across the globe (taking control of hundreds of thousands of PCs capable of sending out an estimated 1.5 billion spam messages) before Microsoft was able to obtain the necessary legal injunctions to shut down the command and control servers.[33]

Cyberaggression is a problem because it could cause the breakdown of essential infrastructure systems or significant financial damage. Cybercrime is unlikely to pose this kind of systemic risk because the attacks are uncoordinated. The real threat it poses is that the inconvenience created for individuals will drive them from open and flexible machines such as PCs to more limited machines and discourage experimentation on the Internet.[34] The result will be less innovation, and the gains to connectivity will not be maximized.

The distinction between cyberaggression and cybercrime is becoming increasingly blurred. New forms of cybercrime, such as cyber espionage or cyber spying—the practice of secretly obtaining information or industrial secrets from other individuals, groups, or rivals—is likely to be on the rise. Such practices are highly secretive and usually illegal, although they may not involve any straightforward financial payoff. Other forms of cyberaggression are also on the rise—including cyberbullying and even cyber extortion.[35] Cyberbullying typically takes the form of escalating online abuse directed at an individual with the potential for catastrophic consequences for those that are the victims of these actions.[36]

Traditional tools for discouraging aggressive and criminal behavior are ineffective in cyberspace. The Internet allows attacks to be conducted under conditions of near-perfect anonymity. It is very hard to trace the source of a particular security breach because attacks are often conducted from compromised computers belonging to innocent bystanders. Even when an attack has been successfully traced, the evidence can be destroyed by a sophisticated cybercriminal. The damage can be compounded by the ability of a cyberattack to promote misinformation that can potentially be used to cause panic, influence markets, and generally cause instability.

Deterrence is also rendered ineffective because such crimes are generally multijurisdictional. An attacker residing in Russia can use compromised computers based in the United States to launch an attack on Estonia. Even if authorities in Estonia managed to trace the attack back to Russia, how would they prosecute the criminal? Unless Russia wished to cooperate, whether by extraditing the individual or prosecuting under its own laws, deterrence would be impossible. Unfortunately, cooperation is often denied—in fact, Russia did deny Estonia cooperation following the attacks of 2007 despite evidence that many of the attackers were Russian.

These two factors combine to render traditional security measures largely useless in the cyber realm. As the number of Internet users increases, the financial returns for cybercriminality seem set to grow as rapidly, drawing more individuals into the lucrative field. The problem of cybersecurity is therefore twofold: How can we minimize the risk of systemic breakdown due to cyberaggression? And how can we limit cybercrime while ensuring that the innovative capabilities of information and communication technology are preserved?

The complexity of cyber risk transcends national boundaries and leaves all countries vulnerable. Although cybersecurity is emerging as a critical concern in the twenty-first century, there is currently no central governance agency focused on cybersecurity issues. We need a unified front in international policy and associated governance to monitor the growing evidence of cybervulnerability, deter cyber risks, and offer support when attacks are successful. New models for understanding and measuring the relative effectiveness of protection strategies are needed, as well as global platforms through which to share best practices and data associated with cyberattacks.

In parallel to the dangers associated with innovation in financial crises—and, as we will show, in pandemics—innovation is the key to the success of computer viruses and worms. Dangerous viruses use vulnerabilities in common programs and operating systems to gain access or cause damage to a machine. Once these viruses have been released, they can be analyzed and their exploits, which are a sequence of commands that take advantage of the vulnerabilities, can be fixed. However, this process can take a while. By the time a software update is released, effective viruses have often infected millions of machines, and because users do not update their programs regularly, these viruses can continue spreading for months afterward.

Reliance on the Internet also creates other points of vulnerability. Large underwater cables carry much of the digital information sent between continents. Damage to these cables has the ability to cause widespread "Internet blackouts" across entire regions. In 2008 Internet services to the Middle East and South Asia were disrupted following the apparent breaking of the cables near the Suez Canal by ships' anchors. The following year, damage to a cable resulted in a complete loss of Internet service to several countries in West Africa, and in subsequent years there have been a number of similar outages. We take for granted the ability to use networked computers. Finding global solutions to the growing vulnerability of these new arteries of global and national commerce and public services is essential if they are to continue to be a driving force of globalization and development.

Complexity and Cyber Risk

The complexity of cyberspace means that it is susceptible to unintended mistakes. In January 2009, the uncertainty surrounding the Internet was manifested when a "human error" at Google brought down its website for about 40 minutes, causing panic among Internet users who feared "serious implications for internet commerce."[37] Six months later, the death of singer Michael Jackson and the subsequent "inundation" of the search engine with his name caused Google to falter again, while social networking services such as Facebook and Twitter experienced spikes in the volume of traffic and slowdowns.[38] Developments in the cyber domain will continue to change the fundamental nature of connectivity across the globe.

The Google, Twitter, and Facebook examples imply another kind of infrastructure risk in the cyber domain. The reliance of significant Internet systems on server hubs operating at high capacity in a relatively small number of geographical locations makes them vulnerable to failure. Facebook, for example, has become the most visited site on the Internet.[39] It relies on a remarkable and rapidly growing network of servers. Data Center Knowledge, a website that provides news and analysis on information technology innovation, reports, "Technical presentations by Facebook staff suggest that as of June 2010 the company was running at least 60,000 servers in its data centers, up from 30,000 in 2009 and 10,000 back in April 2008."[40] Firms such as OVH (with 120,000 servers as of April 2012), Akamai Technologies (105,000 servers as of March 2012), SoftLayer (100,000 servers as of December 2011), Intel (75,000 servers as of August 2011), or 1&1 internet (more than 70,000 servers as of February 2010) are relying on an even more complex system of physical infrastructure.[41] Here there is a trade-off with geographical diversification, which requires more concerted management effort.

These networks are over-reliant on a limited number of clusters of servers and are vulnerable to the links between them, as in the examples of the severing of Internet cables between regions noted above. To cite a slightly different example, in October 2011 British Telecom was unable to provide Internet services to more than a quarter of a million customers after an interruption of power supplies. The liability of Internet providers to meet any compensation claims, particularly from companies potentially exposed to a loss of business or damage to their systems, remains unclear.[42] These failures reinforce the point that failure in the physical infrastructure supporting the Internet can rapidly become systemic because so much of the economy today relies on that infrastructure to function. Overuse of sole network cables or servers also quickly leads to problems when one overconnected node fails, as our examples show.

Social Risks

In chapter 7 we examine social risks of the Internet in more detail. Here it is worth noting that the Internet has the potential to increase

Billions of users

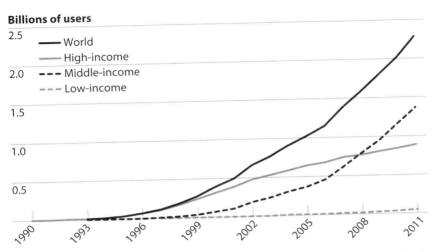

Figure 4.9. Number of Internet users by income bracket, 1990–2011. World Bank, 2013, *World Development Indicators*, World DataBank, accessed 12 February, http://databank.worldbank.org/data/home.aspx. Used with permission.

inequality due to the digital divide in access and affordability to connections. As the Internet developed, its transformative effects did not reach all regions equally. Figure 4.9 shows that the worldwide number of Internet users is rapidly increasing in the aggregate; the growth rate is higher in high- and middle-income countries than in low-income countries. In a world that increasingly relies on Web-based businesses, Internet sales platforms, and other Internet communication, this discrepancy increases inequality by disadvantaging societies and individuals who are not connected.

The Internet–income disparity deepens economic divides. It also creates risks in cybersecurity for low-income countries. Disparity in Internet access goes hand in hand with disparity in knowledge and familiarity with the World Wide Web. Those who are regularly exposed to the advantages and disadvantages of the Internet are better able to protect themselves from risk. Figure 4.10 demonstrates this by showing the development of secure Internet servers over the first decade of the twenty-first century. As can be seen, the numbers are far higher in North America and the EU, with regions like Latin America, the Middle East, and North Africa lagging behind.

Per one million users

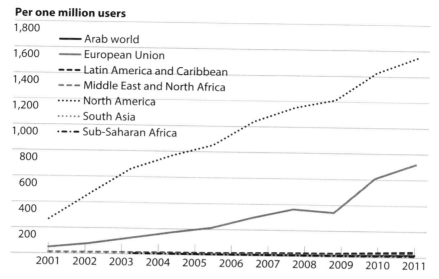

Figure 4.10. Secure Internet servers (per 1 million people), 2001–11. World Bank, 2013, *World Development Indicators*, World DataBank, accessed 12 February, http://databank.worldbank.org/. Used with permission.

LESSONS FOR GLOBAL INFRASTRUCTURE

This chapter has characterized various risks for systemic failure within global infrastructure. This infrastructure is a composite system made up of numerous networks. These include the transport and energy grids that have enabled international trade and global supply chains but equally the physical structure that supports the Internet. We have shown that these individual systems require strengthening.

Governments are for the most part responsible for critical infrastructure, even if the distribution and servicing of this infrastructure can be privatized or, in the case of the Internet, be managed by a nongovernmental organization. In terms of the *general* lessons for mitigating infrastructure risk, we suggest two approaches. First, we need more concerted efforts globally to understand complex infrastructure systems and detect systemic vulnerabilities. Second, legitimate and authoritative institutions are required to devise and implement policy quickly in the face of rapidly changing circumstances.

Lesson 1: Increasing the resilience of infrastructure underpins global integration and provides the foundation for globalization

Our analysis in chapters 2 and 3 showed that the world structures for finance and trade are increasingly complex and globally interconnected. In this chapter we have provided a number of illustrative examples of how the infrastructure that underpins these networks is similarly complex. Infrastructure systems have evolved into complex networks that span numerous jurisdictions, and for these and the other reasons we have outlined, the consequences of disruptions are becoming more difficult to anticipate. Failures have repercussions that transcend national borders and enter domains supervised by regulators of all nationalities. We are *all* mutually benefiting from the integration that infrastructure has facilitated. Oil pipelines, servers, and airports transport fuel, information, and people around the globe at high speed. These systems rely on global actors. Currently their management has devolved to national governments, but if we are to be effective in mitigating systemic risks, the management of these risks must be undertaken in coordination by *different* nations. Understanding this necessitates coordinated regional or global governance with respect not only to financial regulation or the administration of trade flows but also to the design of efficient and resilient physical networks for other global systems. Policy making requires *systemic* thinking with a network-oriented approach to supervision and risk management at both the national and the regional and/or global level.

Lesson 2: Data and analysis are required to understand network dynamics

Taking a systemic approach requires the collection of relevant information. In the context of food security, Ross A. Hammond and Laurette Dubé emphasize policy makers' role in shaping and promoting an interdisciplinary research environment but also the "need to develop integrative longitudinal databases on key processes and outcomes . . . that are expected to have single and combined effects."[43] The "mapping of within- and cross-boundary knowledge is also a critical step toward realizing a systems approach and transdisciplinary tools," and these efforts should begin "with a concrete understanding of existing knowledge about connections within and between systems."[44] These authors' insights apply equally to the realm of global infrastructure and to the global governance of systemic risks in general. We need data and maps of critical systems in order to understand the key linkages and nodes and their evolution.

Lesson 3: There is a need to develop resilience in critical national and global infrastructure

The identification of key pathways and critical nodes provides the basis for creating a more robust and resilient infrastructure. Various options may be explored to build resilience. Regulation and competition policy have key roles in this regard. These policies should be concerned not simply with considerations such as the size of firms but also, importantly, with geographical location. The development of national transport and energy infrastructure to ensure that alternative supplies and systems are developed should be seen as a national priority. This includes using policy levers to distribute not only airports and energy generation and distribution systems but also the necessary backup capacity. The lessons of the Japanese tsunami, Hurricane Sandy's devastating impact on the U.S. East coast, and the Icelandic volcano need to be learned. These include, for example, the need for geographic diversification of backup routes, the stress testing of contingency plans well beyond historic experience, and diversification in fuel, communication, and other critical systems so no one source or node becomes uniquely critical for millions of people.

Lesson 4: Global cooperation is required to protect the integrity of the Internet and tackle cybercrime

The risk of hardware failures due to dependence on critical server systems and cables has been emphasized in this chapter. We have also highlighted the threat posed by cyberaggression and cybercrime, which threaten to overwhelm the Internet, leading to what could be "the end of the Internet."[45] Ensuring that the Internet is not overwhelmed requires global cooperation, which is currently lacking. In this as in a number of other areas, globalization and technological change have raced ahead of institutional capacity. This requires urgent attention by all our national leaders as well as by businesses and civil society, because all are vulnerable and have roles to play in ensuring the integrity of a trusted and open cyber system.

5

⊙⥿⊙

Ecological Risks

Our consideration of systemic risk has dealt with the instability of finance, trade, and infrastructure, which are all the products of economic development. We have touched on possible risks to these structures from natural disasters, and we have seen how events such as floods and storms can cause disruptions and overwhelm infrastructure and fragile supply chains. Typically, environmental hazards are described as "metarisks." Environmental disasters are classified as natural and unavoidable events, exogenous to the fragile systems we have analyzed. In this chapter we take a different view, analyzing environmental risk as an endogenous or integral consequence of globalization. This is because the severity, frequency, and impact of environmental hazards are increasingly shaped by the forces of globalization. In this sense not only the consequences, but also at times the causes, of natural disasters may be described as negative externalities of globalization.

Increasingly, the distinction between "natural" and man-made disasters is being blurred. Not only the causes, but also the implications, of virtually all disasters are the results of human action, as the differential impacts of hurricanes in Haiti and its neighbor the Dominican Republic (which shares the same island) attest. Similarly, the impact of Hurricane Sandy reflected the peculiarities of urbanization and investment in New York and New Jersey.

We draw a distinction between risk *from* and risk *to* the environment and examine each in turn. Natural systems and the environment do not respect national borders, and managing environmental systems requires action at all levels—global, national, and local. It has been argued that environmental degradation ought to be understood in "a global structural context." This reflects "increasing inadequacy of nation-state-centric theories in explaining the dynamic linkage between *global* capitalism and *local* environmental degradation."[1] One example is that we all individually need to make a contribution to lowering our carbon emissions, reducing our demand for energy, or recycling our waste. In this sense, all environmental actions, like political ones, are local and require individual choice.

The frequency and cost of what are defined as natural disasters appear to have increased markedly throughout the 1990s and 2000s (figure 5.1). The link between globalization and environmental risk appears intuitively obvious; more rapid economic growth requires more resource and energy use. The development of integrated production lines and the global fragmentation of supply chains have moved pollution to locations where it is increasingly hard to monitor and control, effectively outsourcing environmental degradation alongside production. On further examination, however, it is apparent that the relationship between globalization and environmental degradation is more complicated, as this chapter shows.

THE NATURE OF ENVIRONMENTAL RISK

Environmental risk can be understood in two distinct ways: it describes risks to the world ecosystem but also risks ensuing from it. We draw a distinction between the environment as a *source of risk* and the

Figure 5.1. Frequency of natural disasters (A) and associated financial costs (B) since 1960. A "disaster" is registered by CRED (the Centre for Research on the Epidemiology of Disasters) if at least one of the following has occurred: 10 or more fatalities, 100 or more people "affected," a call for international assistance, or the declaration of a state of emergency. Nicole Laframboise and Boileau Loko, 2012, "Natural Disasters: Mitigating Impact, Managing Risks," IMF Working Paper 12/245, International Monetary Fund, Washington, DC, 6 and 8, accessed 12 February 2013, http://www.imf.org/external/pubs/ft/wp/2012/wp12245.pdf.

A
Number

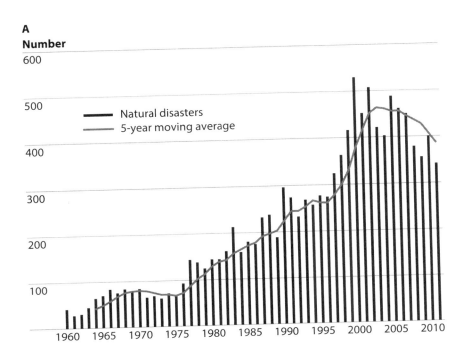

B
US$ (billions)

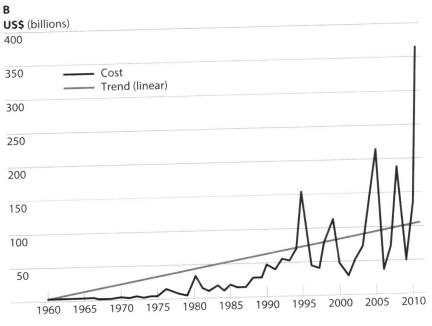

environment as a *system at risk*. To an extent, this was a separation used implicitly in some of our earlier chapters. Having such a multifaceted perspective on risk is an inevitable consequence of the connectivity and complexity that characterize the twenty-first century.

Separating the two aspects of environmental risk is becoming more complex. When Hurricane Sandy led to destruction on the U.S. East coast, it was clearly the result of risks arising from the environment. Yet a number of climate scientists, and indeed the mayor of New York, also attributed this destruction to climate change, reflecting human impact on the environment. Climatic events appear to have become more unstable and unpredictable as well as more frequent. Such trends are increasingly likely to translate into greater human and economic costs.

The impact of environmental and other events is affected by population growth and economic growth as well as by government policies that have sought to protect individuals and society from risk. Although specific policies and measures serve reasonably well within predictable limits, they may be increasing the cost of tail risks in an uncertain world. Examples include the Japanese tsunami, which breached a sea wall designed to keep out the ocean, and a similar breaching of sea defenses in New York by Hurricane Sandy.

Income growth means that the value of property and business is rising and any one impact has a much greater effect. Population growth means that there are many more people, and the pressures on land mean that in poor and rich countries alike, more and more people are locating themselves in flood plains, on valley floors, beside mountains, and along the coasts. In Europe and the United States, the migration of individuals to arid lands (such as southern Spain, Phoenix, or Las Vegas) has defied and compounded environmental pressures. This is testimony both to rising incomes (that allow the drilling of ever-deeper wells and water transmission over greater distances) and the deregulation of planning constraints (which defy long-term sustainability). To the extent that globalization is a key driver of wealth and development, it has increased both our risks from the environment and those to the environment.

In the United States, the implications of extreme weather events such as hurricanes are exacerbated by the perverse impact of flood and storm insurance. Legislation that compels insurance companies in the United States to smooth insurance premiums across different localities means that individuals and firms do not see or pay premiums for the true risks associated with their behavior. Town planning and insurance regulation that effectively encourage people to engage in more risky behavior means that more people are vulnerable to environmental risks as they locate properties on vulnerable shorelines or flood plains.

Environmental risk is different from risks arising from finance in that it is characterized by the interaction of man-made and natural systems. Our primary concern with man-made networks is that they reliably continue to work so that the structures they support will continue to run. In the case of environmental risk, the task of repairing networks and developing resilience in them is much more challenging given the complexity and long-term evolution of the systems. We cannot reproduce fossil fuels or recapture carbon as easily as we rebuild a bridge or re-erect a power line. We also do not understand the complex interactions between, for example, biodiversity and food or among the atmosphere and oceans and our weather systems. Our concern, therefore, should be with *preserving* rather than *recreating* or *replacing* existing systems. The risks to and from the environment have escalated with globalization, not least because, while the spillovers of actions beyond national borders are rising rapidly, the capacity for collective action to address them is lagging further and further behind.

The ecosystem is recognized as a valuable asset in itself, from both a fiscal and a humanitarian perspective.[2] The disruption of natural balances can lead to increased risk for other systems. These risks are not only relevant to "environmentalists" or communities dependent on affected systems: we know that environmental disruptions lead to extreme weather conditions and diseases that originate from the ecosystem and put vital systems (such as those for food and energy supplies, telecommunications, and manufacturing production) at risk. The two aspects of environmental risk are linked; as globalization creates risks to the environment, the resulting ecological disruptions cause risks from the biosphere. Figure 5.2 provides a graphic illustration of these complex interactions with reference to food security. The diagram maps the mutual dependencies between the environmental system and the food system and their links with the health and disease system (we comment on this in chapter 6, on pandemics) and with individual decision making (this relates to our analysis of social risks in chapter 7).

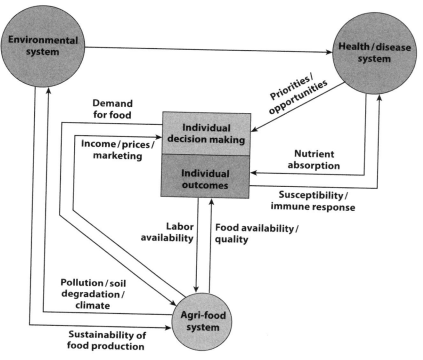

Figure 5.2. A systems framework for food and nutrition security. Ross A. Hammond and Laurette Dubé, 2012, "A Systems Science Perspective and Transdisciplinary Models for Food and Nutrition Security," *Proceedings of the National Academy of Sciences (PNAS)* 109 (31): 12356–12363, image on 12357.

Insofar as ecological stability is a public good, risk to the environment leads to negative externalities and is an example of the global commons problem. To manage these issues, we need to address the free rider problem. Most economists and environmental policy makers tend to agree that those responsible for environmental degradation should bear the costs (the "polluter pays" principle).[3] The problem we face is thus essentially reduced to quantifying the contributions of individual risk components and pricing environmental damage. The challenge faced by governance is mainly practical rather than conceptual, and in this chapter's conclusion we offer some applied lessons for environmental risk management.

RISKS *FROM* THE ENVIRONMENT

The increasing financial severity of natural disasters documented in figure 5.1 has been attributed to population growth and rising per capita incomes.[4] In simple terms, one consequence of globalization and development is more people (with far more to lose financially) living in increasingly confined spaces. This explanation does not capture the full extent of the interactions between either the environment and globalization or the environment and other sectors, but it does highlight the point that as more people accumulate more assets, the costs of disasters rise.

Climate Change and Disasters

Globalization has fueled global warming through development-related emissions. The effect of climate change has been to make the hazards themselves more frequent and of greater consequence in terms of their impact. We urgently need to manage these environmental risks.[5]

Rising water levels resulting from melting ice caps put large numbers of people at risk. More than half of the world's population lives within 60 kilometers of shorelines, and the rising tides are likely to bring flooding, the contamination of groundwater and crops, and the destruction of homes and livelihoods.[6] Previous chapters show how much smaller events have systemic consequences: flooding disrupted supply chains in Thailand; Hurricanes Katrina and Sandy severely disrupted the Gulf and East coasts of the United States, respectively; and storms affected Internet access in Kenya. The effects of such events are often drastic—the World Health Organization (WHO) reports that "approximately 600,000 deaths occurred worldwide as a result of weather related natural disasters in the 1990s."[7]

The direct effects of global warming go beyond melting ice caps. More variable rainfall, temperature, and wind patterns are likely to threaten the supply of fresh water and food, leading to drought, famine, and fatalities. Climate change also brings health risks, and WHO reports that "climate-sensitive diseases [are] among the largest global killers, with diarrhoea, malaria and protein-energy malnutrition alone causing more than 3 million deaths globally in 2004."[8] Furthermore, particularly warm summers have been frequent in recent years, causing an increase in heart and respiratory diseases. WHO references a number of studies suggesting that "the record high temperatures in Western Europe in the summer of 2003 were associated with a spike of an estimated 70,000 more deaths than the equivalent periods in previous years." WHO goes on to argue that rising temperatures have caused increased pollen and air-borne allergen counts, exacerbating the asthma of some 300 million people worldwide. Poor people and poor countries are particularly vulnerable to climate-related food and disease threats. WHO reports "over one third of these deaths occurring in Africa." Climate change has a highly unequal impact and may be anticipated to exacerbate the risks associated with poverty and inequality (see chapter 7).

Public health experts also report that "secondary or indirect impacts . . . may be associated with changes in ecologic systems and human population displacement."[9] The consequences include the destruction of the physical, social, and economic fabric of the affected society. In extreme cases, it may also lead to what can be characterized as "climate change conflicts," as some have argued is the case in Darfur.[10] Environmental risks are systemic not only because of the all-encompassing nature of natural disasters but also because of the potential for "devastating second-round effects" that extend far beyond the original hazard.[11] One specific example of a secondary effect is the changing of weather norms. Although hazards are increasing in number, this is only the tip of the (melting) iceberg. Average weather conditions, too, are changing, and these will have systemic effects on all world systems.[12] In their potential to affect a range of related domains, the risks arising from climate change are systemic. As the Organisation for Economic Co-operation and Development concludes, "Connectedness multiplies the channels through which accidents, diseases, or malevolent actions can propagate."[13] The systemic consequences of environmental hazards extend beyond economic and physical dislocation: the Southeast Asian tsunami of 2004, Hurricane Katrina in 2005, and the 2010 Sahel drought are but a few examples of environmental hazards that posed severe threats to human life.

Exposure to Pressure

A separate aspect of environmental risk emerges from the same considerations that leave finance, supply chains, and infrastructure vulnerable, notably the efficiency imperative. World systems today are more vulnerable to such disasters because they have been stretched and have sacrificed resilience to increase efficiency. Under heightened competitive pressures, firms may choose to locate in particularly risk-prone areas even though this might prove adverse in the long run. We saw in chapter 3 how manufacturing gravitated toward Thailand for its competitive prices, despite the risk. The benefits of lower transportation costs (particularly for bulk traded goods that cannot be efficiently transported by air) and the availability of reclaimed land apparently outweighed the current costs associated with uncertain risks. It is worth emphasizing that the benefits associated with locations near to rivers or low-lying coastal areas are not new, as is evident in the growth of the major cities (such as Amsterdam, Paris, London, St. Petersburg, New York, Los Angeles, Tokyo, Shanghai, and others). However, as we enter an era of rising oceans and an increased risk of flooding, the advantages of these locations may be overshadowed by the escalating need for investments to protect people and systems from flood damage.

The pressures of poverty and growing population density induce farmers, mostly in developing countries, to stretch soil's potential beyond its natural limits and to cut the necessary recovery times of fallow land. Competitive pressures and perverse subsidies that encourage overexploitation of land in Europe and other highly subsidized farming communities compound the problem. Over time, these practices significantly reduce land fertility and erode sustainability.[14] Similar overexploitation of natural resources applies to forestry and fisheries. An example of this is seen in Chile, where the dangers posed by market pressures extend to overmining and seriously threaten sustainable development.[15]

Physicist Tom Murphy maintains that the depletion of fossil resources constitutes an even greater threat to the global system than does climate change. In a recent interview he suggested that eventually growth will become unsustainable, because there will be no more resources left to deplete.[16] This is a contentious and simplistic interpretation of the resource challenge. But it does raise the key questions of the sustainability of growth and our assumptions regarding continued resource extraction and use. These need to be radically reappraised, taking into account both the externalities associated with current use and the sustainability of economic growth as the primary and often the only goal of economic policy.[17]

Degrading Biodiversity

The value of biodiversity can be summarized simply: "Diversity expands the number of potential interactions inside a system and therefore offers, on average, higher stability and resilience."[18] This is true for diversified portfolios in finance, for modular supply chains in global production, and also for our ecosystem. It therefore follows that a loss of biodiversity implies heightened instability and a reduced capacity to withstand shocks. It is worth emphasizing that such threats are not merely hypothetical. According to one study, the spread of invasive species and pathogens constitutes "the clearest link between biodiversity and human health."[19] Indeed, risks are already materializing in many domains; the Food and Agriculture Organization of the United Nations estimates that "over 70% of the world's fish species are either fully exploited or depleted," posing a "major threat" to the food supply of millions of people.[20]

Empirically, declines in biodiversity are typically "followed by an increase in the incidence of diseases and in the presence of invasive species."[21] Furthermore, biodiversity has also been identified as instrumental to medical research and even to commercial agriculture. It provides "numerous goods and services to humanity, including genetic material used in the design of new medicines or in crop and livestock breeding."[22] In other words, decreasing biodiversity leads to threats to human health both direct (diseases) and indirect (food supplies, medical research). Attempts to express the monetary value of an intact and diverse biosystem reach into the trillions of dollars. Often the greatest contributions come from small incidents: Swiss bee colonies, for example, have been shown to ensure "a yearly agricultural production worth about US\$ 213 million by providing pollination," and the value of an improved microclimate from 400,000 trees planted by local authorities in Canberra has been estimated at between US\$20 and US\$67 million.[23]

A loss of biodiversity contributes to global risk in two ways. First, it increases the severity of shocks through homogenization: if local biotas become less diverse and more similar, previously confined damage (such as that caused by diseases, vermin, or predatory species) will spread more easily. Second, a loss of biodiversity increases systemic vulnerability by weakening responsiveness to unforeseen risk events such as climate change, storms, and other disasters. In this context, a study from

BioScience makes the point that although the first epidemiological transition resulted in a shift from hunting to agriculture and the second took place during the Industrial Revolution, we have now entered a third stage of transition, which has arisen as "globalization and ecological disruption appear to be associated with newly emerging infectious diseases as well as re-emerging infections previously thought to be under control."[24]

RISKS *TO* THE ENVIRONMENT

Environmental instability can trigger broader systemic risks in food systems, health systems, and, as we see in the case of climate change, cities and nations. These are risks from the environment, but, as we have highlighted, they are part of a feedback loop in which we create risks to the environment. Environmental instability is not new. Indeed, there is evidence to suggest that environmental disasters over 50,000 years ago nearly led to the virtual disappearance of homo sapiens and precipitated our migration for survival across Africa. Since then we have been migrating across the earth and affecting the environment in many ways. There may have been long lags between when humans have had an impact and when they have become aware of the consequences of their choices, let alone done anything about them. It has taken over two hundred years since the Industrial Revolution to discover that our carbon and other atmospheric emissions are having a greenhouse effect, and it has been only in the past 20 years or so that this has been scientifically linked to climate change. We realized it is too late to reverse the trend but have yet to act decisively to stop the negative impact from having compounding consequences. In part, this is because accelerated emissions of greenhouse gases are part and parcel of the process of globalization and are bound up in the economic growth of emerging markets and the associated rapid rises in incomes and energy consumption.

Globalization and Environmental Risk

The conceptual link between globalization and increasing emissions is not hard to grasp. The global advances of recent decades have been associated with a dramatic increase in energy use. Rising levels of fuel and electricity consumption have resulted in increased carbon dioxide release as fossil fuels have been burned, releasing greenhouse gases (figures 5.3 and 5.4). The link between rising greenhouse gas emissions and increasing global temperatures has been both theoretically demonstrated and empirically verified. For our analysis we thus take rising levels of carbon dioxide and releases of other greenhouse gases to constitute a direct environmental risk. Lord Stern has estimated that the sum of about 2 percent of world GDP would be required to mitigate climate change; this appears to be broadly equivalent to the amounts of other precautionary investments and a reasonable cost for averting potentially devastating and irreversible damage.[25]

Figure 5.3 shows a correlation between energy usage and carbon dioxide levels, thus remaining ambiguous about causality, but figure 5.4 shows that the increase in emissions has been greatest in developing countries—exactly what we would expect if economic growth brings increased emissions. As a direct result of technological advancement and increased connectivity in the twenty-first century, more countries are now able to compete on the world stage. The emission-creating growth of industrialization has "gone global." These figures do not mean that developing countries are less concerned with environmental responsibility than are their industrialized counterparts; they mean only that developing countries are now rapidly climbing the energy curve that the advanced economies have long since climbed. Indeed, 15 percent of managers in developing economies identify "growth of environmental concerns, including concern about climate change" as a defining element of their business

Figure 5.3. Global greenhouse gas emissions, 1990–2005. (A) By gas. HFCs, hydrofluorocarbons; PFCs, perfluorocarbons; SF_6, sulfur hexafluoride. (B) By economic sector. Emissions from international transport (aviation and marine) are separate from the energy sector because they are not part of individual countries' emission inventories. For consistency, in both panels emissions are expressed in millions of metric tons of carbon dioxide equivalents. These totals do not include emissions due to land-use change or forestry because estimates are not available for the most recent years. EPA (Environmental Protection Agency), 2010, *Climate Change Indicators in the United States* (Washington, DC: U.S. Environmental Protection Agency), 12, accessed 5 February 2013, http://www.epa.gov/climatechange/pdfs/CI-full-2010.pdf.

A
Emissions (millions of metric tons of carbon dioxide equivalents)

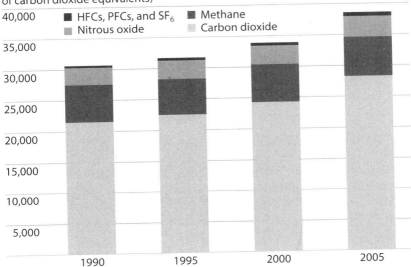

B
Emissions (millions of metric tons of carbon dioxide equivalents)

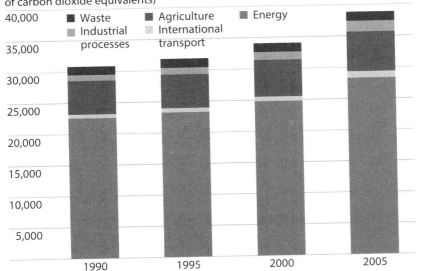

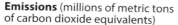

Emissions (millions of metric tons of carbon dioxide equivalents)

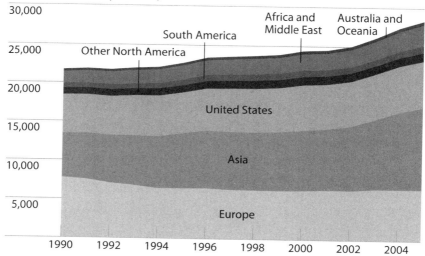

Figure 5.4. Global carbon dioxide emissions by world region, 1990–2005. These data do not include emissions attributable to land use, land-use change, or forestry. EPA (Environmental Protection Agency), 2010 *Climate Change Indicators in the United States* (Washington, DC: United States Environmental Protection Agency), 13, accessed 5 February 2013, http://www.epa.gov/climatechange/pdfs/CI-full-2010.pdf.

strategy compared to only 11 percent in Europe and even fewer (10 percent) in North America.[26] One obvious reason is that, as we have seen, the impact of climate change can be felt most severely in developing countries. Indeed, this may be an unfortunate result of the "polluter pays" paradigm.

The analysis corroborates the direct link between rising emissions of CO_2 from developing countries and the most recent wave of globalization. It has been shown that there is a close relationship between economic growth and environmental externalities, with the various emissions and pollutants peaking at different stages of development.[27] With the help of a theoretical model and a rich cross-country data set on sulphur dioxide concentrations, environmental economists Werner Antweiler, Brian Copeland, and Scott Taylor investigated how integration with international markets affects pollution levels.[28] They found that "a 1-percent increase in the scale of economic activity raises pollution concentrations by 0.25 to 0.5 percent for an average country." They summarize their findings by writing that "income gains brought about by capital accumulation raise pollution."[29] Matthew Cole and Robert Elliott confirmed this finding with their 2003 study of nitrogen oxide and carbon dioxide emission. Their work also reports a negative "scale" effect.[30] Adopting the methodology of Antweiler, Copeland, and Taylor, Junyi Shen studied Chinese provincial data on a variety of pollutants. He also concluded that "for air pollutants (SO_2 and dust fall) increase in trade leads to more emissions."[31]

Biodiversity

We have previously seen how a loss of biodiversity constitutes both a direct risk to human health and an indirect problem through the loss of medicinal and agricultural potential. Human interference with biodiversity, even if small, can put the stability of the ecosystem at risk, thereby incurring uncertain but potentially highly significant costs for society. Empirically, researchers have concluded that "globalization and the transfer of exotic organisms have resulted in widespread biotic homogenization—the replacement of local biota with non-indigenous species."[32] They have emphasized that "these exotic species can cause extinctions of local taxa, resulting in the loss of diversity at many levels, from genetic variation to species number."[33]

Increasing physical connectivity is perhaps the single most important human contributor to globalization's impact on biodiversity. Entomologists have found that "human-aided transport is responsible for the arrival and spread of most invasive vectors, such as anthropophilic fleas, lice, kissing bugs, and mosquitoes."[34] The exact channels through which these invasions occur are diverse, which makes it difficult to prevent such transfers. A major contributor appears to have been the arrival of container ships, in particular those with water-holding freight.[35]

Biodiversity is *indirectly* at risk through globalization's effect on production systems, not least in agriculture. The concentration of land use on monocultures has contributed to ecological homogenization, the loss of biodiversity, and chemical pollution of land and water resources. Agricultural subsidies in Europe, the United States, and Japan have compounded the problem by encouraging excessive application of chemical fertilizers and pesticides. Policies that reward investment in key commodities, which are protected through perverse subsidies in certain OECD countries, notably maize, oilseeds, sugar, and cotton, have led to intense pressure to increase yields and have reduced the incentive to rotate crops and rest the land. The subsidies, which in recent years have averaged US$250 billion, have been reflected in higher land, labor, and other prices, resulting in increased mechanization and chemical applications.[36] Meanwhile, the protectionist policies that prevent the export of these crops to the major markets compel developing-country agricultural producers to concentrate on those products that are not protected in their major export markets, further increasing the tendency to increase the production of monocultures such as cocoa and coffee.

CAN GLOBALIZATION BE GOOD FOR THE ENVIRONMENT?

Globalization does not have only negative consequences for the environment; there are also positive consequences in the form of *technique* and *scale* effects. The next section goes on to evaluate the scope of these possible benefits.

Antweiler, Copeland, and Taylor's landmark study, referred to previously, also suggests that economic growth "drives *concentrations* down by 1.25–1.5 percent via a technique effect."[37] The authors concluded that "trade-induced technique and scale effects imply a net reduction in pollution from these sources," meaning that "freer trade appears to be good for the environment."[38]

Ian Goldin and Alan Winters, on the other hand, along with Cole and Elliott, stress that the net effect can be different depending on the characteristics of the pollutant: in addition to the detrimental net effects of nitrogen oxide and carbon dioxide, Cole and Elliott report that "technique effects are dominating scale effects for SO_2 and BOD."[39] Thus we see that in the case of some pollutants, "pollution declines with per capita income," though the authors stress that this is not universal.[40] In the same spirit, and in contrast to his findings with respect to air pollutants, Junyi Shen observes that "for water pollutants (COD, arsenic, and cadmium) trade liberalization decreases emissions."[41]

Using an instrumental variables approach to address estimation issues related to the endogeneity of trade, Jeffrey Frankel and Andrew Rose show "that trade tends to reduce three measures of air pollution" and, more precisely, that "statistical significance is high for concentrations of SO_2, moderate for NO_2, and lacking for particulate matter."[42] Like Antweiler, Copeland, and Taylor, they conclude that "there is little evidence that trade has a detrimental effect on the environment."[43] Arriving at a similar conclusion, André Dua and Daniel Esty report that, for the Asia–Pacific region, "economic expansion and environmental protection can, in fact, be made mutually supportive."[44] This is an example of the scale effect and relates to what economists term the *intensive margin*. This suggests that as individual incomes increase, average pollution levels decrease because people can afford to have greener preferences and limit their emissions. On the other hand, we must remember that at the lower end of the income distribution an increase in average income enables families to buy their first "white goods" (refrigerators, heaters, air conditioners, microwaves), computers and electronic goods, and cars and to travel and eat increasingly processed food. Here the link between globalization and ecological risk comes from an increase in participation, or the *extensive margin*. The effect of this margin is that the environmental externalities associated with growth accelerate as growth proceeds from low- to middle-income status.

The discovery that globalization can have *positive* effects on emissions has led some to postulate the environmental Kuznets curve (EKC): an inverted U-shaped relation between income (on the horizontal axis) and pollution intensity (on the vertical axis). Supporting the EKC, Daniel Esty reports that "environmental conditions tend to deteriorate in the early stages of industrialization and then improve as nations hit middle-income level, at a per capita GDP of about $5000 to $8000."[45] At around these levels of income, the conversion of every additional dollar earned into the demand for energy, water, and other natural resources is subject to diminishing returns. Thus, although total demand and emissions increase beyond this point, the rate of increase slows down. The coming two decades will see over two billion people go through this income transition, generating a heavy burden in terms of the demand for energy and natural resources as well as the associated environmental costs.

THE EXPORT OF POLLUTION

Thus far we have mainly focused on the link between globalization and environmental risk as related to increased economic activity. Another important concern, and one that has received much attention in public debate, is the tendency of regions with strong "green preferences" (for example, those with restrictive environmental regulation) to outsource either a polluting activity itself or the disposal of accrued waste.[46] Two hypotheses about these "pollution havens" exist. The stronger is the claim that "globalization facilitates the relocation of dirty industry to poor countries" and is known as the pollution haven hypothesis (PHH).[47] A weaker version of the theory instead postulates that "stringent environmental regulation impacts comparative advantage at the margin, but that it does not necessarily lead to a wholesale migration of industry to regions with weaker regulation."[48] This means that although more economically developed countries do have stricter environmental laws, this does not necessarily induce industries to move. This has been labeled the pollution haven effect (PHE). Although it is theoretically convincing, empirical research leads us to doubt the strong PHH in favor of the PHE, which has strong observational data to justify its theoretical claims.[49] There is some evidence that pollution intensity is shifted from strictly regulated to weakly regulated countries, but developed economies still do not outsource their "dirty industries" altogether. Many practical examples of pollution havens exist, and it is important to note that the effect takes place not only between countries but also within countries. California, for example, has a long history of importing power from coal plants in the American West that produce far greater amounts of harmful gases than would be permitted in the Golden State.[50]

The regulatory and enforcement environment regarding pollution typically strengthens as societies develop and incomes increase, so the outsourcing of pollution usually goes from richer to poorer regions. However, environmental risks are often nonlinear; although the sea or a forest can recover from low levels of pollution, contamination beyond a certain threshold can lead to irreparable damage. The erosion of topsoils, for example, can lead to permanent desert landscapes. For this reason, many advanced economies still suffer from the legacy of earlier stages of degradation of their environments.

Pollution havens constitute systemic risk for at least two reasons. First, the tendency to export pollution reduces the incentives for richer countries to invest in cleaner technologies and more effective waste disposal systems. Second, even if poorer countries benefit economically from importing pollution and move along the EKC, there is a real danger of irreparable damage.[51] Pollution havens are obliged to handle additional loads of waste at lower costs and with fewer regulations than are applicable elsewhere and so are less well placed to invest in the most effective waste disposal technologies or enforce stiffer rules.

LESSONS FOR MANAGING ENVIRONMENTAL RISK

In this chapter we have attempted to categorize the most important aspects of environmental risk into two categories: risks *from* and risks *to* the environment. Our account has by no means been complete; other potential risks include genetic modification, urbanization, and the pressure of increased population. We also did not extensively consider fragile ocean and fishery or forest ecosystems or a wide range of other topics, each of which is the subject of many studies and books. These provide additional evidence of the systemic risks associated with environmental risk. Our purpose has been to illustrate the complexity and systemic interactions of globalization and environmental risk and to emphasize both the risks from and those to the environment. The key lessons of this chapter follow.

Lesson 1: Current practices present environmental risk
The tempo of development in recent decades has destabilized the natural ecosystem in many ways. The result will be an increase in disasters, a growing vulnerability to hazards, and the depletion of resources and biodiversity, placing systems and people at risk. This has led experts to predict that "loss potentials among the world's 10 largest cities . . . are projected to increase,"[52] with a forecast of disaster loss potentials ranging from 22 percent in Tokyo to 88 percent in both Shanghai and Jakarta over the period between 2005 and 2015.[53] Because of these predictions, efforts toward improved analysis of the risk and the expansion of investments in disaster risk reduction are urgently needed.

Lesson 2: Robust and resilient responses are required to mitigate environmental risks
The emphasis should be on developing *robust* and *resilient* responses to environmental risks. Robust responses include safeguarding biodiversity,

planting more trees, and strengthening disaster barriers, like the flood breakers installed in Louisiana after Hurricane Katrina and the barriers in Rotterdam.[54] Resilience, instead, can be enhanced, for example, by encouraging wider biodiversity, discouraging monocultures, increasing watershed management, and promoting policies that protect land and manage natural resource depletion. Financial instruments such as catastrophe bonds to prevent environmental disasters from spilling over into the financial sector, weather futures, and others might also provide some insulation to farmers and others and could thus mitigate the systemic consequences of environmental risk events.[55] At the same time, removing perverse regulations—such as insurance policies that encourage people to build in flood plains—and perverse subsidies that encourage fossil fuel consumption, as well as agricultural subsidies in rich countries that lead to excessive production of monocultures and harmful biofuels in Europe and North America, would increase the resilience of the environment.

Lesson 3: The current approach to environmental risk management is ineffective; a coordinated supranational response is needed

Environmental risk management requires interventions at the global, regional, national, and community levels. Globalization has allowed pollution to move to the least protected locations and has encouraged pollution havens. A global carbon tax and the direct payment in production and consumption for externalities associated with our consumption choices would be our preferred options. Failing such global approaches, we believe that border taxes that impose costs equivalent to environmental externalities should be explored at the national or regional (for example, EU) level. A lack of coordination and private-interest lobbying (such as that by the coal industry) has undermined efforts to improve environmental sustainability. Fragmented regulations create the illusion of environmental safeguards and fail to ensure that pollution is not outsourced. In California a seemingly greener track record combined with an increasing demand for energy meant that the net effect on global carbon emissions was much lower than anticipated because energy-intensive products were produced elsewhere. To the extent that regulation has led to the adoption of cleaner technologies—for example, in transport and for domestic use—California did, however, move in the right direction.

The current structures for global environmental management are inadequate. In the context of the "trade–environment divide," for example, "even those who find the promise of sustainable development attractive worry that, in practice, environmental policy tools are not up to the pressures of globalization."[56] Others highlight "the trade-off between allowing governments flexibility to pursue independent environmental policies and constraining the ability of governments in order to close loopholes in trade agreements."[57] In this area, as in others, when it comes to coordinated supranational response, much remains to be done.

Lesson 4: Poor countries and people suffer the most from environmental risk

Citizens of Bangladesh, the Maldives, and other low-lying countries are most threatened by environmental risk, as are those living in arid and fragile lands in Africa and elsewhere. Recent decades have seen growing restrictions on international migration that severely constrain the options of those most affected by environmental risk. The inconsistency between the globalization of production and pollution and the differential costs incurred by different societies compounds inequality and the risks arising from resource degradation. Strategies to address the systemic environmental risks arising from globalization need to take this differential impact into account. It is ethically, politically, and economically counterproductive to slow globalization or arrest growth in emerging markets on account of the environmental spillovers. Many emerging markets, not least China, are already adjusting their growth strategies to reduce carbon intensity and the destruction of their environments. However, much greater attention needs to be given to creating incentives to adopt technologies to encourage greener growth and to building capacity in developing countries to mitigate and to manage environmental risk.

6

⊙↯⊙

Pandemics and Health Risks

This chapter is concerned with the systemic risk of pandemics. Although globalization has brought immense health benefits, it has also led to a number of escalating threats to health. Pandemics, as a result of increasing globalization, can have profound and potentially catastrophic systemic consequences.

When the first case of SARS (severe acute respiratory syndrome) occurred in November 2002 in the Guangdong province of China, the virulence of the disease quickly resulted in an epidemic; incidences were reported throughout Guangdong but mostly remained localized around one epicenter.[1] For most of human history, this would have been the end of the story. But for most of human history cases like that of Liu Jianlun were not possible. Liu, a 64-year-old doctor who had treated SARS patients in Guangdong, checked into Hong Kong's Metropole Hotel on 17 February 2003. While staying at the elite hotel, he came into contact with patrons from all over the world. Having shared elevators and dining halls with Liu, the guests eventually flew home and unwittingly carried the SARS pathogen worldwide. By late June 2003, SARS patients had been identified on all continents, and health experts feared the worst. Over 8,400 cases were reported in 30 countries, and policy makers began to implement quarantines and tried to contain mass panic. Yet, as Larry Brilliant notes, "SARS is the pandemic that didn't occur."[2] Rapid detection on the part of organizations like the Global Public Health Intelligence Network and effective response by the World Health Organization

(WHO) contained what could have been a global catastrophe. Although the deaths from SARS are tragic and the virus has not yet been totally eradicated (the last confirmed case was in April 2004),[3] global action and cooperation prevented global systemic implications.

Experience with diseases such as SARS is what makes the study of pandemics so crucial. In this chapter we seek to understand how globalization has affected health risks and how outbreaks will affect global systems. We do this not only to deal directly with the risk of diseases but also because public health management can teach us important lessons for systemic thinking, as the global system for dealing with disease is among the most developed and the most effective. WHO has, for the most part, successfully kept the threat of pandemics at bay in the period since the Second World War, and newer dedicated agencies such as UNAIDS (the Joint United Nations Programme on HIV/AIDS) have been effective in providing an alternative means to deal with key health challenges that may have been stymied by WHO's sometimes paralyzing politics and bureaucracy.

To learn how to apply the principles of health management to other domains, we first analyze the nature of pandemics and observe their inherent relationship to globalization. We show several ways in which the "increased linkages" characteristic of globalization can facilitate disease transfer. We also look at past pandemics and the responses they elicited, drawing from them lessons for systemic thinking and the management of future pandemics and other systemic risks.

PANDEMIC RISK

Globalization, population growth, and urbanization have facilitated the transmission of infectious diseases. The complexity of global travel and global integration mean that any "patient zero" is now but a few degrees of separation from formerly isolated communities. According to medical experts, more than 30 new disease-causing organisms have appeared in just the past two decades. These have included such deadly pathogens as ebola, hepatitis C, and the human immunodeficiency virus (HIV). In addition, diseases such as cholera, malaria, and the plague, once believed eradicated, have returned with even greater virulence.[4] In the first decade of the twenty-first century, the world was threatened by at least three major pandemics: SARS, H1N1 ("swine flu"), and H5N1 ("bird flu"). The hallmarks of globalization—connectivity and integration—create the potential for negative externalities in the field of health, just as they do in other sectors.

Definition of a Pandemic

Characterizing a pandemic is not a straightforward task, and there is no one agreed definition. WHO provided a formal definition only in 2009, "despite ten years of issuing guidelines for pandemic preparedness" activities.[5] WHO eventually defined a pandemic as an influenza exhibiting "community level outbreaks" and "human-to-human spread of the virus into at least two countries."[6] Immunologists characterize pandemics more generally as exhibiting wide geographic extension, disease movement, high attack rates, minimal population immunity, novelty, infectiousness, contagiousness, and severity.[7] Similarly, the U.S. Department of Health and Human Services lists rapid worldwide spread, overloaded health care systems, inadequate medical supplies, shortage of hospital beds, and disruption of the economy and society as the "characteristics and challenges of a . . . pandemic."[8]

Although the exact definition of *pandemic* is important, for our purposes it suffices to say that it relates to a virus that *spreads easily among humans* and has *infected patients worldwide.*[9] The key term here is "worldwide," and this is what separates pandemics from epidemics. An epidemic is seen to affect a "large number of individuals within a population, community, or region," and thus differs from a pandemic in the limited geographical distribution of infections.[10]

A Systemic Risk

There are many examples of the connection between globalization and pandemics. Increased integration fosters both the nascence and the proliferation of diseases. The health risks are inevitably systemic, so any pandemic or growing disease will have consequences for other sectors. One of the best ways to illustrate this is through the example of smallpox—"the greatest killer in history"—which is reported to have taken the lives of many world leaders including Pharaoh Ramses V of Egypt, Emperor Marcus Aurelius of Rome, Holy Roman Emperor Ferdinand IV of Spain, Emperor Fu-Lin of China, Queen Mary II of England, King William II of Orange, Tsar Peter II of Russia, and King Louis XV of France.[11] Clearly, infectious diseases can affect anyone anywhere, even the most powerful and most protected among us.

There is a significant probability that a pandemic will strike a financial center such as New York or London and, through disease, quarantine, panic, or the collapse of secondary services (transport, energy, information technology, or other), lead to at least a temporary isolation of major players in the global system. A pandemic also could isolate Washington, Whitehall, Brussels, or Beijing. Many experts believe that it is a question of when, not whether, such events will occur. It is for this reason that the study and prevention of pandemics is so vital to safeguarding all world systems.

GLOBALIZATION AND HEALTH RISKS

Connectivity

The density and intensity of connections between humans, and also between humans and animals, are primary determinants of the development and spread of pandemics. When in 1967 Stanley Milgram conducted an experiment to quantify global connectivity, he found that people were, on average, just six degrees of separation away from each other.[12] By sending packages to random individuals in Omaha, Nebraska, and Wichita, Kansas, Milgram sought to measure how many "friends of a friend" would be needed to pass the parcels on to individuals in Boston, Massachusetts. Although the experiment was remarkable at the time, the connectivity it measured was limited to the continental United States, and the six mutual friends through whom the packages passed were all U.S. residents. In the globalized world of the twenty-first century, integration has far exceeded Milgram's findings. In 2011 Facebook analyzed its 721 million users *worldwide* to find how many steps would be required to connect any two individuals on the planet. They found that, on average, just 4.7 "mutual friends" separate any one Facebook user from another, even if thousands of miles lie between them physically.[13] The combination of population growth and travel, as well as the commercial and inadvertent movement of animals (rats in ships or mosquitoes in airplanes), has rapidly increased the risks of spreading infectious diseases. As we saw in the case of Chinese doctor Liu Jianlun, the "superspreader" of SARS, connections can be dangerous. A virulent pathogen often requires just brief contact to infect someone and spread. This turns airplanes and international journeys into disease vectors.

Concentration

By 2025 the fraction of the world's population living in cities is expected to rise to 70 percent.[14] With Tokyo's population density as high as 5,847 persons per square kilometer and with 1 in 25 people already living in a megacity, it is inevitable that "new approaches for surveillance, preparedness, and response will be needed [to deal with pandemics]."[15] This is important everywhere but especially in overcrowded or unhygienic conditions, where people live close to animals, and where water is easily contaminated. These incubators for the development and spread of infectious diseases are expected to grow particularly rapidly, because virtually all the growth in megacities will be occurring in developing countries over the coming decades and because many of them have shantytowns and other communities in which people are living in poor conditions. Inequality within cities and the exclusion of parts of their populations from the basic benefits of sanitation, clean water, and medical care are thus sources of potential pandemic risk.

The risk of concentration also amplifies the risk of connectivity both within the urban conglomeration and globally, not least because major airport hubs tend to be located alongside these cities. If a disease originates in a metropolis, it is nearly impossible to prevent it from spreading around the globe. Megacities are typically also home to particularly mobile migrants and business people with connections on all continents.

Information Management

Information and rumors can now spread almost instantaneously through the Internet and social media. With this ability, the risk of panics linked to infectious diseases has increased dramatically and the complexity associated with managing pandemics has multiplied. Information management is essential, because hysteria can escalate danger systemically as citizens seek to acquire and stockpile medications or masks and as governments' attempts to control the movement of people, medicines, and vital services are overwhelmed by the public's response. In attempting to prevent mass hysteria, governments may also be tempted to engage in the dangerous repression of vital information. In the context of social networks in the financial world, there is evidence that "individual decision makers often pay attention to the actions, decisions, and even beliefs (such as risk perceptions) of others to whom they are linked socially."[16] It is precisely in this sense that we believe innovation and technology have also shaped the risk from contagious diseases; in addition to the physical channels of transmission, we need to be aware of the risks related to "'social' contagion."[17]

An additional challenge is managing the dissemination of information about sensitive research. An example has been the debate surrounding the decision by the U.S. government to request that the leading scientific journals *Nature* and *Science* withhold the publication of research regarding the evolution of the H5N1 influenza virus. Although the studies were eventually published, according to Medical News Today, a website reporting news from the health sector, they "were held back because of international concerns that making such data public would make it easier for terrorists to make bioweapons."[18] (We further examine the risk of bioterrorism in chapter 7.)

A different link between informal and social networks and the risk of pandemics relates to the role of public health in preventing the spread of diseases. One study, for example, has analyzed the interaction between the state of public health and the influenza pandemic of 1918 (the "Spanish flu"). It concludes that at the time "the epidemic was an unwanted reminder of the limits of the new public health" but goes on to argue that "the public health techniques of a previous era still had relevance and even the power to stem disease."[19] Precautionary measures can be instrumental in preventing a pandemic and central to the development and implementation of solutions for the containment of such diseases. In our tightly integrated world, these precautionary measures require worldwide monitoring, timely detection, and effective intervention to prevent the spread of pandemics.

CASE STUDIES

Our case studies reveal key lessons for pandemic management. By looking at specific examples we can better understand the theoretical risks we have identified and maximize our ability to react to future threats. Recent research has indicated that influenza pandemics follow a cyclical pattern, with similar viruses appearing every 10–15 years.[20] This would make the world long "overdue" for a pandemic. Our case studies shed some light on the possible origins and implications.

Historical Pandemics

The first recorded transnational epidemic dates back to 430 BC. This disease, which became known as the Athenian plague, started in what is now Ethiopia before being transmitted into Egypt via troop movement during the Peloponnesian War.[21] Since then, waves of "extensive epidemics" have been associated with the internationalization of trade.[22] Starting in 1347 with the bubonic plague, also known as the "Black Death," increased commerce meant that merchant trade lines could act as conduits for the spread of pathogens.[23] During the seventeenth century, globalization aided the spread of infectious diseases through European colonization, which exposed local populations to viruses such as influenza, measles, and smallpox.[24] By the twentieth century, trade had reached all but the most remote parts of the world, and extensive epidemics were becoming *pandemics*.

The Spanish Flu

The global influenza pandemic of 1918, also known as the Spanish flu, is normally given as a prime example of the devastating impacts of viral infections. It has been deemed "uniquely virulent" and the "deadliest public health crisis in human history."[25] Spanish flu killed an estimated 17 million people in India alone and between 50 and 100 million worldwide.[26] The disease came in three increasingly deadly waves with nine-month intervals between them. Tragically, Spanish flu was particularly dangerous for the young, and half of all fatalities were among those aged between 20 and 40.[27] Although the exact origins of the flu are still unknown, there is some evidence that the virus arose from "genome adaption" rather than from "gene reassortment" between humans and animals. This would mean that its precursor was "hidden in an obscure ecologic niche" before it began to affect humans.[28] Spanish flu did not start in Spain, nor was its incidence greatest in the country that has been saddled with the name of the pandemic. Rather, because Spain had relatively open media and did not ban reporting, it became identified with the flu.

Within a few weeks of its initial outbreak, Spanish flu affected the majority of the countries in the world.[29] In part, this was the result of troop movement during and in the aftermath of World War I and the poor sanitary conditions of military life.[30] Although these circumstances were exceptional for the time, such travel was slow and fragmentary compared to that currently. A then-extraordinary exercise in logistics shuttled soldiers around the world and concentrated large volumes of people in small areas. Today movement on (or above) the scale of that in post–World War I Europe is the norm, and economic considerations have driven human beings into megacities and slums that pose even graver threats in terms of the development and spread of pandemics.

The Asian Flu (H2N2) and the Hong Kong (H3N2) Influenza

The Asian flu of 1957 and the Hong Kong influenza of 1968 have been seen as descendants of the 1918 Spanish flu.[31] Together, these three outbreaks are typically listed as the major pandemics of the twentieth century. Not only did the pathogens themselves share physical features but the distribution patterns of all three crises also resembled each other. The 1957 flu seems to have displayed the same multiple-wave structure as its predecessor nearly 40 years earlier.[32] The first wave came in February 1957, when the first outbreak of the H2N2 virus was reported in Asia. By May the virus had reached the United States, and the U.S. government started the mass production of vaccines. Infection rates peaked in October, and by December it seemed as if the worst was over. In February 1958, however, a year after the initial outbreak, a second wave of infections rose up. Most of the American deaths from Asian flu—approximately 70,000—occurred during this unexpected second coming.[33]

A decade after the Asian flu, another pandemic arose from the Far East. The "Hong Kong flu" was first detected in the eponymous city-state in early 1968 and did not reach the United States until September of the same year. As in the case of the Asian flu, the rate of its initial spread was thus much slower than that of the 1918 Spanish influenza. Deaths related to H3N2 peaked between December 1968 and January 1969, but unlike those in the previous two "great" pandemics, primarily affected those aged 65 and over. Again, however, the virus returned in subsequent outbreaks, with a second and a third wave in 1970 and 1972. The total number of fatalities in the United States was 33,800, making it the "mildest flu pandemic in the 20th century."[34]

According to the U.S. Department of Health and Human Services, timing is a determining factor in the severity of a pandemic's impact. Outbreaks that occur during the school term are far more likely to have devastating consequences. This can be taken as strong evidence that connectivity can result in the generation of pandemics, because mass contact in schools is typical of globalized interaction.

The *response* to the Asian and Hong Kong pandemics also greatly curtailed their impact. Edwin Kilbourne, the scientist responsible for leading the fight against the pandemics, reports that it was media outlets, not governmental organizations, that discovered and reported the early instances of these diseases.[35] News groups were responsible for drawing public attention and the interest of policy makers to the threat of the pathogens. This suggests that informal reporting networks will be vital elements in containing the spread of pandemics in the future. In turn, this idea implies that modern technologies such as mobile devices or social networking sites will be crucial for pandemic management in the twenty-first century, just as we have already indicated that they pose a threat in terms of stirring panic and possibly counterproductive responses.

HIV/AIDS

We believe that HIV/AIDS, as one of the most devastating diseases of recent decades, deserves special attention.

HIV/AIDS is frequently termed an epidemic rather than a pandemic. The reasons for this, however, are unclear. Although definitions vary, the following characteristics typically distinguish the concepts: epidemics are generally caused by seasonal outbreaks of a virus subtype already in circulation, whereas pandemics are typically caused by a new virus strain or subtype (to which the population has little or no immunity); epidemics involve more than the average "outbreak" (because the number of infections exceeds what would normally be expected), but epidemics relate to a given community or region; pandemics involve heightened infection on a global scale and are far more costly in terms of life, social disruption, economic loss, and general hardship.[36]

With more than 25 million global fatalities from HIV/AIDS since 1981 and 33 million more people living with the disease, we believe that the crisis is nothing short of a pandemic.[37] A harrowing 1.8 million individuals died as a result of HIV/AIDS in 2010 alone, and 2.7 million new infections were reported that year.[38] Furthermore, with 67 percent of those infected living in the poorest regions of Africa, it is also clear that the disease is contributing to the problems of global inequality that we discuss in chapter 7.[39]

Despite these daunting figures, there are positive lessons that can be learned from the world's campaign against HIV/AIDS. It has been observed that the AIDS pandemic breached the public discourse only after "famous people became infected."[40] This is part of the reason for the delayed response of global aid networks; WHO did not launch a campaign until 1987, a full six years after the first cases had been identified and after the disease had spread to the United States and Europe. Until the beginning of the 1990s, action was focused on prevention, because health professionals did not have treatments that could be useful in limiting transmission and extending life expectancy.[41] From these mistakes we can see how vital it is that future pandemics be met with rapid and effective action in order to avoid situations like that we face today with HIV/AIDS. Because the world took so long to act, prevention, care, and treatment are still not available for most of those infected, and the fight against HIV/AIDS must continue.[42]

Pandemics of the Twenty-First Century

So far, the twenty-first century has experienced three pandemics. As we have seen, the connectivity and geographical "coming together" that characterize globalization today have resulted in an increased risk of such crises.

SARS

In February 2003, Dr. Carl Urbani of WHO reported the first case of SARS. Writing from China's Guangdong province, he termed it "the first severe infectious disease to emerge in the twenty-first century." Urbani wrote that it "poses a serious threat to global health security, the livelihood of populations, the functioning of health systems, and the stability and growth of economies."[43] The SARS outbreak can be considered "bursty" and "stochastic" and was therefore inherently hard to control.[44] Figure 6.1 provides data on daily infections and the corresponding growth rates, as well as the initial underestimation of the number of cases.

In July 2003, four months after its first detection, SARS had spread internationally and looked set to plunge the world into crisis. More than 8,000 SARS cases were reported in 26 countries, with 774 deaths. The disease caused "significant social and economic disruption" through its effects on travel capability (see, for example, figure 6.2).[45] By October 2003, academics such as Dr. Anarfi Asamoa-Baah of WHO were arguing that SARS demonstrated some of the negative aspects of globalization and connectivity. As we noted earlier, however, SARS was "the pandemic that didn't happen." Hand in hand with fears about globalization should come hope; Dr. Asamoa-Baah, in particular, has emphasized that "SARS has shown that it is possible to contain a new disease with traditional public health methods."[46] Coordinated efforts from WHO and the Global Outbreak Alert and Response Network (established in 2000) led to a "technical collaboration of existing institutions and networks."[47]

These efforts pooled both human and technical resources for the rapid identification of incidents and coordination of responses.[48] Effective action meant that incidents of SARS reached into the thousands, not the hundreds of thousands.

The Bird Flu

The second pandemiclike event of the twenty-first century was the outbreak of H5N1, the much-feared bird flu. WHO has characterized H5N1 as "highly pathogenic," and the virus first infected humans in 1997 during

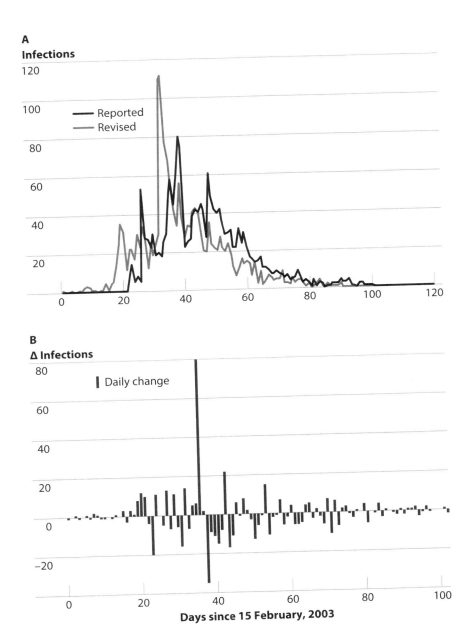

Figure 6.1. The SARS outbreak in Hong Kong, 2003. Michael Small and Chi K. Tse, 2005, "Small World and Scale Free Model of Transmission of SARS," *International Journal of Bifurcation and Chaos* 15 (5): 1745–1755, image on 1746. Used with permission.

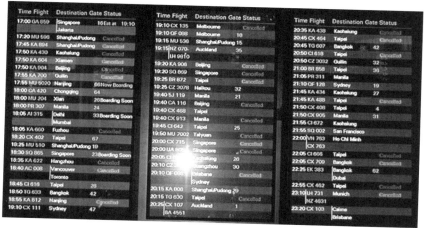

Figure 6.2. Photo of an airport flight board showing flight cancellations in Hong Kong during the SARS outbreak, 2003. David M. Bell, 2012, "Global Trade Security Depends on Implementation of the Revised International Health Regulations," PowerPoint presentation, Centers for Disease Control and Prevention, Atlanta, 8, accessed 25 August, http://iom.edu/~/media/Files/Activity%20Files/Global/USandGlobalHealth/Bell.pdf.

a poultry outbreak in Hong Kong. After that, the pathogen spread from Asia to Europe and then to Africa, becoming endemic in world avian populations. In total, there have been "millions of poultry infections, several hundred human cases, and many human deaths."[49] By March 2007 there were 167 reported fatalities, with 277 confirmed cases of human infection (implying a death rate of at least 65 percent).[50] Although to some extent the virus's spread has slowed, there remain significant concerns that the pathogen could acquire the ability to spread from human to human (so far it has been passed only from birds to humans).[51] The fear is that close contact between humans and birds might allow the virus to mutate and to develop this transmissibility. The risk of this happening is far higher in concentrated megacities and their surrounding slums.

Because H5N1 originates in bird populations, it is a natural fear that migrating birds flying over long distances could spread the virus. This could lead to an even more rapid spread of the disease and would likely render containment virtually impossible. Scientific studies indicate that migratory wildfowl have the potential to carry H5N1 but suggest that "the likelihood of . . . virus dispersal over long distances . . . is low" and "estimate that for an individual migratory bird there are, on average,

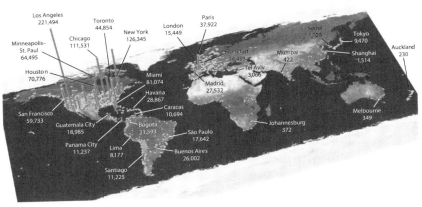

Figure 6.3. Destination cities and corresponding volumes of international passengers arriving from Mexico, 1 March–30 April 2008. Kamran Khan et al., 2009, "Spread of a Novel Influenza A (H1N1) Virus via Global Airline Transportation," *New England Journal of Medicine* 361 (2): 212–214. © 2009 Massachusetts Medical Society. Used with permission.

only 5–15 days per year when infection could result in the dispersal of H5N1 virus over 500 km."[52] The transfer of live birds and animals by airfreight and ships, however, means that these pathogens can now travel faster and farther than before and do not have to rely on the long-distance migration of birds. In short, modern technologies significantly heighten the risk of global pandemics.

Swine Flu

The third disease to have achieved pandemic or near-pandemic status in the twenty-first century is H1N1, widely termed "swine flu." Although the 2009 outbreak was comparable to the 2003 bird flu pattern, its relationship to globalization was even more evident due to the role of airline "hubs."[53] Having emerged in Mexico City and New York in early April 2009, the novel S-OIV virus, a strain of H1N1, spread to 30 countries worldwide within a matter of weeks by the vector of human-to-human transmission.[54] This is interesting because, in contrast to SARS and bird flu, the pathogen originated in two of the world's most connected regions rather than in remote East Asian provinces. This might explain the virulence and severity of the influenza and thus should demonstrate how dangerous supercities can be in terms of health risks.

Estimates of fatalities vary widely, from initial estimates of 12,799 deaths to those of more recent research, which suggests that globally over 570,000 were killed by the disease.[55] The role of globalization in the spread of the disease is evident in the close connections reflected in figure 6.3.

West Nile Virus

West Nile virus is not associated with a pandemic but is included here because it illustrates the risks identified in the previous sections. Marm Kilpatrick writes that "many of the invasive species that have been spread through the globalization of trade and travel are pathogens."[56] Drawing on the example of the West Nile virus, he argues that globalization is a significant contributing factor to the nascence of pandemics. He reports that West Nile virus, having been identified for the first time in Uganda in 1937, was introduced to North America in 1999, reaching the West coast within four years and causing regional epidemics in 2002 and 2003. By 2010 the virus had infected 1.8 million, caused 360,000 illnesses, and killed 1,308.[57] The situation deteriorated in 2012, with the U.S. Centers for Disease Control and Protection reporting that the virus had spread to 48 states in the United States and by December had caused a record 286 deaths.[58] With millions of dead birds, the impact on wildlife has been even more severe, contributing to more than US$120 billion of annual damage.

The reason that the West Nile virus was so damaging is that the urbanized and agricultural habitats generated by globalization enabled it to thrive.[59] This means that the outbreaks can be considered a direct result of world integration; the disease was able to survive in environments artificially created by human activity. Moreover, because the concentration and connectivity of developed regions like North America allow viruses to spread with unprecedented speed, their effects are even more deadly. For many in Africa, the slow spreading of the virus meant that up to 80 percent of those aged 15 or older developed antibodies as a result of long-term exposure to the virus.[60] In places with high degrees of connectivity and urbanization, peoples' immune systems did not have enough time to develop these protective measures, meaning that rates of fatalities were higher than they might otherwise have been.

Based on experience with the West Nile virus, Kilpatrick asserts that the world's biota are "more connected than at any time in Earth's history" and that many "biogeographic barriers" have been removed.[61] This has resulted in the introduction of new species to unprepared habitats, sped by developments in transport and the growth of international trade. For instance, Kilpatrick observes that air traffic into New York City is a "likely pathway" for the introduction of foreign organisms to the United States.[62] He concludes that "continual introduction of pathogens to new regions is inevitable in our globally connected planet."[63]

NONINFECTIOUS DISEASES

Although the main focus of this chapter is on pandemics and diseases whose spread can be linked with human-to-human transfer, it is also worth commenting on the impact of globalization on health risks more generally. These fall into two general categories: risks from the spread of dangerous practices in the "developed" world to developing countries and risks from the integration of cultures more generally.

One general health risk ensuing from globalization reflects how internationalization has changed the nature of marketing and widened "target groups" for advertising campaigns. One example is the worldwide spread of smoking and the resulting rise in lung cancer as well as other smoking-related diseases. This effect can also be seen in the globalization of brands such as McDonald's or Coca-Cola; fast food chains have been among the most successful firms in exporting their products around the world. Changing diets have led to rising levels of obesity, diabetes, and heart-related illnesses in places like China and Japan, where such afflictions were previously rare. Much as in the case of the "export" of measles and smallpox during periods of colonization, Chen, Evans, and Cash argue that global marketing has led to the export of lung cancer and obesity.[64] Consistent with this hypothesis, WHO predicts that noncommunicable diseases will exceed maternal, perinatal, and nutritional diseases as the most common causes of death in Africa by 2030.[65] Although globalization *does* foster development, and with it the information and medicine that can save lives, it is also worth bearing in mind its responsibility for the spread of "lifestyle" diseases to the developing world.[66]

A second kind of noninfectious disease risk comes from the movement of people, as opposed to pathogens, around the world. Arhin-Tenkorang and Conceição report that genetic disorders seem to exhibit the same pattern of global spreading as infectious diseases. Their research uses the example of sickle-cell disease, a condition that was originally brought to the United States on the ships that carried thousands of Africans to America and into abject slavery. Although the disease was originally confined to African-American communities, it has now spread to far wider demographics as a result of interracial relationships. Today about 10 percent of *all* Americans are at risk from the condition.[67] The authors use their insights to argue that the "excessive disease burden in developing countries" should be perceived as a problem for global governance. The warning that Arhin-Tenkorang and Conceição convey is that in the twenty-first century, no disease can remain a solely local or national problem.

GLOBAL COOPERATION AND DISEASE CONTROL

Arhin-Tenkorang and Conceição claim that "health concerns have triggered systematic international cooperation for more than 150 years" and that international cooperation on health issues is older and runs deeper than military cooperation or collaboration in areas such as trade and finance.[68] This suggests that there are lessons to be learned from this chapter in terms of how global governance can develop over time to address other systemic risks associated with globalization.

A Brief History

Arhin-Tenkorang and Conceição discuss the case of a cholera pandemic in the early nineteenth century.[69] They document how, after its nascence in India in 1826, cholera took just one year to spread to Russia. From there, within five years the pathogen had reached Germany, Hungary, and Austria. Within the next year, it hit Paris, London, and eventually New York. Just seven years after its initial outbreak, in a world where trans-Atlantic transportation was limited to ships if it occurred at all, cholera had enveloped the U.S. Pacific coast and Mexico. In an effort to stem the spread of the disease, public policy in the United States began to favor strict quarantines of foreign arrivals. These were enacted at major ports, often imposing significant costs and slowing trade. However, it soon became obvious from the continuing proliferation of cholera that these isolated quarantines were having little effect; lack of coordination meant that they could not achieve their goals, and the restrictions on commercial travel imposed a substantial and ineffective burden on the U.S. economy.

Following the failure of national governments to deal with the cholera pandemic, in 1834 the French issued a call for international coordination. Though laudable, this appeal was largely unanswered and cholera continued to spread, culminating in further pandemics in 1848 and 1849. As the effects of these new cholera outbreaks rippled through the world, governments started to realize the essential value of international cooperation in fighting the disease. This realization eventually led to the first global sanitary conference in 1851, with subsequent assemblies held in 1859, 1866, and 1874. Although these gatherings of national representatives provided a forum for discussion, it was not until 1902 that the first international health body was founded—the International Sanitary Bureau (a precursor to the Pan American Health Organization). In 1907, when the effectiveness of a multinational approach to health management had become clear, the International Office of Public Hygiene was initiated in Paris. A decade later, the Health Organisation of the League of Nations, the first organization to openly embrace global governance, was eventually established in the aftermath of the First World War.

These initial organizations focused on coordinating border controls and sharing information. Most early twentieth-century bodies were not explicitly concerned with influenza pandemics. Policy makers before World War II seemed to understand that their scientific knowledge and disease-fighting capability were inadequate to combat the virulence of infectious diseases. With the discovery of penicillin in 1928, however, and the creation of WHO two decades later, the international bodies raised their ambition to that of "eliminating all communicable disease at their sources."[70] WHO's early campaigns to eradicate infectious diseases met with some success. In what was the largest-scale international health engagement in history, an army of doctors, health professionals, and willing volunteers set out to eradicate smallpox in 1968. Dr. Larry Brilliant—one of the pioneers—notes that the operation involved "doctors of every culture, nation, race, or religion," and the team he led made over one billion house calls to smallpox sufferers throughout Southeast Asia and beyond.[71] At the campaign's start in 1967, smallpox was endemic in 37 countries worldwide. Within three years, targeted efforts had reduced this number to 18. By 1974, just six years after WHO launched its "audacious mission," smallpox was limited to five countries.[72] Today smallpox has been eradicated from the planet, and the lessons from WHO's successful campaign have been applied by public health professionals in many parts of the world, including in the campaign to eradicate river blindness in Africa. Although these achievements are remarkable, it is worth noting that they have been far from universally successful. Continued efforts to eliminate malaria have failed; there are still over 220 million cases and an estimated 2,000 deaths per day. In all, communicable diseases continue to account for one-third of the global disease burden and are still one of the leading causes of premature death.

Nobel Laureate Joshua Lederberg has noted that with developments in health management have come new challenges. In 1997 he argued that the introduction of antibiotics and the discovery of a vaccination for polio in the early and mid-twentieth century, respectively, provided mixed blessings. Although these advancements gave substantial resources to doctors fighting deadly diseases, they also led to a "national, almost worldwide, redirection of attention to chronic and constitutional diseases."[73] He cautioned against the danger of neglecting infectious diseases in favor of research on noncommunicable illnesses. According to Lederberg, "It is fortuitous that retroviruses had already been studied from the perspective of cancer etiology," because otherwise "we would have had no scientific platform whatsoever for coping with HIV and AIDS."[74]

The Twenty-First Century

The twenty-first century has brought new resources but also new challenges for disease control. The factors that determine how pandemics occur are "frequently complex and poorly understood."[75] This appears typical of the negative externalities that arise from globalization.

In his 1997 article Joshua Lederberg recognized that the coming new century would bring new challenges.[76] He pointed to several specific instances in which the corollary of progress is risk. To Lederberg, a global perspective on health management is a prerequisite for sustainable development, and he argued for investments in public health and agricultural microbiology and also in research into new ways to fight diseases. Hand in hand with these investments, he considered capabilities to rapidly share information to be essential and cleanliness and education to be mandatory. Lederberg recognized that governments must be ceded power from the individual and wrote that "in the triumph of individual rights, the public health perspective has had an uphill struggle in recent pandemics." This struggle emphasizes the need for debate and heightened awareness of the "social context for constraints."[77]

Chen, Evans, and Cash also highlight that globalization is the source of both solutions and new challenges. They argue that infectious disease surveillance itself is a public good and suggest that "globalization may be shifting the balance of health to a global public good."[78] As early as 1999, they spoke of an "inherent tension between global health equity and social exclusion" and asserted that "globalisation [was] blurring the traditional line between public and private in health."[79] These authors, all eminent public health experts, saw that the corollary of this good might be a "third wave of health threats" that includes public *bads*. These, they argued, would come in the form of emerging infections but also new noncommunicable diseases and the consequences of pollution and other environmental threats we examined in the previous chapter. They attempted to assign responsibility for new epidemics in developing countries (for example, for cholera in Latin America), for local infections in previously protected populations (for example, for cyclospora, or so-called traveler's diarrhea, in the United States), and for novel health fears (for example, for "mad cow" disease, in Europe). The source of pandemics, they argued, could be found in the same "acceleration of international trade" that had brought economic benefits and growth but through various means had also spawned new health challenges.[80]

Chen, Evans, and Cash point out that coordination of international efforts might run into conflicts of interest. A diversity of involvements and priorities leads almost inevitably to different actors' having different perspectives and views on how to address global coordination arising from their different material interests. The authors conjectured that although more affluent economies might primarily be concerned with preventing and eventually containing the spread of a new global virus, developed economies might prefer to focus their scarce resources on understanding the transmission patterns of more common but still fatal diseases such as diarrheal or respiratory diseases.

LESSONS FROM PANDEMIC MANAGEMENT

David M. Bell et al. contrast the measures taken to deal with the H1N1 virus (swine flu) in Mexico City and New York in 2009. In Mexico the government invoked its emergency powers on 24 April in anticipation of widespread panic. These allowed the authorities to engage in an intensive media campaign, as well as to put measures in place for social distancing and the dissemination of antiviral drugs. In an attempt to control the spread of the virus through the education system, the government instigated the screening of all schoolchildren throughout the country. The fragmented nature of Mexican health care, however, meant that the government had difficulty coordinating its actions among the three major health care systems. As a result, laboratory capacity in Mexico was too limited to deal with the crisis, and estimates of the overall bill are over US$2.3 billion, the equivalent of 0.3 percent of Mexico's GDP.[81]

In New York, on the other hand, the public campaign was associated with only the occasional closure of schools and instead put emphasis on existing health mechanisms. The emergency stocks of vaccine compiled by local authorities were in the end not needed because "normal distribution channels" continued to function sufficiently.[82] The problems in New York instead related to individuals who lived, worked, and commuted through different administrative jurisdictions. This should emphasize that although the ability to respond to threats in a flexible manner is required, the importance of preplanning and preparation cannot be overstated.

Picking up on this same message, Marguerite Pappaioanou, professor of infectious disease epidemiology at the University of Minnesota, advocated "basic strategies" to minimize pandemic risk. These primarily involved limiting human exposure to animals, particularly among high-risk groups such as farmers, vendors, and those involved in the transport of live animals.[83] Coupled with this, Pappaioanou wrote that she considered vaccination the most effective preventive approach to pandemic risk and hence advocated "continued virologic and disease surveillance of Avian influenza virus in humans, poultry, and swine." This, she argued, is "essential" to monitor pandemic risk and to properly prepare for outbreaks.[84] In her conclusion Professor Pappaioanou cited WHO's "five priority actions for optimal pandemic prevention and preparedness," with respect to bird flu specifically:

- Reduce human exposure to the virus.

- Strengthen early warning systems.

- Intensify rapid containment operations.

- Build coping capacity.

- Coordinate global research.[85]

Although these specific actions relate to H1N1, we can see that their usefulness is far more general. Larry Brilliant has summarized the two simple principles involved: "The key to eradicating smallpox was *early detection, early response.*"[86] In sum, there are three crucial lessons to be learned for systemic thinking regarding the health risks arising from globalization.

Lesson 1: To identify risks, mechanisms for early detection are essential
The difficulty associated with managing pandemics grows exponentially with the number of people affected. The key is to locate the pathogen at its source, then isolate and contain it. As Dr. Brilliant has stressed, "You can't cure or prevent what you don't know is there."[87] The Web provides global search engines that could be set up to browse millions of Web-based activities across different languages in order to detect pandemic outbreaks. These could both intuitively and empirically bear results much faster than institutions such as WHO that rely on reporting by individuals with long lead and lag times. During the SARS outbreak, WHO itself was alerted to the problem by the Web-based Canadian Global Public Health Intelligence Network (GPHIN).[88] GPHIN's Web-based search, along with those of similar systems, like the European Media Monitor or the Google-supported Innovative Support to Emergencies, Diseases, and Disasters, allows for early warnings and has the advantage

that information is easily collected across language barriers, circumventing slow-moving institutional structures.[89] Engaging civil society to support these activities and establishing the necessary technologies—including evolving sensors embedded in mobile phones—provides the global ability to locate and contain pandemics at their source.

Adding the capabilities afforded by new technologies is not a substitute for more effective coordination between countries. Overcoming concerns regarding the capture of intellectual property to ensure that those who share information on potential threats are able to benefit from the subsequent development of drugs to manage the pandemic is key. So, too, is providing the necessary skills and laboratory and other capacity in all regions of the world to adequately monitor and identify potential pandemics, not least in rural areas and the poorer neighborhoods of cities.

Lesson 2: Once a pandemic is detected, mechanisms for early response must be enacted

Identifying the source of a pandemic is the first necessary step. The isolation and eradication of the pandemic is the necessary next step. The establishment of national, regional, or global capabilities in this regard is vital. The equivalent of special weapons and tactics (SWAT) teams with the medical and other capacity to mobilize rapidly (without lengthy authorization procedures) and engage anywhere in the world is vital. Such capacity is required for pandemics nationally and globally. Once a pathogen has skipped from the countryside to a megacity or from a megacity to a major airport, there is no bringing it back. Although the immediate response should be medical, the broader implications also need thinking through. For example, if the emergency requires the culling of all the poultry or pigs on which people depend for their livelihoods and nutrition, alternative mechanisms to support the population need to be put in place immediately, with the costs of this response to a potential global emergency underwritten by WHO or another global institution.

Lesson 3: Systemic risks require systemic responses

The international coordination on HIV/AIDS, SARS, and other recent pandemics highlights the vital role of research, coordination, and global action. Pandemics have no respect for national borders, and, given the incubation period for all known threats, it is fanciful to imagine that the threat can be contained at a national border. Any pathogen that is carried through a major airport hub will be global within three days at the most. There is an urgent need, therefore, to (1) deepen investment in research, including on vaccines and other protective interventions; (2) develop monitoring and surveillance at the national level that is globally integrated; (3) establish SWAT teams for bio risks, with at least one team ready to act at each major intercontinental hub; (4) develop national and global cascading scenarios based on the worst experiences of the past; (5) rapidly escalate attention to the creation of lethal pathogens, including the possibility that these may be developed through increasingly affordable DNA sequencing and new chemical synthetics; and (6) pay increasing attention to antibiotic resistance and curtail antibiotic applications. The permissive use of antibiotics needs to end if we are to ensure their continued efficacy. The distribution of over-the-counter antibiotics that do not require prescriptions and the use of antibiotics in nonhuman applications need to be restricted. With over half of the antibiotics made allocated to animal husbandry to increase factory farming efficiencies and the growing use of antibiotics in other applications (such as the painting of ships' hulls to reduce the growth of barnacles), we are at growing risk that when we need antibiotics for our survival, they will have become ineffective.

7

⊛

Inequality and Social Risks

Globalization has led to growth in inequality both within countries and between countries. It has been the most powerful force in history in raising incomes for poor people. But not everyone has benefited equally. Within countries, the educated and the most physically and virtually connected have benefited most. Across countries, the majority of emerging markets are growing at three to five times the rate of the richer countries, leading to what has been dubbed "convergence, big time."[1] However, up to 20 of the poorest countries—the failed states, states in conflict, and those such as North Korea—are isolated as a result of their crises or have turned their backs on globalization. These countries are stagnating or even getting poorer, leading to a widening spectrum of incomes when we compare the richest and the poorest countries.

In *Globalization for Development* Ian Goldin and Kenneth Reinert examine the relationship between globalization and inequality and provide a systematic account of the policies that may lead to more inclusive growth.[2] In *The Butterfly Defect* our concern is with systemic risk, so our focus is on the relationships among globalization, inequality, and systemic risk. Our view is that this triad is unstable and that without addressing questions of social cohesion none of the issues identified in the preceding chapters will be addressed. We believe that *inclusive* globalization is required to address systemic instability. Our analysis thus far has focused on facilitating globalization that is "resilient" and "robust." In this chapter we discuss the fact that "sustainable globalization" requires a consideration of social factors, as well as the more technical concerns elaborated in previous chapters.

A cohesive society is as crucial to sustainable globalization as functioning physical and virtual infrastructure. Political instability and polarization constitute metarisks that are as threatening as risks from floods or infrastructure collapse. Failure to avert these crises will have repercussions across many domains and can impair global integration and connectivity. It may even provoke a reversal of globalization altogether. The mismanagement of globalization runs the risk of undermining the benefits it has brought about. When citizens see globalization as a source of threat rather than opportunity and seek to reverse it through protectionist, nationalist, and xenophobic policies, the developments that have benefited so many could be sacrificed. For poor people and those who have yet to fully benefit from globalization, this would have particularly negative consequences.

We begin by examining the state of global inequality today. We investigate how these disparities arose and see the channels through which risks are created. Some of the threats we discuss, specifically those related to governance, resemble the problems that Harvard Economist Dani Rodrik identified in a 2002 article in *Harvard Magazine* and later expanded on in his 2011 book *The Globalization Paradox.*[3] We end the chapter by drawing lessons for global governance.

GLOBAL INTEGRATION AND INEQUALITY

Even among those who are doubtful about the benefits from globalization it is recognized that, on average, poverty has decreased during decades of global integration.[4] The number of people in the developing world who are living on less than US$1.25 (in terms of purchasing power parity, or PPP) per day was as high as 1.9 billion in 1990 but had dropped to 1.29 billion by 2008; the poverty headcount ratio decreased from 43.1 to 22.4 percent over the same period.[5] Even looking at higher income levels, it is predicted that "by 2030, roughly 50% of the world population [will] fall into the $6,000–$30,000 bracket, up from around 29% currently (and around 24% in the 1980s)."[6] In fact, during the 20 years prior to the 2007/2008 financial crisis, "real disposable household incomes increased in all OECD [Organisation for Economic Co-operation and Development] countries, by 1.7% a year, on average."[7] Furthermore, there is evidence that the link between globalization and poverty reduction is not coincidental and that increasing integration and openness are indeed responsible for reducing global poverty.[8]

Figures like these are overly simplistic, and the debate about the relevant development indicators to consider and the appropriate ways of measuring them remains a concern for many development economists. An important qualification, particularly in view of questions related to governance, regards the distinction between inequality across and within countries. Consistent with the traditional view in the literature on economic growth and development, it seems to be the case that overall inequality at the global level is decreasing as most developing countries are enjoying rapid income growth.[9] Despite the still very wide absolute differences in incomes, there is convergence *between* the average incomes of most, but certainly not all, developing countries and the more advanced OECD economies. However, *within* virtually all countries, rich and poor alike, inequality is increasing.[10] Globalization is part of the explanation. The ongoing crisis in the Eurozone and the aftermath of the global financial crisis have fueled this development further. We elaborate on these patterns below.

Within-Country Inequality

The OECD reports that income inequality was increasing in most OECD countries from the mid-1980s to the late 2000s; exceptions were Turkey and Greece, where inequality decreased, and France, Hungary, and Belgium, where the degree of inequality remained stable throughout the late 2000s (figure 7.1). For Anglo-Saxon countries like the United States or the United Kingdom, the increase in inequality is the continuation of a trend that started in the 1970s; the fact that countries like "Denmark, Germany and Sweden, which have traditionally had low inequality, are no longer spared from the rising inequality trend" constitutes a more recent phenomenon.[11]

These inequalities can partly be explained by changes in wages and, more specifically, by the accelerating growth of salaries among top earners.[12] Yet there are also more structural explanations: reduced

**Gini coefficients
of income inequality**

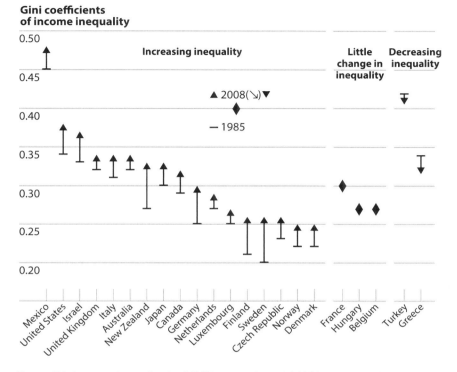

Figure 7.1. Income inequality in OECD countries, mid-1980s and late 2000s. The data for the mid-1980s refer to the early 1990s for the Czech Republic and Hungary. OECD (Organisation for Economic Co-operation and Development), 2011b, *Growing Income Inequality in OECD Countries: What Drives It and How Can Policy Tackle It?*, OECD Forum on Tackling Inequality, Paris, 2 May, 6, accessed 3 February 2013, http://www.oecd.org/els/socialpoliciesanddata/47723414.pdf. Used with permission.

working-time arrangements, for instance, are more prevalent among low-wage earners, and the more frequent use of such arrangements causes the income gap to widen even when wages remain unchanged. Due to improved opportunities for transport and communication as well as increasing competitive pressures, usage of such arrangements has indeed become more widespread[13]—in particular for those jobs that are more readily transferred to lower-wage locations. This reproduces a structural link between globalization and income inequality at the national level. Technological change over recent decades, in particular the development of the Internet and the automation and innovations in logistics, has also increased inequality. We discussed in chapter 3 the dimensions associated with the new international division of labor and the ability to relocate labor-intensive production to lower-wage economies. The substitution of capital invested in machines for workers in the higher-wage economies has also contributed to rising inequality. As the returns to capital expressed in profits have risen, those with assets and income have benefited relative to those who do not have such endowments. As the OECD has observed, "Globalisation, skill-biased technological progress and institutional and regulatory reforms" are among "the most important impacts on widening inequality in OECD countries."[14]

Figure 7.2 shows that measures of trade integration, research and development expenditures, and especially financial openness rose rapidly in the period when innovations in communication technologies became affordable for individuals and small businesses. Although this affordability offered new opportunities for those able to employ these technologies, the take-off of new technologies left behind those who were not sufficiently skilled or could not afford the necessary training and equipment. In the words of the OECD, "These changes have brought higher rewards for high skilled workers and thus affected the way earnings from work are distributed."[15] Highly skilled employees were paid a higher premium for their skills while returns to low-skilled laborers stagnated—if not in absolute terms, certainly relative to skill levels. Evidence of such a skill premium is provided, for example, by World Bank researcher Branko Milanović, who reports that wage differentials between rich and poor cities are higher for low-skilled earners (table 7.1). The OECD also finds evidence of a wage gap "between skilled and unskilled workers."[16] Based on comparable evidence, Martin Rama of the World Bank concludes, "If exposure to international trade and foreign direct investment increase the wage premium to skill, access to education for all should be a priority."[17]

Although the effects of globalization on within-country inequality differ between countries,[18] in most cases integration into the world economy increases income inequality. China, for example, has experienced a moderate but persistent increase in income inequality—as measured by the GINI index—since the 1980s.[19] Even India, which has benefited from low and stable levels of inequality over the same time period (with a GINI index hovering around 31.0), exhibits a small increase if the latest

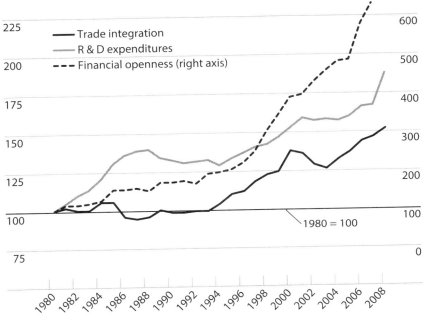

Figure 7.2. Economic integration and technological innovations (1980 = 100), 1980–2008. The figure shows the Organisation for Economic Co-operation and Development countries' averages for developments in trade integration, financial openness, and technologic change and assumes the use of paid workers of working age. Trade integration is defined as the sum of imports and exports as a percentage of GDP. Financial openness is defined as the sum of cross-border liabilities and assets as a percentage of GDP. R&D expenditures refer to business-sector expenditures on research and development as a percentage of GDP. The data for the mid-2000s refer to 2000 for Belgium and France. Those for the mid-1980s refer to the early 1990s for Austria, the Czech Republic, France, Greece, Hungary, and Ireland. OECD (Organisation for Economic Co-operation and Development), 2011b, *Growing Income Inequality in OECD Countries: What Drives It and How Can Policy Tackle It?*, OECD Forum on Tackling Inequality, Paris, 2 May, 9, accessed 3 February 2013, http://www.oecd.org/els/socialpoliciesanddata/47723414.pdf. Used with permission.

(post–financial crisis) data points are included.[20] Figure 7.3 highlights some of the within-country income inequalities in the United States as well as in Brazil, Russia, India, and China.

Despite such intriguing evidence, the effect of technological progress and global connectivity on within-country levels of inequality is not

Table 7.1
Wage Differentials, Skilled versus Unskilled Laborers (US$), 2009

City / rich versus poor	Building laborer[a]		Skilled industrial worker[b]		Engineer[c]	
	Nominal after-tax wage	Real food wage	Nominal after-tax wage	Real food wage	Nominal after-tax wage	Real food wage
New York	16.6	16.6	29.0	29.0	26.5	26.5
London	15.4	9.7	19.0	30.4	22.1	35.2
Beijing	1.3	0.8	2.3	3.8	5.8	9.5
Delhi	1.7	0.5	2.1	6.9	2.9	9.1
Nairobi	1.5	0.6	2.0	4.7	4.0	9.2
Rich versus poor (unweighted ratio)[d]	10.9	20.4	11.0	5.8	5.8	3.3

Notes: Food prices are estimated from a basket of 39 food products with weights reflecting West European consumption patterns. New York food prices are set equal to 1. The real food wage (in New York food prices) is estimated by dividing the nominal after-tax dollar wage by the food price index (not shown here). The annual number of hours worked is equal to the weekly number of hours of work given for each profession and country separately, multiplied by 52 weeks and reduced for the number of official and paid vacation days per year for each country.

[a]Unskilled or semiskilled laborer, about 25 years of age, single.

[b]Skilled worker with vocational training and about 10 years of experience, working in a large company in the metal-working industry, approximately 35 years of age, married, two children.

[c]Worker employed in an industrial firm in the electrical engineering sector, a university or technical college graduate with at least 5 years of experience, about 35 years of age, married, two children.

[d]The rich are in New York and London; the poor are in Beijing, Delhi, and Nairobi.

Source: Branko Milanović, 2011, "Global Inequality from Class to Location, from Proletarians to Migrants," Policy Research Working Paper 5820, World Bank, Washington, DC, 15, accessed 3 February 2013, http://www-wds.worldbank.org/servlet/WDSContentServer/WDSP/IB/2011/09/29/000158349_20110 929082257/Rendered/PDF/WPS5820.pdf. Used with permission.

Global percentile

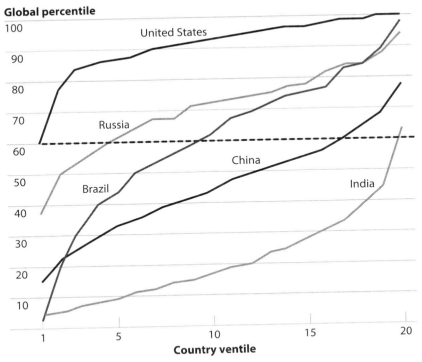

Figure 7.3. Income distribution, United States versus the BRIC countries, 2005. Based on national household surveys, with people ranked by per capita income or per capita consumption adjusted for price differences between the countries using the most recent purchasing power parity figures. BRIC denotes the emerging market economies of Brazil, Russia, India, and China. Each value on the horizontal axis indicates 5 percent (a ventile) of the population. The value 1 corresponds to the poorest 5 percent, 20 to the richest 5 percent. Values on the vertical axis correspond to the global percentile position of each national ventile; for the poorest 5 percent of the U.S. population (1 on the horizontal axis), the value is 60 (the location of the dashed line in the figure), implying that the poorest 5 percent in the United States are better off than 60 percent of the world population. Branko Milanović, 2011, "Global Inequality from Class to Location, from Proletarians to Migrants," Policy Research Working Paper 5820, World Bank, Washington, DC, 8, accessed 3 February 2013, http://www-wds.worldbank.org/servlet/WDSContentServer/WDSP/IB/2011/09/29/000158349_20110929082257/Rendered/PDF/WPS5820.pdf. Used with permission.

straightforward from the point of view of economic theory. Improved availability of information, heightened mobility of labor as well as goods and services, and increasing degrees of competition should, in a world of perfect markets, be expected to increase efficiency and thereby the marginal product of labor (wages). Even in a world of heterogeneous abilities, these efficiency gains should lead to an increase in "the size of the cake" and—with the appropriate social policies in place—ultimately to higher living standards. Orthodox trade theory, nevertheless, also predicts that increased trade could lead to increasing wage differentials in developed economies[21] while reducing inequality in developing countries. This, however, is inconsistent with evidence on heightened inequality globally, including in poor countries.[22] World Bank researcher Branko Milanović and economist Lynn Squire show that innovation has an adverse initial impact among those who are constrained in their ability to profit from it, that is, people with lower levels of skill and initial investments.[23] However, some dispute that global integration unequivocally leads to growing income inequality. Some studies, for example, appear to show that "rising imports from developing countries are associated with declining income inequality in advanced countries."[24] This finding refers specifically to the effect of trade openness. It also serves as evidence that thoughtfully managed integration has the potential to bring about decreasing inequality and the aforementioned improvements in living standards, especially when the detrimental effects of financial integration can be contained.[25]

Global Inequality

In contrast, the evidence of the relationship between globalization and global income inequality appears to be ambiguous and, more important, sensitive to the choice of the sample. As Figure 7.3 shows, at the individual level there are wide income differentials, even between the citizens of countries that would not necessarily be at the bottom of the income distribution when ranked by country averages. Owing to their static nature, however, these comparative data have little to say about the development of individual inequality over time, and thus about the causal impact of globalization. Commenting on the corresponding dynamics, Branko Milanović finds that "the world today presents a peculiar picture where some of its parts are immensely richer than ever in history while other parts have an income level about the same as it was 150 or even 500 years ago." He also asserts that "even when we contrast the fast-growing 'emerging economies' of China and India with the rich world, the gap in the first decade of the 21st century is greater than it was around 1850."[26] Based on this evidence, it seems that the picture at the global scale resembles what we have reported for national inequality: more globalization seems to be associated with a more unequal world. This long-term historical trend is even more remarkable if we acknowledge that the rapid growth and integration of some of the poorest and most populous economies (most notably those of China and India) have actually reduced global inequality and encouraged convergence in recent times.[27]

Analyzing slightly higher income brackets, Goldman Sachs researchers Dominic Wilson and Raluca Dragusanu present evidence that might help explain the apparent "convergence" in recent times. They observe that the global middle class is "exploding" and the global income distribution is "narrowing."[28] They are confident that "by 2030, roughly 50 percent of the world population [will] fall into the $6,000–$30,000 [income] bracket, up from around 29 percent currently (and around 24 percent in the 1980s)."[29] In absolute terms, Wilson and Dragusanu expect poverty levels to decline even though "Africa's share of the global poor may continue to rise."[30] In contrast to the analysis by Milanović, their take on the data suggests an overall trend toward a narrower global income distribution (figure 7.4). The Goldman Sachs data suggest that the effects of globalization on the global income distribution are primarily driven by an increase in the average incomes of several developing economies—not by structural changes in the developed countries.[31]

Even though Milanovic's data (see figure 7.3) suggest that there is often substantial heterogeneity within countries, the comparison of country averages seems to exhibit the same qualitative features as the analysis at the individual-country level. As the Goldman Sachs study indicates, there has been a rise in average incomes in developing countries; a few stagnating or contracting low-income economies are the exceptions rather than the norm. Table 7.2 also shows that although the group of low-income countries witnessed faster economic growth than the group of high-income countries during the first decade of the twenty-first century, the even more

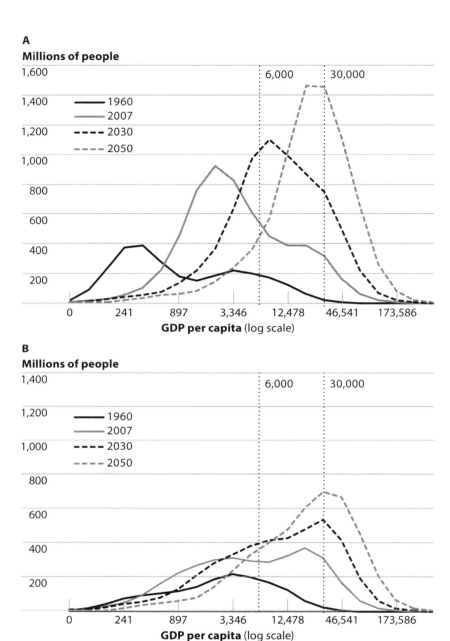

A

Millions of people

6,000   30,000

1,600
1,400 ——— 1960
          ——— 2007
1,200 ----- 2030
          ----- 2050
1,000
800
600
400
200

0   241   897   3,346   12,478   46,541   173,586

GDP per capita (log scale)

B

Millions of people

6,000   30,000

1,400 ——— 1960
          ——— 2007
1,200 ----- 2030
          ----- 2050
1,000
800
600
400
200

0   241   897   3,346   12,478   46,541   173,586

GDP per capita (log scale)

Figure 7.4. (A) Global distribution of income and (B) global distribution of income excluding China and India, 1960–2050. Dominic Wilson and Raluca Dragusanu, 2008, "The Expanding Middle: The Exploding World Middle Class and Falling Global Inequality," Global Economic Papers 170, Goldman Sachs, New York, 5, accessed 3 February 2013, http://www.ryanallis.com/wp-content/uploads/2008/07/expandingmiddle.pdf. Used with permission.

TABLE 7.2
GDP PER CAPITA, SELECTED REGIONS AND COUNTRIES (CURRENT US$), 2000–2011

Income level/Region	GDP per capita (current US$) 2011	GDP per capita growth rate (%) 2000–2011	Ranking by GDP per capita (current US$, 2011)[a]
High-income	41,095.47	63.15	
Middle-income	4,570.30	253.32	
Low-income	580.74	125.13	
North America	48,639.67	43.25	
Sub-Saharan Africa (all income levels)	1,444.90	180.80	
Selected countries (ranked by slowest growth in 2000–2011 to fastest growth)			
Gambia	624.57	2.98	20
Bahamas	22,431.03	5.52	145
Antigua and Barbuda	12,595.51	21.88	126
Japan	45,902.67	23.09	160
Belize	4,133.48	24.09	81
Micronesia	2,851.84	30.75	61
United Arab Emirates	45,653.09	32.73	159
Guinea	501.99	34.59	12
Hong Kong SAR, China	34,456.96	35.79	153
United States	48,441.56	38.08	164

[a]Ranking is from lowest to highest; that is, the United States (with the highest rank) has the highest per capita income in the group, Guinea the lowest.

Source: World Bank, 2012a, "GDP per Capita (Current US$)," *Data*, accessed 3 September, http://data.worldbank.org/indicator/NY.GDP.PCAP.CD/countries. Used with permission.

rapid growth among middle-income countries has contributed to a widening gap at the bottom of the income distribution. And although there is some evidence of convergence (North American income grew 43 percent between 2000 and 2011, whereas the growth rate in Sub-Saharan Africa was 180 percent), the table also shows that, at the bottom of the income distribution, some countries have been left behind.

As countries become wealthier, their population growth rates typically slow, so one should expect the per capita gap between rich and poor countries to be even more pronounced than the gap in total income at national levels. Because the developing countries have grown much more rapidly than the rich economies in recent years, the average per capita income in most developing countries has also risen rapidly. Convergence across countries is one of the central predictions of the early growth literature, and this has indeed, to a certain degree, been evident in recent years. Not all developing countries have enjoyed rapid economic growth, though; as some have stagnated or contracted, there has been a divergence of economic prospects when all countries are taken into account. Specific policies are therefore required to reduce inequality between countries as well as within countries.[32]

THE CHANNELS OF INEQUALITY

As the marginal costs of using innovations decrease, new technologies can improve the living conditions (and incomes) of poor people. A good example is the cost of mobile phones or the Internet. By means of higher connectivity and by improving access to education and information, technologies such as the cell phone and the Internet may contribute to closing the income gap. A wealth of research shows that education and the flow of information play crucial roles in enhancing female income and employment prospects, improving nutrition and health, and reducing the isolation of rural and marginalized communities.[33]

Another channel through which globalization may affect the distribution of incomes is the interplay of global competition and regulatory reform. In the case of the labor market, for example, it has been argued that more flexibility (for example, weaker employment protection for temporary workers) has led to more pronounced earnings differentials while also improving employment levels.[34] Other prominent examples that are linked to the competitive pressures from globalization include tax competition (specifically with respect to corporate taxes and taxes on capital income) as well as environmental and financial regulation.

Examples of tax competition were highlighted in the British media in November 2012. They focused on the low levels of taxes paid by global firms such as Starbucks (which paid £8.6 million in corporation taxes in 14 years on U.K. sales of £3 billion, a rate of under 1 percent), Amazon (which paid no corporation taxes on its £3.3 billion of sales in the United Kingdom), or Apple (which paid US$713 million in taxes on its overseas profits of US$36.8 billion, a rate of 1.9 percent), highlighting the tension between globalization and national sovereignty.[35] The following June the G8 pledged to "make a real difference" in addressing tax avoidance by sharing information across borders, reforming tax rules, and obliging companies to report profits and taxes paid (no matter where) to all tax authorities.[36] A month later this pledge was followed by the announcement of a G20/OECD 15-point action plan for "aligning tax with substance" by ensuring that all taxes are paid where corporations make sales and profits.[37]

THE RISKS OF INEQUALITY

In this section we build on previous observations by discussing the different ways in which inequality puts the benefits of globalization at risk. Our central theme is that a lack of cohesion and the growing frustration of those who are unable to participate undermine the foundations on which improved global living standards rest. Within countries this frustration exposes the mismatch between global challenges and local governance structures. Politicians think and respond nationally, although the key issues that will determine our future arise from forces that are beyond our borders.[38]

Social Cohesion and Political Stability

A recent book hints at two forces—opposing forces—concerning the link between globalization and social cohesion.[39] On the one hand, "cultural homogenization" and the increasing ability to share information, as well as a wide array of problems with almost everyone on the globe, should be expected to foster social cohesion. On the other hand, globalization makes the welfare state more difficult and more expensive to maintain, suggesting that the challenges that come with global integration may impair social cohesion.

The distinction between within-country and across-country inequalities is an important one, although both are important when considering the sustainability of globalization. For many, a key concern and measure of the impact of globalization is whether it results in a decline in inequality for the world population as a whole (as some forecast[40]). This neglects an important political dimension in that sustainable global arrangements require stability and operable institutions at the national level as well.[41] If nation-states look inward and seek to reverse globalization, this process cannot become more inclusive or better able to deal with the questions of the global commons and global systemic risks.

It follows that avoiding excessive inequality at the national level is a precondition of any policy intending to tackle global inequality. This raises an important challenge for global governance. If electoral incentives and institutions are designed to respond to national conditions (perhaps, for example, by providing incentives for politicians to pursue protectionist policies to reduce unemployment or curb migration), there is a risk that global achievements may be sacrificed. The same is likely to be true if the polarization of income and the growing disparity of social conditions enable relatively small, powerful elites to set the policy agenda by squeezing the capacity of the middle class (often seen as "the bastion of social values"[42]) to mount an effective challenge.

Dani Rodrik argues that sustainable globalization requires addressing the trade-off between harvesting the benefits of globalized competition and preserving stability at the national level with stronger national institutions.[43] Although we agree with his diagnosis, the fact that "the global perspective is not well represented politically" remains.[44] Rodrik's approach of strengthening national institutions would not necessarily resolve this problem and could even impair the efforts toward global representation that we have identified as essential.

Wilson and Dragusanu provide a different perspective on these issues by focusing on a growing *global* middle class. Figure 7.5, taken from their study, exhibits an S-shaped relationship between household income and oil demand on the one hand and car ownership on the other. The two curves exhibit the steepest slope within the US$6,000–US$30,000 income bracket. This is precisely the range of incomes of those who are expected to account for about 50 percent of global income recipients by 2030. Even though the slope seems to be mitigated when individuals reach the US$25,000–US$30,000 threshold, the data suggest that the peak demand for and potential conflict over natural resources will arise over the coming 20 years. The difficulty with this, in the words of Wilson and Dragusanu, is that "there is no doubt that the kinds of demands and pressures that the Expanding Middle could put on global resources and the sorts of changes it may set in place are likely to generate tensions within and across countries."[45]

This difficulty only reinforces the need for strong global institutions. Without coordinated global policies, these pressures will be hard to manage; yet, if it is true that "inequality within some countries remains high or rises further," the politicians in charge will have incentives to focus on national policies first and to put the required adjustments at the global scale second.[46] There is a growing risk that policies designed to meet national interests will undermine the potential long-run benefits of global integration at the expense of the short-run alleviation of national problems related to unemployment or inequality.

Clearly the relationship between globalization and social stability is complex. Moreover, the nature of inequality itself has changed. In the past, income was determined by social class or, even more directly, by land ownership. In a fascinating study, François Bourguignon and Christian Morrisson found that location determined income inequality in 1820 to only a small extent (11.7 percent of the explanation was between-country differences), while social class was significantly more important (within-country differences accounted for 88.5 percent of income inequality as measured by the Theil index). By 1992 the study found that location accounted for as much as 60 percent of inequality, while class explained only 40 percent.[47] Using data from 2005 and Gini coefficients to measure inequality, other studies have found the relevance of class even further reduced (explaining only 15 percent of the Gini coefficient) and that of between-country differences further elevated (to 85 percent).[48] In fact, Milanović implies that this development has

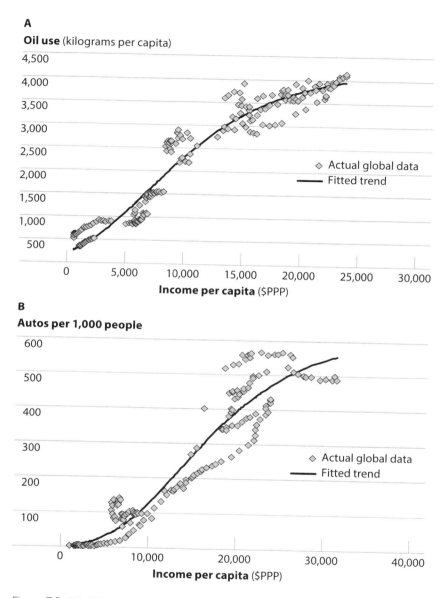

Figure 7.5. (A) Oil demand and (B) car ownership by income level. PPP, purchasing power parity. Dominic Wilson and Raluca Dragusanu, 2008, "The Expanding Middle: The Exploding World Middle Class and Falling Global Inequality," Global Economic Papers 170, Goldman Sachs, New York, 17, accessed 3 February 2013, http://www.ryanallis.com/wp-content/uploads/2008/07/expandingmiddle.pdf. Used with permission.

weakened global cohesion because members of the working class across countries now have less in common with one another economically and may even have "conflicting" interests.[49] Unskilled laborers in rich cities receive higher incomes and are now much better off than their counterparts in the world's poorer regions (see table 7.1). This makes it harder to coordinate and to form global coalitions to support their interests, and it runs counter to the improved technological opportunities for organizing such coalitions. Whether communities that may be gaining membership will be able to translate diverse local interests into a cohesive global agenda to promote real change in global policies and institutions remains an open question. Individuals across the world now share their concerns, but there is a complexity and diffusion of responsibilities that means that the achievement of political mobilization and consequences, particularly in a sustained manner, is often lacking.

There may no longer be an alliance of the global working class, but there are new global challenges to globalization as articulated, for example, through Attac, Anonymous, the Indignados, or the Occupy movement.[50] Instead of protesting against the terms and conditions of work, protesters are concerned by the opacity of global institutions and the negative consequences of what many see as the systemic failure of globalization to deliver jobs and a sustainable environment. By making the world more complex and risks harder to trace back to their origins, globalization has divided global society into groups that are prepared and able to embrace the corresponding benefits on the one hand and, on the other, people who are overwhelmed with the complex causalities, the often incomprehensible influences on their lives, and their inability to identify political or institutional responsibilities.

New levels of connectivity expose global differences in living standards and opportunities and, for individuals around the world, present stark evidence of a global system that many have no desire to engage with and in which many feel they have little chance of succeeding. As the example of the Occupy movement shows, such concerns are particularly prominent among younger people, who feel increasingly disenfranchised. In many countries and cities around the world, "they have now been joined by protesters who believe that they are bearing the brunt of a crisis for which they have no responsibility, while people on high incomes appear to have been spared."[51]

Part of the problem is that for many the globalized system seems to stifle social mobility and prevent talented, hardworking people from achieving the rewards they deserve. Countries in which the lack of "intergenerational . . . mobility" is particularly pronounced include Italy, the United States, and the United Kingdom. A lack of prospects and upward mobility translates into unequal opportunities and frustration. It "breeds social resentment" as well as "political instability," and "it can . . . fuel populist, protectionist, and anti-globalization sentiments" and induce "people [to] no longer support open trade and free markets if they feel that they are losing out while a small group of winners are getting richer and richer."[52]

Increasing frustration with complexity and the divergence of incomes and opportunities constitutes the central political risk of the twenty-first century.[53] There is a real risk that the ethical and moral basis of globalization is eroding as it fails to fulfill its promise of improving living conditions and opportunities for increasing numbers of people in both the developing and the richer countries. This, in turn, makes it more likely that populism and extremism will find fertile soil and that democracies will be destabilized as a result of their electorates' desire to fight complexity by becoming more insular.

Unequal Opportunities, Migration, and Right-Wing Crimes

In a world in which television and the Internet constantly expose the inhabitants of poorer regions of the world to the better living conditions in the richer countries and cities, such differences create desires and aspirations that many cannot realize except through migration. This is not a risk in itself, and migration, in fact, constitutes one of the most promising solutions to persistent global inequalities. Milanović sees it as "the most powerful tool for reducing global poverty and inequality" and, "in the absence of significant acceleration of growth in poor countries," identifies it as "a great 21st century mechanism of adjustment."[54] Like us, he is furthermore convinced that "aid and migration ought to be regarded as two complementary means for achieving [a reduction in global inequality and global poverty]."[55]

However, in view of recent events and elections in Europe (including in Austria, the Netherlands, Hungary, Greece, and the United Kingdom), we emphasize that the successful management of the migratory approach to reducing global inequality remains more elusive than ever. When the receiving countries suffer from growing inequality and endure economic crises, they appear to be even less willing than on other occasions to accept immigrants.

The threats to stability and the political consequences that follow are real. It is already possible to witness a tendency toward the reversal of globalization. Commenting on developments in Eastern Europe and specifically in Hungary, the Romanian political scientist Cristian Pârvulescu observes "a return to populism and nationalism" following widespread disappointment with EU entry. He warns that "the developments in Hungary should serve as an alarm signal for Brussels."[56] In France, too, it has been observed that "both the far left and the far right find their core constituency among the vast number of French who feel economically insecure and politically disenfranchised—in essence, all those who perceive themselves as having no opportunity in an open society."[57] Similar considerations apply to countries such as Austria, Finland, Greece, and the Netherlands that have exhibited a surge in support for nationalist candidates, suggesting that "the real energy of populism in Europe comes from people who feel that their hands have been taken off the levers of controlling government and [who] want to get them back on somehow."[58] The link with the complexity and the perceived risks associated with globalization is immediate.

A noteworthy study compares the complex factors driving policy responses to the global financial crisis and climate change. It points to the sheer number of actors with divergent interests, the interaction of multiple causal factors that encourage lobbying activities, and nonlinear dynamics that create both a false sense of security and behavior that contributes to the tipping points that can arise endemically in complex systems and generate systemic risk.[59] What is good on a global scale may therefore conflict with what is best for a nation itself. For example, contributing to climate stability by reducing CO_2 emissions is good on the global scale but can hurt short-term growth at the national level. Because causality is difficult to establish in such complex processes, there is room for lobbying activities, as is evident in financial industry lobbyists opposing reform or the coal industry opposing measures to reduce carbon emissions. With simple and clear causality, lobbying for any policy that is not fostering financial stability would be more difficult and would be regarded as socially and politically unacceptable. Because the dynamics are such that a buildup of systemic risk is slow and often remains "under the radar," policy makers do not feel a sense of urgency to act before a crisis unravels. In this sense, one could argue that globalization, as well as the complexity it involves, facilitates the undermining of fundamental elements of democratic systems. It follows that the urgency with which questions of "social systemic risk" need to be addressed cannot be underestimated.

The Eurozone crisis has also shown that frustration with complexity is not the only potential source of social risk. In addition, there is also the risk that the political elites (those who wish to protect the benefits they derive from globalization) will be tempted to put democratic values aside in order to enable a timely and decisive political response. Unelected prime ministers, for example, have been installed in Italy and Greece, "in large part as a result of pressure from outside creditors." This may reveal a "democratic deficit at the heart of [European] integration."[60] This deficit has led to protests. Less aggressive but no less dangerous is the alternative protest "at the ballot box." Only 3 of the 27 democratically elected leaders who were in office at the beginning of the financial crisis in 2007 were still in office five years later. According to the *Economist*, within two years of the beginning of the euro crisis in 2010, "no fewer than nine of the [Euro] zone's 17 national leaders [had] been ejected from office."[61] So-called fringe parties have had unprecedented success in countries such as Finland, the Netherlands, Greece, and France, often as a result of voters' protesting the "opaque, complex and remote" European governance structures.[62]

The lesson to be taken away for integration at the global scale is that policy makers need to be aware that the growing sense of a blizzard of complexity and unequal sharing of benefits is provoking a reaction that threatens the foundations of globalization. The potential to participate and consider alternative policies and their implications is central to individuals' sense that their future remains in their own hands and is not simply determined by a remote and opaque institution that they can neither control nor hold accountable. As a government official states, "The weakness of the system is not about spending and how to promote growth, but about legitimacy."[63] Achieving the balance between

**Percentage of
total electorate**

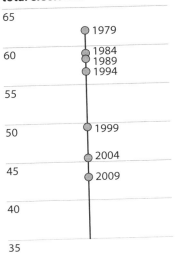

Figure 7.6. Turnout in elections for the European Parliament (percent), 1979–2009. *Economist*, 2012b, "The Euro Crisis: An Ever-Deeper Democratic Deficit," 26 May, accessed 28 January 2013, http://www.economist.com/node/21555927. Used with permission.

maintaining democratic legitimacy and the ability to respond in a timely manner is a vital and extraordinarily challenging task.

In Europe the tension among national, regional, and global accountability has become acute. Figure 7.6 illustrates the erosion of trust in the European Parliament. In part this is because, as a French government official asserts, "The (European) Commission was technically and politically unprepared and therefore unable to take the lead and act swiftly" when the euro crisis struck (a similar development is evident at the national level).[64] The European debt crisis and the failure of European institutions to manage it successfully has led a number of commentators to argue that "the best way to organise the necessary limitation of national power is obviously not through the current approach resting on a bewilderingly complex and fragile array of atypical political bodies, rules and sanctions."[65] As the German journalist Christian Wernicke puts it, "What we're doing at the moment is we're turning Brussels or Europe into something that looks pretty closely to what the IMF [International Monetary Fund] used to be in the '80s for Latin America."[66] This cannot be a sustainable model for democratic governance.

A failure to restore trust will almost certainly play into the arms of "politicians with a simple message: our countries have had enough of . . . tutelage and belt-tightening; the time has come to return to . . . national values and interests."[67] For many, the lesson to be learned is that integration was too rapid and inadequately prepared for the pressures of global competition. In Hungary, for example, expectations associated with global integration could not be met and citizens have reacted by retreating into nationalism and protectionism. In the words of journalist Keno Verseck, "After the turn of the millennium, Hungary became the first Eastern European victim of globalization, as many foreign companies moved further east. Large chunks of the country's economy, such as the agricultural and food industries, were too underdeveloped to survive the country's accession to the EU in 2004."[68]

The Hungary example is indicative of a wider concern that if exposure to global complexity and competition is too sudden and too overwhelming, reversal may well follow. Such reversal may be abrupt and accompanied by a radicalization that is borne out of disappointment and the fear of losing identity. In this context, it has been observed that "questions of community and identity [are] clearly more important than economic grievances," implying, for example, that "in Austria and Switzerland, the electoral success of right-wing populist parties among workers seems primarily due to cultural protectionism: the defense of national identity against outsiders," whereas "in Belgium, France, and Norway, cultural protectionism is complemented by deep-seated discontent with the way the countries' democracies work."[69]

The European debt crisis is partially responsible for the radicalization of politics in a number of the EU member states (table 7.3). The combination of economic distress and austerity with the impression of an apparently "arbitrary" and opaque foreign intervention in the national economic and political space has provided an excuse for politicians who seek to externalize their failures and has reinforced prejudices against regional or foreign institutions. The occasional paralysis of the European governing body and its failure to resolve the crisis have strengthened populist politics, even among traditionally more centrist voters. The degree to which this has happened has varied considerably in different countries, reflecting national and cultural differences as well as the severity of the crisis and the nature of the political and media debate.

TABLE 7.3.

ELECTION RESULTS OF RADICAL RIGHT-WING PARTIES (PERCENT), NATIONAL ELECTIONS (AVERAGES), AND EUROPEAN PARLIAMENT (EP) ELECTIONS, 1980–2009

Country	1980–84	1985–89	1990–94	1995–99	2000–2004	2005–9	EP 2009
Belgium	1.1	1.7	6.6	11.6[a]	13.8	14.0	10.1
Denmark	6.4	6.9	6.4	9.8	12.6	13.9	14.8
Denmark	0.2	0.6	2.3	3.3	1.0	2.1	1.7
German Federal Republic	0.4	9.9	12.7	14.9	12.4	4.7	6.3
France	—	0.6	0.9	—	0.2	0.7	8.3
Great Britain	6.8	5.9	17.8	15.7	4.3[b]	8.3[b]	10.2[b]
Italy	4.5	8.4	6.0	15.3	14.7	22.5	—
Norway	5.0	9.7	19.6	24.4	10.0	28.2	17.8
Austria	—	—	4.0	—	1.5	3.0	3.3
Sweden	3.8	6.3	10.9	9.3	1.3	30.0	—
Switzerland	2.8	5.0	8.7	13.0	7.2	12.7	—
Average							

Notes: The following parties were included in the calculations: Belgium—Vlaams Blok, Front National; Denmark—Fremskridtsparti, Dansk Folkeparti; France—Front National, Mouvement National Républicain; Germany—Republikaner, Deutsche Volksunion, German National Democratic Party; Great Britain—British National Party, National Front; Italy—Movimento Sociale Italiano, Alleanza Nazionale, Movimento Sociale–Fiamma Tricolore, Lega Nord; Netherlands—Centrumpartij, Centrumdemocraten, List Pim Fortuyn, Party for Freedom; Austria—Austrian Freedom Party, Bündnis Zukunft Österreich; Sweden—Ny Demokrati, Sverigedemokraterna, Nationaldemokraterna. Dashes indicate no data.

[a] This figure (and the corresponding average) has been corrected based on data derived from http://electionresources.org/, accessed 21 July 2013.

[b] Without Alleanza Nazionale but including Lega Nord, Movimento Sociale–Fiamma Tricolore, Mussolini, and Rauti.

Source: Michael Minkenberg, 2011, "The Radical Right in Europe Today: Trends and Patterns in East and West," in *Is Europe on the "Right" Path? Right-Wing Extremism and Right-Wing Populism in Europe* (Berlin: Friedrich Ebert Stiftung Forum), 37–55, data on 44. Used with permission.

This partly explains why the radicalization of German voters has not (yet) progressed to levels that were achieved by the Front National in France or by Jobbik in Hungary.

To avoid radicalization, thoughtful management and inclusion are of the utmost importance, potentially even at the risk of incurring higher short-term economic and political costs. Global integration needs to be coordinated and painstakingly prepared for, and it needs to be transparent. We now have the technological means of achieving it, but we do not yet have the institutions necessary to manage it.

Although the link between democratic responses and economic hardship remains unclear and requires further study, the relationship between declining economic conditions and crime is better understood. The evidence indeed appears to suggest that right-wing extremist crimes (RECs) can be seen as a proxy for antiglobalization and antimigration sentiments. It has been shown, for example, that there is "a significantly positive relation between state level unemployment and the incidence of RECs."[70] Interestingly, this finding holds only for nonviolent crimes, not for violent ones. The underlying study also suggests that total unemployment is a better predictor of RECs than is youth unemployment, indicating that right-wing sentiments, in particular in the face of economic distress, are a problem of the entire society. This conclusion is also consistent with the conjecture that "the normative pressure against right-wing criminals may deteriorate in a high unemployment environment."[71] Yet another study corroborates the general insight that "the likelihood of harassment . . . is aggravated by poor economic circumstances."[72]

Analyzing the determinants of right-wing voting decisions, sociologists find that right-wing voters are driven by immigration scepticism rather than by "genuine" xenophobia.[73] This suggests there are political factors alongside the economic factors that may drive voters toward radical parties.[74] It also shows that politicians and institutions are bearing some of the responsibility for the shifts toward these fringe parties and that more inclusive policies might have been able to avoid some of the political problems surrounding the ongoing European debt crisis, as is evident, for example, in the turmoil in Greek politics. The crisis has heightened concerns regarding globalization, and these now threaten European integration and the cohesiveness of European societies. At the global level, policy makers should monitor these developments closely, because the European experience may well have lessons for other societies grappling with global integration.

Globalization and the Threat of Destabilization

In the previous section we discussed how within-country inequality and the competitive pressures of globalization can lead to stress in the societal order and to a radicalization of voters. A similar pattern arises on the global scale, where—as we have seen—some countries and some regions are "left behind." Citizens who feel unable to catch up with global developments and are without the resources (both physical and educational) to exploit the wealth of new opportunities that globalization provides can feel that the system has nothing to offer them and indeed may be the source of their difficulties. Together with the clash of often very different cultures, situations like these create the potential for discontent, and thus for instability.

New technologies and notably the Internet provide an opportunity for aggrieved individuals to have a great impact with limited resources. Cyberspace has very low barriers to entry and hence can be the site of a great deal of tension. For the overwhelming majority of citizens, the Internet provides a forum for expressing views and nurturing or joining (online) communities. A small minority of individuals, however, are able to benefit financially and in other ways from the new opportunities for cybercrime, although individuals, groups, or even nations are also able to use the Internet for cyberaggression. As Lieutenant General Harry D. Raduege Jr., chairman of the Deloitte Center for Cyber Innovation, has pointed out, "In the 21st century, Americans use cyberspace to run industries, share information, control machinery, purchase items, move money, and perform essential government services."[75] Our lives and livelihoods are highly dependent on virtual connectivity around the globe. Research from the EastWest Institute emphasizes that even in China, where the Internet remains highly controlled, "vital individual, business, and even national interests are threatened" by the risks of destabilization from the Internet.[76] We have shown that cybercrime is widespread and especially difficult to detect, prosecute, and deter (chapter 4). For these reasons, the management of the physical infrastructure and abuse of the Internet requires coordination not only between countries but also between governments and private sectors. As Raduege suggests, "To protect our information networks against espionage, crime, and attacks in cyberspace, we need an unprecedented private–public partnership."[77]

In extreme cases, the risk of high-impact, low-cost threats may extend beyond the Internet to bioterrorism. Jeffrey L. Arnold notes that with the anthrax letter attacks in 2002, the beginning of the twenty-first century witnessed the largest-ever bioterrorist attacks, which left five dead and necessitated the provision of prophylactic antibiotics to over 32,000 individuals.[78] The risk of manufactured biological threats, however, stems from states as well as malevolent individuals. Many countries invest substantial sums in the development of biological warfare agents, implying that they voluntarily create and hoard infectious agents. Countries that have been reported to accumulate, or try to accumulate, such reserves in recent years include fragile states such as Iraq, Libya, North Korea, Sudan, and Syria.[79] In a world where countries like these are struggling with unstable political leadership and growing economic frustration, the existence of biological weapons is a major risk, as recent events in Syria demonstrate.[80] The risks, however, are by no means confined to fragile or hostile states. As Arnold has noted, "The last known case of smallpox in the world resulted from a laboratory accident in 1978," and the anthrax strain used in the letter attacks was found to be originally from a U.S. Defense Department laboratory as well.[81]

The Internet provides individuals and small groups with a wealth of information that includes instructions on how to build bombs or experiment with pathogens or chemical materials.[82] The sarin gas attacks of the Aum Shinrikyo cult in the Tokyo subway in 1998 illustrate the threat that the wrong materials, in combination with sufficient information, can pose in the hands of terrorists. Releasing the deadly gas in five trains, the cult killed 13 people and severely injured more than 5,000.[83]

The low cost of accumulating information and assembling the materials for such deadly weapons, combined with a high population density in extremely concentrated urban areas and with the high frequency of travel and trade, provides dangerous individuals with easy access to high-impact weapons.

Globalization has made these kinds of risks all the more dangerous. There are very few alternatives to enhanced monitoring and control.

This is increasingly likely to raise concerns regarding privacy. To contain the impact that rogue individuals or states have at their disposal, greater attention should be given to resilience and mitigation measures. Individual actors or small groups who, for political, religious, economic, or psychotic reasons, wish to attack society can gain leverage from the information, supplies, and high-impact nodes that are characteristic of globalization. Building resilience requires an appreciation of the corresponding vulnerabilities. The aim should thus be to minimize the threats but also to ensure that no individual action could lead to cascading risks. Ensuring that individuals or small groups cannot cause a bank run or the collapse of a key transport, cyber, energy, water, or other vital hub should be a priority of all governments concerned with the stability of the "ecosystem" that provides the foundation for our globalized society.

LESSONS FOR CHALLENGING GLOBAL INEQUALITIES

Three key policy lessons for managing global inequalities follow from the discussion in this chapter.

Lesson 1: Global governance must be transparent, even at the cost of operability and flexibility

In the introduction to his most recent book on the role of inequality in a global world, Nobel Laureate Joseph Stiglitz proclaims, "The problem . . . is not that globalization is bad or wrong but that governments are managing it so poorly."[84] Stiglitz is particularly concerned with growing inequality around the world and within countries, and he explains how this is accompanied by the increasing influence of special-interest groups. Wealth leads to power, and the fact that a smaller and smaller proportion of citizens are holding an increasingly large share of global wealth threatens democratic principles. As the most powerful firms and individuals operate across borders, the influence of their actions and lobbying efforts is often difficult to discern at the national level. Because perceptions matter, if individuals *feel* unrepresented they may become alienated and blame this on forces beyond their control or on globalization. Improving transparency is vital to avoid untargeted frustration and a sense of anomie. Making policy choices comprehensible to ordinary citizens and giving them a say in decisions that affect their lives are essential to the creation of more inclusive globalization and to the mitigation of the systemic risks arising from growing inequality.

Two practical measures are, first, to ensure that tax payments and receipts are paid in the countries where the value is added, as was discussed at the June 2013 G8 meeting and the July 2013 G20 meetings, and, second, to restrict the power and role of lobbyists so that wealthy individuals and firms do not cement their privileges through their greater access to regulatory and legislative processes.

Lesson 2: Reducing inequality at the national level is a prerequisite for the continued success of globalization

The second lesson we draw from our earlier discussion about ways to ensure inclusivity at the national level is that widening inequality must be tackled directly. The stability of globalization requires that most, if not all, of society has to feel that globalization is beneficial to them. If a sizable minority of the population feel that globalization is eroding their living standards and poses a greater threat than an opportunity, they will make further integration increasingly difficult to achieve and will support protectionism and greater isolation. It is necessary to focus on greater equality of opportunity. A wide range of measures are required that focus particularly on the most disadvantaged groups in society. Widening opportunity requires investment in education to ensure equal access to quality education at all levels, from preschool to university; a greater focus on skills and (re)training; determined efforts to overcome health and nutrition deficits; increased geographical mobility through the provision of housing, transport, and information; and the provision of vital infrastructure, including national access to broadband capability. To ensure that these investments have the desired outcomes, learning from global best practices and the introduction of randomized trials can be helpful. Higher expenditures on opportunities to reduce inequality in an age of budget deficits necessarily imply the need to raise revenues through taxes. Greater social solidarity is required to sustain globalization.

As the IMF has concluded, "Globalization and technological changes increase the returns on human capital." These findings are "underscoring the importance of education and training in both developed and developing countries."[85] Prioritizing investment in human capital can thus accelerate the beneficial effects from global connectivity. According to the OECD, the role of education in reducing global inequalities is even greater than the individual contributions of technology or institutions.[86]

Lesson 3: Reducing inequality at the global level is a prerequisite for the continued success of globalization

The frustrations that will destabilize national societies will have the same kinds of effects at the international level. In *Globalization for Development*, Goldin and Reinert show that the roles of trade and aid are particularly important in this regard.[87] A sharp reduction in rich countries' agricultural protectionism, for example, is long overdue.[88] The subsidies given to European and U.S. farmers are economically unfounded, environmentally destructive, and highly regressive in terms of incomes, even within the rich countries. Policies that provide cows in Europe with double the average income (in terms of their daily subsidies and cost) of over 500 million African people must be urgently reformed. Meanwhile, because developing countries are better managed than ever and rich countries are richer, the commitment made 40 years ago to devote 0.7 percent of OECD income to aid should finally be implemented.[89] Such policies would go a long way toward reducing global inequality and demonstrating a shared commitment to a more inclusive globalization. Coherence between aid and trade policies is vital, but perhaps even more significant are policies with respect to international migration. Historically, this has been the way that people have escaped dire poverty and other threats. The current phase of globalization is characterized by sharp increases in all cross-border flows, but, as a share of national or global populations, migration is being curtailed to levels that are far below those of the age of mass migration over a century ago. Too many people are trapped in poverty and are unable to benefit from the opportunities provided by a globalized world. As Goldin, Cameron, and Balarajan show in their book *Exceptional People*, migration is the orphan of the global system. This needs to be remedied by policies developed to increase the number of migrants accompanied by regularization and policies to ensure that migrants accept the responsibilities that go with their rights.[90]

8

⊶✛⊷

Managing Systemic Risk

The world we live in is markedly different from that of just a couple of decades ago. Goods, services, people, and ideas travel across borders more rapidly than ever before. This connectivity has brought about unprecedented improvements in average living and health standards. It has enriched our lives with more information, more choices, and more opportunities. It has also contributed to the mitigation of political tensions. The ending of the Cold War, the opening of China, and the sustained period of peace in Europe, as well as the fall of authoritarian regimes in over 60 countries in Africa, Latin America, and Asia, are part of this extraordinary process, of which the Arab Spring has been the latest manifestation. Connectivity has also accelerated the spread of innovations that have changed the lives of millions for the better. For most of the world's growing number of inhabitants, globalization—greater connectivity—has been a blessing.

Many, however, see globalization as a curse. They worry about growing inequalities and about those who are excluded from the benefits of closer integration. They also point to systemic risks, including financial crises, environmental destruction, pandemics, cyberattacks, and other cascading threats. We share these concerns. The complexity of the world that we have built may well have escaped our models and cognitive abilities. We are overloading the global networks; we are stretching their capacity beyond what prudence recommends, and—as we have shown—too often we neglect the accumulation of a large variety of risks and the geographical concentration of activities in a small number of pivotal nodes.

The primary lesson of our analysis is that sustainable globalization requires careful management, ensuring *transparency, inclusivity,* and *resilience* as guiding principles. The many networks and mechanisms on which global integration relies cannot be allowed to outgrow the capacities of their governing institutions. There is an urgent need for greater investment in policies and institutions that build resilience at the national level. Because systemic risk and globalization specifically refer to relationships that transcend national borders, this necessarily also implies the reform of regional and international institutions. With a few notable exceptions, these are unfit for twenty-first-century purposes and are the legacy of the Second World War and the subsequent Cold War. The required renewal is wide ranging and includes a fundamental reassessment of the mandates, shareholding and governance structures, skills, conceptual models, and operating procedures that guide the work of the international system. This renewal cannot be a one-time process; given the speed of the evolution of challenges, flexible structures need to be created that allow regular monitoring, evaluation, and refreshing of skills and mandates. It implies that there needs to be less of a permanent civil service–type model, with expectations of permanent careers, and greater consideration of institutional models focused on task-based capabilities, more akin to what is seen in the private sector. The danger of successful institutions' attracting further funding and concentrating power also needs careful consideration. The international financial architecture did not suffer from a lack of power, people, resources, or data. The International Monetary Fund, the Bank for International Settlements, and other global financial institutions and their national counterparts— the treasuries, finance ministries, and central banks—were the strongest global and national institutions. Their core purpose is global and national financial stability. Yet because they adopted uniform formulas for financial management and failed to keep abreast of technological and other changes, their advice allowed problems to fester and eventually to lead to a cascading crisis. As indicated above, an intellectual revolution as well as an institutional revolution is required to make financial governance, like other aspects of global governance, fit for twenty-first-century purposes.

Globalization has been associated with a growing complexity of relationships and interconnections that have made the attribution of cause and effect more difficult and at times apparently impossible to discern. Citizens feel that they are no longer in control of their destinies. Meanwhile, politicians and others in positions of responsibility are able to hide in the maze of globalized, entangled networks. The sense of diminished control leads people to seek to bring responsibility home and to be more local. The desire to make politics and decision making less remote is one effect and is giving rise to the fragmentation of previously united countries. In the United Kingdom the decision of Scotland to hold a referendum in 2014 on Scottish independence is one manifestation of this fragmentation, as is the decision by the British cabinet to hold a referendum on the United Kingdom's membership in the EU. In the local elections held in May 2013, some 23 percent of the votes were for the U.K. Independence Party.[1] Overwhelmed by global complexities, citizens and politicians resort to local thinking and short-termism. This not only impairs local and global economic progress and innovation; it also opens the doors to nationalist ideologies and threatens the peace and the relative global political stability that have been painfully achieved in recent decades.

Globalization is worth preserving, and even deepening. But it must be nurtured and shaped in a manner that ensures that it will be more inclusive, transparent (to provide a better understanding of its complexities and ensure greater accountability), and resilient. Policies are required at the local, national, and global levels to ensure that globalization works for, not against, development. These policies are the subject of three previous books by Ian Goldin,[2] and they require urgent attention if globalization is to be sustained.

MOVING FORWARD, NOT BACKWARD

This book provides ample evidence of a simple but important fact: the world is connected; individuals are connected, firms are connected, and governments depend on each other more than ever. We can neither halt nor reverse this development; the physical flow of goods and services may still be interrupted by borders and regulations, but virtual exchange overcomes such obstacles easily. The world has experienced what Robert Keohane and Joseph Nye term "complex interdependence."[3] Insufficiently managed globalization might drive us toward a world of overly complex interdependencies, with the resulting cascading shocks and lack of accountability encouraging more local rather than more globally connected politics.

Global integration can be slowed down, and this can sometimes be advisable, but we can no longer hope to rely on national governments alone to manage global challenges. These challenges transcend the borders that nations rely on for their sovereignty. We have a common responsibility for the world and cross-border problems, and we can recognize this responsibility only if we learn to coordinate and to cooperate globally—not alone, not bilaterally or even regionally—although all these levels of engagement are vital building blocks of global agreement. We need responsive, proactive, and to a certain degree autonomous global capacity. Global institutions need to be more accountable and transparent, but they also need to be given mandates and resources that are relatively immune to the constant buffeting of political tides. These need to be adequately resourced in order to meet the challenges of our time. U.S. President Barack Obama recognized this global responsibility in his 2009 speech at the University of Cairo:

> When a financial system weakens in one country, prosperity is hurt everywhere. When a new flu infects one human being, all are at risk. When one nation pursues a nuclear weapon, the risk of nuclear attack rises for all nations. When violent extremists operate in one stretch of mountains, people are endangered across an ocean. And when innocents in Bosnia and Darfur are slaughtered, that is a stain on our collective conscience. That is what it means to share this world in the 21st century. That is the responsibility we have to one another as human beings. . . . Given our interdependence, any world order that elevates one nation or group of people over another will inevitably fail. . . . Our problems must be dealt with through partnership; progress must be shared.[4]

President Obama highlighted the urgent need for global action to manage collective challenges. In practice, however, the United States remains a major stumbling block to international agreements in a number of critical areas, not least on climate change and deep reform of the international financial architecture.

In *The Globalization Paradox* Dani Rodrik argues for greater national control and the ceding of less power to international institutions. The principle of "subsidiarity," according to which decisions are made as locally as possible (by the lowest practical authority) so they reflect the decisions of citizens and communities, is one we ascribe to. However, the interdependencies arising from globalization mean that a greater share of decisions require coordination. Interdependence is at the heart of globalization, and in many, but certainly not all, areas it cannot be reversed without undermining the benefits that integration and connectivity bring. National governments alone cannot respond to many of the challenges ahead. The financial crisis of 2007/2008 and the example of Europe have shown this, and so have the responses to swine and bird flu, to the Fukushima crisis and the Eyjafjallajökull volcano, to global warming, and to the war on terror and cybercrime. The forces of globalization require active management at the global, national, and local levels.

Not all issues require global collective action. The principle of subsidiarity must apply, because many of these issues are resolvable at the national, regional, or bilateral level or by nongovernmental actors such as organizations in the private sector or civil organizations.[5] Global management must be considered only where public action pursued by governments in cooperation with one another is necessary to address a problem. Not all actors need to be involved in every global negotiation, and a principle of selective inclusion should be adopted, with the key actors most able to effect solutions but also the countries most affected engaged.

CONFRONTING A NEW CHALLENGE?

The realization that global connectivity requires global policy coordination is not new; the Great Depression of the 1930s led to the coordination of monetary policy (the gold standard), and in the aftermath of World War II policy makers were pressed "to find a common measure, a common standard, a common rule applicable to each and not irksome to any."[6] At the Bretton Woods conference of 1944, the leaders of the time responded to this challenge by agreeing to revive monetary policy coordination and establish the International Monetary Fund and the International Bank for Reconstruction and Development (World Bank). These institutions have continued to play an important role. However, they were designed for a different time and, as noted above, need to be radically reformed if they are to meet current challenges. The financial crisis, and the connected world that we have outlined in the previous chapters, demand a "Bretton Woods moment" for the twenty-first century. This would offer a fundamental reorganization of global governance.

The financial crisis opened a window of opportunity for institutional change, not only because it unveiled the insufficiency of current structures but also because it made the enormous costs that a global crisis can impose vividly evident around the world. People everywhere are suffering the impact. We all have learned firsthand how quickly systemic risk can spread and how unexpectedly it can materialize. We have seen how failure in a relatively small financial market, concentrated on the American West coast, was able to propagate across the continent to New York, then overseas to London and to financial centers on all continents. The collapse of these centers led to domestic economic crises and destroyed the savings portfolios and the jobs of hundreds of millions of people. The experience has turned systemic risk into a palpable concept. It is the responsibility of politicians and business and other leaders to communicate that this kind of risk is not confined to the world of finance. Globalization needs to be carefully nurtured and managed if it is not to overwhelm us.

Systemic risk is no longer an abstract concept but is now something that every investor, every small business in search of funding, and every person with a savings account can relate to. Tragically, so can the unemployed, those concerned about their job security, and those searching for new employment opportunities. The same applies to those on fixed-income pensions and other benefits. A heightened sense of awareness and an improved safety culture have already been achieved following the failure to manage financial risk. Although the lingering crisis has deepened the dialogue between the private (financial) sector and public institutions, trust has not been restored. Opportunistic behavior on the part of banks and hard regulatory proposals have reinforced mutual mistrust. The danger is that, with a return to apparent calm in the markets, the regulatory reforms will be diluted. At the time of this writing, the efforts to achieve regulatory reform appear to have been insufficiently undertaken globally and to have failed to take account of crucial dimensions of systemic risk, such as the colocation of vulnerable financial institutions and cyber and other systems within concentrated national geographies. The Basel III and other regulations that are currently being implemented would most likely not have prevented the financial crisis of 2007/2008; in our view they are even less likely to prevent future systemic crises.

As far back as 1997, the Group of Thirty (an international private consultative group composed of senior representatives of the private and public sectors and the academic world) had already outlined a model for cooperation between the public and the private sectors to manage systemic risk. In a report titled *Global Institutions, National Supervision, and Systemic Risk* they demanded the "creation of a standing committee to promulgate and review global principles for managing risk" as well as to consider "the full range of risks in a global firm." They suggested that multinational corporations be subjected to an "expanded review by a single, independent, external audit firm or firm group, and [that there be] more consistent and meaningful disclosure of financial and risk information on a global, consolidated basis."[7] The idea of a global review process for identifying risk exposure, especially that of multinational firms, provides a promising practical model for transparency and risk assessment through public–private cooperation.

So far there has been much too little reform even in the area most affected, finance. This has extended the impact of the current crisis and heightened the risk of further crises. The window of opportunity is closing; disappointed and alienated by the failure to address the crisis, citizens (and their governments) are turning to the streets and to local rather than more globally connected solutions. Politicians and commentators need to be as clear as possible regarding the causes and consequences of the crisis. As our future is increasingly influenced by forces beyond our borders, some sacrifice of national decision making in favor of cooperative outcomes is required. We do not know where the next shock will come from. If a central purpose of governments is to protect us, the precautionary principle is a good basis for policy. This implies that in the face of uncertainty we need to invest in areas of potential threat and to build capabilities to react and adapt. To explain the benefits of global governance, the threats arising from its absence must be identified. Global governance has a considerable cost in terms of both the loss of national sovereignty and the financial burden. The benefits must be justified as outweighing these costs.

The world is increasingly subject to geographical concentration rather than diversification, which is vital for resilience. A multinational corporation with offices, assets, and human talent located in different regions will be better able to withstand a natural disaster or an infrastructure failure than a company that has all its valuable resources concentrated in one location. If we cannot predict where the next disaster will strike and in what form, firms should prudently diversify their centers of knowledge and leadership. Although this will increase their exposure to local risks, it will also increase their resilience because when a local failure occurs, the majority of the network will remain operable. Such diversification, however, requires global coordination. Multinational companies must be supervised in such a manner that they are not all beyond the reach of national jurisdictions. In 2012 the extent to which leading international brands, including Google and Starbucks, were optimizing their tax residency to reduce their payments to the British exchequer became a source of intense media scrutiny, reflecting the need to manage the systemic risks associated with globalized firms and the tensions that can arise at the local and national levels.

Because of their international dimensions, many problems cannot be tackled by national governments alone, so in addition to greater coordination across borders, greater coordination is required with the private sector and civil society. For example, the European Aviation Safety Agency may be competent in dealing with the risk from a volcanic ash cloud, but it has no expertise in securing the supply of organs for transplant if air traffic is interrupted. Similarly, the New York Fire Department and the Pentagon may be able to provide a first response to terrorist attacks such as those on 9/11, but they have no knowledge of mitigating the financial repercussions of a closed New York Stock Exchange. Interdisciplinary institutions and task forces that are able to coordinate the responses to such cascading risks are necessary to avoid costly economic and social losses and even chaos.

As we have seen, the nature of these problems is not necessarily new. What is new is the breadth and depth of the links involved and their growing complexity. Interconnectedness has turned into complex inter-dependence. This reflects the number of countries, people, and objects that are connected and the speed and extent of connections that permeate all aspects of our lives and economy.

THE NEED TO REFORM GLOBAL GOVERNANCE

The entire system of global governance needs to be reassessed to identify the needs of our time. There are critical orphan issues that have no institutional homes—among them climate change, cyberspace, and migration. Other issues have international homes, such as the World Health Organization, which is responsible for pandemics and public health, but, like those that have responsibility for finance and poverty reduction, these institutions require urgent renewal.[8]

New rules and institutional frameworks are required to allow policy makers to be prepared for, and respond to, systemic risk and cascading crises. If managing Hurricane Katrina or the Fukushima disaster was a challenge for the United States and Japan, respectively, the situation is even more complicated when international coordination is required either because the disaster spills over borders or because the society is poor and unable to sufficiently respond, as in the case of the catastrophic earthquake that hit Haiti in 2010. The United Nations Office for the Coordination of Humanitarian Affairs, for instance, still needs to coordinate efforts and funding between countries every time it responds to a humanitarian crisis; the case of the 2010 Haiti earthquake offers an unfortunate example of what this can imply for those in need.[9] The nature of the French intervention in Mali beginning in January 2013 also reflects the slow-moving character of coordinated international responses. The United Nations passed the relevant Security Council resolution authorizing action on 20 December 2012. Yet the army of 3,300 soldiers from the Economic Community of West African States (ECOWAS) earmarked to confront the Islamist extremists in the Malian north a month later were still negotiating the precise terms of military assistance with the Malian army.[10] The general problem seems to be that our current institutions fail to be prepared for the fact that *low risk is not no risk.*[11] They have been set up to respond to certain risks but fail to be prepared for circumstances that are unpredictable by nature or that are considered highly unlikely.

Cohesive societies are best able to support the successful management of global challenges. But such societies have to rest on stable foundations: secure information highways, reliable infrastructure, an intact environment, an efficient production sector, a supply of affordable credit, effective education and health systems, and other types of basic social and physical infrastructure. These foundations, in turn, require effective governance at both the local and the global levels. We need institutions that are able to identify the most crucial interdependencies but that also understand the need to equip society for unpredictable failures.

This task requires maintaining governance structures that are *simple*, *transparent*, and *flexible*. The need for less complexity and greater simplicity has been recognized by regulators lately.[12] Regulation itself might have become too complex; we need to resort to simpler, more robust regulatory frameworks in order to prevent arbitrage.[13] Our governance structures also have to become more transparent, which will help to ensure their accountability and legitimacy. Without an engaged public, politicians will be unable to find the majorities they need to make the difficult and potentially costly decisions required to make globalization sustainable. This implies that governance structures have to become more flexible and responsive to the rapid evolution of technologies and societies. Although some progress has been made in terms of reforming financial governance institutions and the regulatory framework, the same cannot be said of preparations to deal with other forms of systemic risk. The next big threat might stem from disease, cyberterrorism, climate change, or some new, unforeseen catastrophe.

Buffers, safety nets, and emergency procedures are also necessary. For governments and firms to adopt a prudent approach to risk management they should consider backup structures as more than "dead capital" or redundant investments. Lean management can be beneficial when things go well. More spare capacity, however, is required in an increasingly interconnected, interdependent, and riskier world. We believe that the benefits of investing in resilience should be seen as sources of strength on balance sheets rather than merely as other costs to be cut. Working capital allocated to risk management or backup strategies is not always a liability and in worst-case scenarios may be an organization's greatest asset. In the case of public utilities, resilience is often eroded by accounting rules that discourage the maintenance of stocks. These include anything from the bandages, antibiotics, and vaccines that complement the services of doctors and nurses to the supplies of grit and salt that are essential to keep roads open during extended icy snaps.[14] The result of lean management in such cases is an excessively tight and brittle system that is not only "lean and mean" but ill prepared to respond to shocks.

Many of the risks discussed throughout this book share the common feature of being hidden for a prolonged period before materializing suddenly and with a vengeance. In other words, they are *low-frequency, high-impact* events. Kunreuther and Useem focus on these types of risks and identify six aspects of risk management:

- Risk forecasting
- Communicating risk information
- Economic incentives
- Private–public partnerships
- Reinsurance and other financial instruments
- Resilience and sustainability[15]

Among these points it is easy to recognize some of our central lessons from earlier chapters, even though we would rank the items listed differently. On top of our list has been the insight that global connectivity must be built on *resilient* and *sustainable* foundations. Physical, virtual, and social networks need to be constructed in ways that allow them to withstand, and respond to, the novel challenges of our time. They have to be flexible and organic rather than static, and their capacities cannot be stretched to the limit.

We have also emphasized, notably in chapter 7, the need for *transparent communication* of policy alternatives. In the complex world that we have outlined, achieving transparency is not a trivial task. The full range of consequences that policy choices entail often remains unknown—even to those who have all the information *available*. This makes it all the more important to be explicit about uncertainties and unknowns[16] and to motivate choices in a comprehensible fashion. False promises of manageability may alleviate the pain in the short run, but they undermine credibility and legitimacy if they are continuously broken. The ongoing crisis of the European Monetary Union provides an unfortunate testimony to the corrosive effect of failed promises. It also highlights the need to implement and ensure the enforceability of agreements if they are to be credible. It was the failure to adhere to the Maastricht Treaty of 1992, which set strict fiscal guidelines for the countries of the EU, that led to the spiraling debts across Europe, starting with France and Germany and then extending in a less sustainable manner to Southern Europe. Heightened transparency in finance and other areas offers the additional benefit of allowing intentionally malevolent behavior to be more easily identified; this serves to lift the cover of complexity that too often conceals the opportunistic behavior of those with the means and the influence to benefit from their privilege.

Risk forecasting translates into improving risk measurement in the context of global governance. Greater efforts are required to understand twenty-first-century risks while recognizing the limitations of such efforts in a rapidly evolving and increasingly complex environment. Improving risk measurement is essential for identifying uncertainties but also for improving accountability and for communicating policy choices. Resolving systemic risk requires that we rectify economic incentives and internalize the failure of policies to account for externalities.

WHY REFORM HAS BEEN SO SLUGGISH

International organizations have been slow to recognize the fundamental changes in globalization and the nature of systemic risk. The 2003 report of the Organisation for Economic Co-operation and Development (OECD), *Emerging Risks in the 21st Century*, is exceptional in that it examines "the underlying forces driving change" in natural disasters, technological accidents, infectious diseases, terrorism-related risks, and food safety.[17] The report identifies "the challenges facing OECD countries—especially at the international level—in assessing, preparing for and responding to conventional and new hazards" and "sets out a number of recommendations for governments and the private sector as to how the management of emerging systemic risks might be improved."[18] The report was issued preceding the biggest financial crisis since the Great

Depression and did not identify issues of systemic risk. Nonetheless, its general conclusions remain valid. They consist of the following five points as to how to meet the challenge of future hazards:

- Adopt a new policy approach to risk management.

- Develop synergies between the public and private sectors.

- Inform and involve stakeholders and the general public.

- Strengthen international cooperation.

- Make better use of technological potential and enhance research efforts.[19]

Some of these recommendations reiterate well-known elements such as coordination and research. The call for involving stakeholders and the general public—while also requiring transparency—relates to the education aspect that we identified earlier. The emphasis on fostering synergies between private and public actors involves the development of "risk awareness" and a "safety culture." It also aims to "enhance dialog" and to "build trust" among the actors from both domains.

As we have seen, over fifteen years ago the Group of Thirty recommended "[improving] the capabilities of supervisory agencies to understand complex financial products, assess sophisticated risk management systems, and deal with crisis management in global markets." The group's report recommended strengthening "laws regarding:

- enforceability of netting

- enforceability of collateral contracts

- speedy and unsure insolvency procedures

- protection of customer assets, funds and positions on exchanges."[20]

These recommendations are aimed at defining contingencies and clarifying (legal) responsibilities. They promote strong and responsive governance and also formulate the need for an improved regulatory understanding of (financial) complexities. Reading through these conclusions after the 2007/2008 crisis, one cannot help but think that more efforts toward translating them into action would have mitigated the damage.

The question of why financial reform has been so sluggish naturally arises. One answer can be found by appealing to theories of international relations. The liberal view is that cooperation among states is feasible and will grow over time. Institutional theorists such as Robert Axelrod and Robert Keohane draw on game theory to analyze how and why states cooperate.[21] They put special emphasis on the role of learning to facilitate cooperation. In their view, institutions allow states to have continuous interactions with each other and to learn from past experiences. International organizations thus facilitate cooperation.

The pace and depth of globalization, however, have changed radically in just a few decades. Now, in the early twenty-first century, states face new problems and types of risks that make it difficult, if not impossible, to draw on past experience. Many of these problems have the potential to spread more rapidly and widely than ever before. A rogue trader can bring down a global company at the touch of some buttons. A computer virus or cascading crash can knock out entire networks across continents. And a new infectious disease can become global in less than three days. Such fundamental changes help explain why reform might be slow from a liberal perspective.[22]

Hans Morgenthau, like Kenneth Waltz, puts a much stronger emphasis on the role of sovereign states in pursuing their national interests.[23] Both men are skeptical of the potential for international cooperation. Given the large number of influential international organizations and the importance of nonstate actors such as nongovernmental organizations and multinational corporations, it is difficult to view international policy from a simply statist standpoint. We have considered the nationalist tendencies surfacing in many countries as a consequence of the financial crisis. These tendencies will strengthen the viewpoint that states act in their own interest and limit the potential for collaboration. The lessons for policy reform we draw below are therefore particularly important to overcome nationalist tendencies and enhance the potential for collaboration among states.

With global risks now emerging within and across many different domains, we cannot afford to neglect the lessons derived from analyses of systemic risk (as demonstrated in the financial crisis) a second time. As we have discussed, the consequences may well be more serious, even more costly, and potentially more fatal the next time around.

Our conclusions therefore include recommendations to prepare for contingencies (define a lead coordinator and formulate common standards), as well as to define—and enforce—unified legal responsibilities (even if complexity will not always allow these rules to reflect the "true" responsibilities).

LESSONS FOR GLOBAL POLICY REFORM

Six lessons for global policy reform follow from our discussion.

Lesson 1: Promote resilience and sustainability: geography and accounting
Public and private leaders should be aware of the increasing unpredictability of risk and prepare to face unforeseen challenges with resilient organizational forms. This preparation should include, in particular, fostering flexibility and avoiding over-reliance on single channels and mechanisms. Sustainability requires taking into consideration the broader context and longer time horizons. Systemic risks can be triggered even by inconspicuous choices; being aware of this will reduce risk and thereby long-term costs, even though the investments in resilience may raise costs in the short term.

In practice this means that geography and the location of activities need to be given much greater attention in government and business decision making. The concentration of economic activity in a small number of critical nodes is raising the prospect of systemic risk. The global and national distribution of vital infrastructure, including that for energy, cyber, and transport, should be designed to withstand the potential impact of any one node's becoming inoperative. This may be for reasons associated with a pandemic, a cyber- or bioattack, an energy failure, or an unexpected event, such as the spread of dust from the Icelandic volcano or the Japanese tsunami. Geographical dispersion should be considered in light of the potential risks, and the distance between critical nodes should be maximized wherever possible, taking into account the correlation of risks—avoiding, for example, a separation of services that would be equally vulnerable to flooding, airport closure, or a pandemic. In finance, for example, regulations should ensure that financial institutions in London or New York back up their systems in locations that are geographically distant and robust against attacks on the operational cyber systems of those institutions.

In their regional and town planning, governments should seek to ensure greater resilience not only through focusing on flood defenses and other investments but also through seeking to encourage the dispersion of vital nodes. Regulations or fiscal policies that create perverse incentives—such as those evident in the U.S. home insurance market, which insulates individuals from a significant part of the risk of home ownership in the most vulnerable parts of Florida or other flood areas or agricultural subsidies in the rich countries—are particularly counterproductive.

Competition policy has a vital role to play in reducing systemic risk by ensuring not only that no one firm is too big to fail but also that no one location is too important to fail in terms of the national economy. Greater awareness of the risk of geographical concentration would change the nature of the regulatory debate in many areas, including in finance, where there has been a focus on the sizes of institutions and their systemic importance but not on their locations. A group of banks that are co-located in a major financial district, such as Wall Street or Canary Wharf in London, poses a systemic risk if they were to be collectively affected by a major risk event, even if no one institution alone would be systemically significant. The same concentration risk applies to server farms, vaccine stores, and any other vital parts of the global production or management chain. For governments or large firms, the implication is that no one location, individual or co-located group of people, or information system should be required for the continued operation of the business.

Accounting and management policy has a strong influence on decision making in both the private and the public sectors. We have argued that mark-to-market accounting and the preoccupation with quarterly and short-term reporting have contributed to a decline in resilience. The ubiquitous MBA has propagated a culture of "lean management" and the driving down of costs and working capital that may be tied up in spare capacity, stocks, or other investments in resilience. We view the ability to bounce back after a shock and withstand systemic risks as a vital asset for a firm, not a liability. Embedding such a perception in the accounting and management professions and educating shareholders as to the need to think over the longer term about their investments would contribute to lowering systemic risk and building resilience. Here our practical solution is to encourage managers and the accounting profession to see investments that increase resilience as assets on balance sheets. For private firms, for example, this might mean ensuring that there is some backup in terms of the availability of spare parts or flexibility in supply chains. For public utilities such as hospitals, for example, this would imply maintaining higher reserves of medical supplies and treatment capacity. The costs of greater amounts of working capital tied up are offset by the benefits of the ability to respond to unforeseen circumstances. Capital costs can be measured in the short term; the benefits of capital buffers, however, accrue over a longer period through the sustainability of enterprises and the corresponding benefits to society. These benefits are inadequately accounted for in current accounting and management practices.

Lesson 2: Foster the transparent communication of choices, risks, and uncertainties about policy alternatives to address political and attribution challenges

Transparency is being reduced by the increasing complexity and speed of transactions. Private and public leaders need to understand this and respond by increasing transparency. If attribution of responsibilities is impossible, it undermines accountability and liability. Shareholders require information on which to make their decisions, including those with respect to potential sources of instability and risk. Electorates similarly require transparency in order to make rational choices and ensure democratic stability. The uncertainties surrounding political and strategic choices need to be communicated in order to enhance accountability. Communication can also help raise awareness as to why resources need to be set aside for unlikely events and unknown risks. Communicating the complexity of our world and educating the general public about the related difficulties can also prevent the rise of populists with overly simplistic messages. It is better to acknowledge uncertainties than to provide a false sense of security. The weight of past experience may also make forward planning more difficult in a rapidly changing world. The decisions of governments to allocate around 2.6 percent of expenditures to the military in the United Kingdom or 4.7 percent in the United States are regarded by most of the electorate as appropriate, while the allocation of less than one-hundredth of this amount to preventing a pandemic is regarded as excessive, even though we estimate that the threat to the population from pandemics is at least one hundred times greater than the threat from war.[24]

Lesson 3: Improve risk measurement

Due to rising complexity and interdependency, we are reaching our limits in terms of correctly assessing cross-sector and cross-border risks. This does not imply, however, that we should abandon our efforts; rather, we should redouble them. In particular, we should invest in understanding complexity and "big data," where very weak signals are embedded in vast amounts of data. Examining highly complex, massive data sets is familiar territory for astrophysicists, climate scientists, pandemic modelers, neuroscientists, and others, and we believe that learning across these areas how to model and map risk holds promise for the modeling of complexity and risk.[25] Improving risk management also implies acknowledging the uncertainties that surround our calculations. We have to be careful not to be over-reliant on sophisticated risk measurement and to acknowledge that some risks may still escape our attention. Improved risk measurement can guide the efficient allocation of resources, but it should not prevent us from also preparing for the unexpected and the (seemingly) unlikely. In the case of climate, we advocate the creation of the equivalent of a CERN (the European Organization for Nuclear Research), with a significantly stepped-up investment in a centralized global computing and research center where top climate scientists from around the world can pool their information and modeling expertise.[26] The aim would be to increase our knowledge of climate change and its likely consequences, not only to improve our understanding of the urgency and relative significance of different mitigation strategies but also to ensure that we are able to prioritize our required investments in adaptation.

Lesson 4: Rectify economic incentives

Research in economics, specifically behavioral and empirical research, has an important role to play in political responses to the complexities of our times. Salaries, taxes, insurance payments, and markets and prices have an important influence on the choices of millions. These choices can harm the environment, create financial risk, or make us vulnerable to infrastructure failures or other risks, including those arising from the virtual domain. Governments need to invest in understanding how the incentive and legal frameworks that they provide shape the decisions not only of their electorates but also of citizens around the world. They need to combine this understanding with the knowledge obtained in medical research, environmental research, or risk measurement and seek to design incentive schemes that align private incentives with those of the public. These models need to be applied with caution and, where possible, evolve from a variety of pilots or experiments. Badly designed instruments—for example, a too-low carbon tax—may increase the problem rather than attenuating it. The effects of policy changes need to be carefully studied, and policy makers need to be prepared to adjust their choices if their initial design is found to be faulty.

Among the possible policy implications could be policies that are designed to nudge consumers toward choices that address individual or national needs, like those developed to encourage people not to smoke. Incentives to embody the costs of externalities in choices are also important, for example, carbon and other pollution taxes. Lowering the discount rates that are applied on investments to the levels that are applied by leading firms and governments would raise the value attached to sustainability and the future. Competition, accounting, and remuneration policies that place a greater emphasis on longer-term performance would similarly encourage investments in resilience and sustainability.

Systemic risks such as those arising from the housing bubble in the United States or from badly designed incentives in part reflect the undue influence on policy makers of misguided economists who placed undue faith in market signals and notions of economic rationality as expressed in prices. Underway is the development of more pluralistic economics in which cooperative and sustainability concerns are given greater weight and economics tools are used to solve real-world problems such as unemployment, inequality, and complexity.[27] This is vital if the problem of badly designed incentives is to be rectified.

The pressure on businesses and governments to make decisions based on short-term considerations has increased greatly in recent decades for reasons that are spelled out in the report of the Oxford Martin Commission for Future Generations titled *Now for the Long Term*.[28] Among the many negative consequences of this short-termism is the application of discounting strategies for both government and business investment decisions that inadequately account for uncertainty and risk.

Lesson 5: Prepare for contingencies

In combination with conducting research on risk management, public actors need to work toward designing contingency plans and the capability to respond to unforeseen risks swiftly. This includes setting aside resources, educating risk and disaster management experts, and defining contingencies for times when global political coordination is suddenly required. If supranational agencies that could assume these tasks are not available, as typically they are not, plans for coordinated international cooperation need to be developed. At the same time, firms need to prepare for, and be made aware of, the limitations of public action. During the early stages of the recent financial crisis, a significant part of the problem was the uncertainty surrounding bailouts and governmental interventions (at the time of this writing, this remains the case in the context of the European debt crisis). There were no contingency plans for orderly default—not for systemically relevant financial institutions and not for countries that were defaulting on their obligations. In the same way that private companies need to provide contingency plans, for example, for the failure of a nuclear reactor, multinational firms should be required to prepare for the failure of their supply chains or their ability to provide vital medicine. Contingency plans—if they are expected to be enforced ex post—can also rectify incentives. They allow every actor, every participant, to weigh the benefits against the costs and—if designed correctly—to align their choices with what is best for the common good. In this sense, preparing for contingencies and rectifying economic incentives can be complementary. An additional benefit of a contingency plan is that it can aid the response to unexpected events. In the same way that Joshua Lederberg credited the results from cancer research with providing a platform for studies of the then-unknown HIV virus, and for the same reasons that Professor Pappaioanou perceives that vaccinations against known forms of the flu are the most effective preventive measures against pandemic risk, contingent plans in one domain can also accelerate the response to an event (or a domain) that it was not designed for—for example, by providing orderly procedures for communication and information sharing or by predefining hierarchies and responsibilities.

Lesson 6: Define and enforce unified legal responsibilities

Unifying and enforcing legal responsibilities do not necessarily lead to the assimilation of national legal frameworks. They require, however, that every firm—whether it operates from Taiwan, the Cayman Islands, or the United States—be held to the same standards in terms of its impact on the global stage. A unified global legal system would be one way of achieving this. It is unlikely to be politically feasible in the short term. Europe, however, has shown that supranational legal structures are possible as, for example, in the case of European competition law, and this could inspire international rules and jurisdictions in trade, tax, finance, cyber, and other areas. Unifying legal responsibilities has a range of implications. It enhances accountability because escaping prosecution by moving would become harder. As a result, it also improves incentives. Creating clear and widely adopted rules and regulations reduces complexity and increases transparency, in the process improving risk management and measurement. To this end, the Oxford Martin Commission for Future Generations has proposed a series of initial steps to make progress in cyber, tax, and other areas, which could begin with businesses and governments' forming "coalitions of the working" to share information and agree on codes of practice. Over time, these codes could evolve into treaty-based agreements carrying the force of international law, but meanwhile progress would not be held hostage to the frustratingly elusive quest for international unanimity.

In defining the legal responsibilities of governments, it is vital to recognize that the public sector alone cannot carry the entire burden of managing globalization and systemic risk. This needs to be seen as a cooperative effort between governments at all levels and the rest of society, not least the private sector and civil society. This involves promoting trust and transparency between these sectors and developing an understanding that what may seem profitable to the private sector in the short run can often have enormous public (and private) costs in a wider context. Resilience is a national and global objective. If it is appropriated by governments and seen as the sole legal responsibility of governments or, worse still, certain government institutions or ministers and chief risk officers, it is bound to fail.

MANAGING SYSTEMIC RISK

We have shown that although globalization is the cause of systemic risk, it is ironically also its solution.[29] Only by domesticating globalization—creating a resilient globalization—can the world reap the rewards of heightened connectivity while also reducing its risks. Systemic risk, as we noted in the preface and introduction to this book, is integral to globalization. The benefits of globalization necessarily express themselves in various forms of systemic risk. More connectivity and openness, rapid change, growing populations, and higher incomes bring greater complexity and higher potential for systemic risk. Systemic risk is thus a process to be managed, not a problem to be overcome. The cultivation of a resilient globalization is the best means available to us to manage it. We need to build the national and international institutions that provide the foundations of resilient globalization.

In this book we have sought to identify the key dimensions of this risk and illustrate through our case studies how this risk has evolved. Each thematic chapter has provided a summary of the lessons learned. Together these lessons provide a preliminary set of tools for managing the challenges associated with systemic risk.

Our synthesis above shows that the different areas identified have a number of common characteristics. There is a real danger that failure to address systemic risk will lead to its becoming more frequent and threatening in terms of the human and economic costs. This would also mean that our societies would become more divided because risk affects peoples differentially. The lack of cohesion would make the political challenge more difficult. Already in Europe we see how the financial crisis has led to more fractured politics and greater support for extremist views. We have shown that in part this reflects the desire to hold local politicians or firms responsible for risks that appear to escape accountability. The cascading of shocks across national borders is the inevitable consequence of higher levels of integration and connectivity. Our challenge is to learn how to manage this. Increasing awareness of the issues is the first step toward ensuring that globalization can be made to be more inclusive and sustainable. We have argued that globalization is worth defending because it is the source of the greatest progress the world has known. But it needs to be carefully managed if it is not to be overwhelmed by the forces of systemic risk that it has unleashed. Our purpose has been to raise awareness of the issues and motivate our readers to engage on these issues. Our hope is that we have contributed to an understanding of the extent to which we increasingly live in a global village. With better management there is the potential for all citizens to share in our world's magnificent achievements, the most impressive of which could be yet to come.

Notes

PREFACE

1. Edward N. Lorenz, 1963, "Deterministic Nonperiodic Flow," *Journal of the Atmospheric Sciences* 20 (2): 130–141. The original metaphor referred to the flapping of a seagull's wings. The term "butterfly effect" was coined later by a colleague, Phil Merilees, as the title for one of Lorenz's talks. See Tim Palmer, 2009, "Edward Norton Lorenz, 23 May 1916–16 April 2008," *Biographical Memoirs of Fellows of the Royal Society* 55: 139–155, esp. 145 ff.

ACKNOWLEDGMENTS

1. Ian Goldin and Tiffany Vogel, 2010, "Global Governance and Systemic Risk in the 21st Century: Lessons from the Financial Crisis," *Global Policy* 1 (1): 4–15.

INTRODUCTION

1. We are most grateful to an anonymous referee for suggesting this introduction for the book.

2. See David Ricardo, 1817, *On the Principles of Political Economy, and Taxation* (London: John Murray). Ricardo argued that two countries should specialize in producing goods and services in which they have a comparative advantage in terms of labor productivity. This amounts to saying that two parties should produce whichever goods or services have the lower marginal or opportunity costs in relation to others. Ricardo's theory of comparative advantage shows that as long as the parties specialize according to their relative efficiencies, they will both benefit from trade—even if one party has an absolute efficiency advantage in producing the goods and services traded. In subsequent chapters we refer to this concept as Ricardian efficiency. For further discussion of the principle, see Ronald Findlay, 2008, "Comparative Advantage," in *The New Palgrave Dictionary of Economics*, vol. 1, 2nd ed., ed. Steven N. Durlauf and Lawrence E. Blume (Basingstoke, UK: Palgrave Macmillan), 514–517.

3. This classification follows Ian Goldin and Kenneth Reinert, 2012, *Globalization for Development: Meeting New Challenges*, new ed. (Oxford, UK: Oxford University

Press). For a discussion of the different waves of globalization, see also Dani Rodrik, 2011, *The Globalization Paradox: Democracy and the Future of the World Economy* (New York and London: W. W. Norton); and Richard E. Baldwin and Phillipe Martin, 1999, "Two Waves of Globalization: Superficial Similarities, Fundamental Differences," NBER Working Paper 6904, National Bureau of Economic Research, Cambridge, MA, accessed 4 January 2013, http://www.nber.org/papers/w6904.pdf.

4. We are most grateful to an anonymous referee for this point.

5. Kelly Swing, 2013, "Conservation: Inertia Is Speeding Fish-Stock Declines," *Nature* 494: 314.

6. For an analysis that is aimed more explicitly at the lessons for global governance, see Ian Goldin, 2013, *Divided Nations: Why Global Governance Is Failing, and What We Can Do about It* (Oxford, UK: Oxford University Press).

Chapter 1: Globalization and Risk in the Twenty-First Century

1. Peter H. Diamandis and Stephen Kotler, 2012, *Abundance: The Future Is Better Than You Think* (New York: Free Press), 9.

2. David Held et al., 1999, *Global Transformations: Politics, Economics, Culture* (Cambridge, UK: Polity Press), and Ian Goldin and Kenneth Reinert, 2012, *Globalization for Development*, new ed. (Oxford, UK: Oxford University Press).

3. Goldin and Reinert, 2012.

4. Gordon E. Moore, 1965, "Cramming More Components onto Integrated Circuits," *Electronics Magazine* 38 (19 April), accessed 8 July 2013, http://download .intel.com/museum/Moores_Law/Articles-Press_Releases/Gordon_Moore_1965_ Article.pdf. Moore revised his prediction 10 years later to imply a doubling of transistors every two years. Gordon E. Moore, 1975, "Progress in Digital Integrated Electronics," *Electron Devices Meeting* 27: 11–13. Today Moore's Law is often read as implying a shorter 18-month time horizon for doubling the number of transistors on a computer chip.

5. CII (Chartered Insurance Institute), 2012, *Future Risk: How Technology Could Make or Break Our World*, Centenary Future Risk Series, Report 4 (London: Chartered Insurance Institute), 3.

6. UNFPA (United Nations Population Fund), 2011, *State of World Population 2011: People and Possibilities in a World of Seven Billion* (New York: United Nations Population Fund).

7. Ian Goldin, 2011, "Globalisation and Risks for Business: Implications for an Increasingly Connected World," *Lloyd's 360° Risk Insight* (London: Lloyds, and Oxford, UK: James Martin 21st Century School), 8, accessed 9 January 2013, http:// www.lloyds.com/~/media/Lloyds/Reports/360/360%20Globalisation/Lloyds_360_ Globalisaton.pdf.

8. Many countries, particularly in East Asia, sought to develop through more interventionist state policies instead.

9. These figures are taken from Goldin, 2011, 8, and from Charles Roxburgh, Susan Lund, and John Piotrowski, 2011, *Updated Research: Mapping Global Capital Markets* (New York: McKinsey), August, 1, accessed 21 January 2013, http://www.mckinsey.com/insights/mgi/research/financial_markets/mapping_global_capital_markets_2011.

10. Goldin, 2011, 8. Iran and Iraq are among the largest of the economies that have not joined the WTO.

11. See Ian Goldin, Geoffrey Cameron, and Meera Balarajan, 2011, *Exceptional People: How Migration Shaped Our World and Will Define Our Future* (Princeton, NJ, and Oxford, UK: Princeton University Press).

12. See Stephen Castles and Mark J. Miller, 2009, *The Age of Migration: International Population Movements in the Modern World* (New York: Palgrave Macmillan).

13. Goldin, Cameron, and Balarajan, 2011, 58–63, 85–96, and Castles and Miller, 2009, 2.

14. Many more high-speed rail links are forecast for Asia, Latin America, Eastern Europe, the Middle East, North Africa, and Australia. See UIC (International Union of Railways), 2010, *High Speed around the World*, 15 December (Paris: High Speed Department, International Union of Railways).

15. In 2010 world container port traffic stood at 538 million TEUs. For data on container port traffic, see World Bank, 2013, *World Development Indicators*, World-Databank, accessed 7 January, http://databank.worldbank.org/.

16. See, for example, Jean-Paul Rodrigue, Claude Comtois, and Brian Slack, 2009, *The Geography of Transport Systems* (New York: Routledge), or Goldin, 2011, 11.

17. The question of how economic, political, and technical change interact with and feed off one another is beyond the scope of this book. Nor is it possible to pursue the equally interesting question of how global development might have fared if change had not taken place (or had been fundamentally different) in one of these spheres. For a discussion of the political economy of development that touches on these issues, see, for example, Ha-Joon Chang, 2002, *Kicking Away the Ladder* (London: Anthem); Ha-Joon Chang and Ilene Grabel, 2004, *Reclaiming Development: An Alternative Economic Policy Manual* (London: Zed Books); and Phillip A. O'Hara, 2006, *Growth and Development in the Global Political Economy* (London: Routledge).

18. Cisco, 2011a, "Cisco Visual Networking Index: Global Mobile Data Traffic Forecast Update, 2010–2015," Cisco White Paper, 1 February, 1.

19. Ibid., 2.

20. Where electricity is not supplied through a grid, phones are charged at local stores with generators, at work, or elsewhere; indeed, phone charging is one of the myriad services provided by small businesses in many poor communities.

21. Many areas, particularly in poorer countries, still lack a physical infrastructure capable of handling Internet data. Without significant investment, these areas will continue to be restricted to voice and text messaging.

22. Cisco projects the following compound annual growth rates for 2010–2015: Latin America, 111 percent; Eastern Europe, 102 percent; and North Africa and the Middle East, 129 percent. Ibid., 3.

23. See, for example, Habibul H. Khondker, 2011, "Role of the New Media in the Arab Spring," *Globalizations* 8 (5): 675–679.

24. Richard H. Day, 2010, "On Simplicity and Macroeconomic Complexity," in *Handbook of Research on Complexity*, ed. J. Barkley Rosser Jr. (Cheltenham, UK: Edward Elgar), 195.

25. J. Barkley Rosser Jr., 2009b, "Introduction," in *Handbook of Research on Complexity*, ed. J. Barkley Rosser Jr. (Cheltenham, UK: Edgar Elgar), 3–11.

26. J. Barkley Rosser Jr., 2009a, "Computational and Dynamic Complexity in Economics," in *Handbook of Research on Complexity*, ed. J. Barkley Rosser Jr. (Cheltenham, UK: Edgar Elgar), 22–25.

27. John Horgan, 1997, *The End of Science: Facing the Limits of Knowledge in the Twilight of the Scientific Age* (New York: Broadway Books), 303; see also Neil Johnson, 2009, *Simply Complexity: A Clear Guide to Complexity Theory* (Oxford, UK: Oneworld Publications).

28. Paul Ormerod, 2012, *Positive Linking: How Networks Can Revolutionise the World* (London: Faber and Faber).

29. Ibid., x.

30. Ibid., xi.

31. Malcolm Gladwell catalogs numerous events and trends that occur for seemingly inexplicable reasons. Linking such diverse subjects as fashion trends or crime to the patterns with which epidemics develop, his work illustrates precisely the nonlinear and opaque nature of twenty-first-century risk that we intend to study in the course of this book. See Malcolm Gladwell, 2002, *The Tipping Point: How Little Things Can Make a Big Difference* (London: Abacus).

32. Dirk Brockmann, Lars Hufnagel, and Theo Geisel, 2005, "Dynamics of Modern Epidemics," in *SARS: A Case Study in Emerging Infections*, ed. Angela McLean et al. (New York and London, UK: Oxford University Press), 81–91.

33. Goldin, 2011, 24.

34. Peter Dattels and Laura Kodres, 2009, "Further Action Needed to Reinforce Signs of Market Recovery: IMF," *IMF Survey Magazine: IMF Research*, 21 April, accessed 8 January 2013, http://www.imf.org/external/pubs/ft/survey/so/2009/RES042109C.htm.

35. See, for example, William C. Hunter, George G. Kaufman, and Thomas H. Krueger, eds., 1999, *The Asian Financial Crisis: Origins, Implications, and Solutions* (Norwell, MA: Kluwer Academic).

36. Ortwin Renn, 2008, *Risk Governance: Coping with Uncertainty in a Complex World* (London: Earthscan), vi.

37. Frank H. Knight, 1921, *Risk, Uncertainty, and Profit* (Boston: Hart, Schaffner, and Marx); and Larry G. Epstein and Tan Wang, 1994, "Intertemporal Asset Pricing under Knightian Uncertainty," *Econometrica* 62 (3): 283–322, quote on 283.

38. Epstein and Tan Wang, 1994, 283.

39. For a critical discussion, see Jochen Runde, 1998, "Clarifying Frank Knight's Discussion of the Meaning of Risk and Uncertainty," *Cambridge Journal of Economics* 22 (5): 539–546.

40. UNISDR (United Nations Office for Disaster Risk Reduction), 2004, "Note on Terminology from the WCDR Conference Secretariat to the Drafting Committee (18/11/2004)," United Nations Office for Disaster Risk Reduction, Geneva, 2, accessed 15 October 2012, http://www.unisdr.org/2005/wcdr/intergover/drafting-committe/terminology.pdf.

41. Renn, 2008.

42. Ian Goldin and Tiffany Vogel, 2010, "Global Governance and Systemic Risk in the 21st Century: Lessons from the Financial Crisis," *Global Policy* 1 (1): 4–15, quote on 5; and George G. Kaufman and Kenneth E. Scott, 2003, "What Is Systemic Risk, and Do Bank Regulators Retard or Contribute to It?" *Independent Review* 7 (3): 371–391, quote on 371.

43. The German sociologist Ulrich Beck provides a similar insight: "The speeding up of modernization has produced a gulf between the world of quantifiable risk in which we think and act, and the world of non-quantifiable insecurities that we are creating." See Ulrich Beck, 2002, "The Terrorist Threat: World Risk Society Revisited," *Theory Culture Society* 19 (4): 39–55, quote on 40.

44. Kaufman and Scott, 2003, 371.

45. Domenico Delli Gatti et al., 2009, "Business Fluctuations and Bankruptcy Avalanches in an Evolving Network Economy," *Journal of Economic Interaction and Coordination* 4 (2): 195–212.

46. George G. Kaufman, 1995, "Comment on Systemic Risk," in *Research in Financial Services: Banking, Financial Markets, and Systemic Risk*, vol. 7, ed. George G. Kaufman (Greenwich, CT: JAI Press), 47–52, quote on 47.

47. Robert Jervis, 1997, *System Effects* (Princeton, NJ: Princeton University Press).

48. Robert M. May, Simon A. Levin, and George Sugihara, 2008, "Complex Systems: Ecology for Bankers," *Nature* 451 (21 February): 893–895.

49. A recent example of complexity research's being successfully applied to drawing policy lessons from the financial crisis is Andrew G. Haldane and Robert M. May, 2011, "Systemic Risk in Banking Ecosystems," *Nature* 469: 351–355. See also Felix Reed-Tsochas, 2005, "From Biology to Business and Beyond," *Business at Oxford* (Magazine of the Saïd Business School) 8 (Winter): 4–5, accessed 9 January 2013, http://www.sbs.ox.ac.uk/Documents/bao/BuisnessatOxfordWinter2005.pdf.

50. Bruno Latour, 2005, *Reassembling the Social: An Introduction to Actor-Network-Theory* (Oxford, UK: Oxford University Press).

51. A. Marm Kilpatrick, 2011, "Globalization, Land Use, and the Invasion of West Nile Virus," *Science* 334 (6054): 323–327, quote on 323.

52. BOI (Board of Investment, Thailand), 2012, *Thailand Investment Review* 28 (8): 6, accessed 17 January 2013, http://www.boi.go.th/tir/issue/201208_22_8/TIR -201208_22_8.pdf.

53. Air traffic came to a complete halt between 15 and 21 April, although periodic cancellations continued until the third week of May. Losses are from Oxford Economics, 2010, *The Economic Impacts of Air Travel Restrictions Due to Volcanic Ash*, report prepared for Airbus, 5 January (Oxford, UK: Oxford Economics).

54. Michael Useem, 2011, "Deutsche Bank Case Study: Catastrophic Risk Management during the Fukushima Earthquake in March 2011," presentation at the Sasin Bangkok Forum: Asia in Transformation, Royal Méridien Hotel, Bangkok, 8–9 July.

55. The notion of Ricardian efficiency is explained in the introduction, n. 2.

56. See, for example, Joseph E. Stiglitz, 2006, *Making Globalization Work* (London: W. W. Norton); Anthony B. Atkinson, 2012, "Optimum Population, Welfare Economics, and Inequality," Oxford Martin School seminar paper, revised version, January, University of Oxford, Oxford, UK; François Bourguignon, 2012, *La Mondialisation de l'inégalité* (Paris: Editions du Seuil et La Republique des Idees); and Dani Rodrik, 2012, "Global Poverty amid Global Plenty: Getting Globalization Right," *Americas Quarterly*, Spring, accessed 4 January 2013, http://www.americasquarterly .org/node/3560.

57. For a more detailed discussion of the "governance gap," see Ian Goldin, 2013, *Divided Nations: Why Global Governance Is Failing, and What We Can Do about It* (Oxford, UK: Oxford University Press).

58. See Goldin and Reinert, 2011, 26 and 130.

59. Lars-Hendrik Roeller and Leonard Waverman, 2001, "Telecommunications Infrastructure and Economic Development: A Simultaneous Approach," *American Economic Review* 91 (4): 909–923.

60. Goldin, 2011.

61. Martin Ravallion and Shaohua Chen, 2004, "Learning from Success: Understanding China's (Uneven) Progress against Poverty," *Finance and Development* 41 (4): 16–19.

62. For further evidence supporting the view that the benefits of globalization have exceeded its cost for the majority of the world's population, see Ian Goldin, F. Halsey Rogers, and Nicholas H. Stern, 2002, "The Role and Effectiveness of Development Assistance: Lessons from World Bank Experience," research paper, Development Economics Vice Presidency of the World Bank, Washington, DC; Jagdish Bhagwati, 2007, *In Defense of Globalization* (New York: Oxford University Press); or Goldin and Reinert, 2012, among others.

63. Anthony Giddens, 1991, *The Consequences of Modernity* (Stanford, CA: Stanford University Press), 175.

64. Khaled Fourati, 2009, "Half Full or Half Empty? The Contribution of Information and Communication Technologies to Development," *Global Governance* 15 (1): 37–42.

65. Stiglitz, 2006, and Goldin and Reinert, 2012.

66. Ravallion and Chen, 2004.

67. Alex Evans, Bruce Jones, and David Steven, 2010, *Confronting the Long Crisis of Globalization: Risk, Resilience, and International Order* (New York: Brookings Institute and Center on International Cooperation, New York University), 5.

68. Brian Walker et al., 2004, "Resilience, Adaptability, and Transformability in Social-Ecological Systems," *Ecology and Society* 11 (1): 5, accessed 9 January 2013, http://www.ecologyandsociety.org/vol9/iss2/art5/print.pdf.

69. Goldin, 2011.

70. Kilpatrick, 2011, 334.

71. Rodrik, 2011.

72. William D. Nordhaus, 1994, *Managing the Global Commons: The Economics of Climate Change* (Cambridge, MA: MIT Press).

73. Brian Wynne and Kerstin Dressel, 2001, "Cultures of Uncertainty: Transboundary Risks and BSE in Europe," in *Transboundary Risk Management*, ed. Joanne Linneroth-Bayer, Ragnar Löefstedt, and Gunnar Sjöestedt (London: Earthscan), 126–154.

74. On this issue see Goldin, 2013.

75. John F. Kennedy, 1959, "Education: United Negro College Fund," speech to the United Negro College Fund, Indianapolis, Indiana, 12 April, 2, accessed 10 July 2013, http://www.jfklibrary.org/Asset-Viewer/Archives/JFKCAMP1960-1029-036 .aspx.

Chapter 2: The Financial Sector

1. Ian Goldin and Tiffany Vogel used the term "Golden Decade" in their 2010 article "Global Governance and Systemic Risk in the 21st Century: Lessons from the Financial Crisis," *Global Policy* 1 (1): 4–15, quote on 6.

2. Robert Jackson, 2008, "The Big Chill," *Financial Times*, 15 November, accessed 20 January 2013, http://www.ft.com/intl/cms/s/0/8641d080-b2b4-11dd-bbc9 -0000779fd18c.html#axzz2Cn5IKHoa.

3. Central Bank of Iceland, 2008a, "Economic Indicators," September, 2, accessed 24 January 2013, http://www.sedlabanki.is/lisalib/getfile.aspx?itemid=6451.

4. Central Bank of Iceland, 2008b, "Economic Indicators," November, accessed 24 January 2013, http://www.sedlabanki.is/lisalib/getfile.aspx?itemid=6628.

5. Jackson, 2008.

6. These figures refer to the approximate mid rate for August and the mid rate for 28 November, respectively. They are derived from Central Bank of Iceland, 2013, "Exchange Rate," accessed 11 July, http://www.cb.is/exchange-rate/.

7. Tasneem Brogger and Helga Kristin Einarsdottir, 2008, "Iceland Gets $4.6 Billion Bailout from IMF, Nordics (Update3)," Bloomberg website, 20 November, accessed 5 February 2013, http://www.bloomberg.com/apps/news?pid=newsarchive &sid=a3Zf1f9IBUWg&refer=europe.

8. This figure refers to constant 2000 U.S. dollars from World Bank, 2013, *World Development Indicators*, World DataBank, accessed 7 January, http://databank .worldbank.org/.

9. Directorate of Labour (Iceland), 2013a, "Unemployment 9.3 in February 2010," *Directorate of Labour News*, 10 March, accessed 24 January, http://english .vinnumalastofnun.is/about-directorate-of-labour/news/nr/1031/, and Directorate of Labour, 2013b, "Unemployment 9.3 in March 2010," *Directorate of Labour News*, 20 April, accessed 24 January, http://english.vinnumalastofnun.is/ about-directorate-of-labour/news/nr/1061/.

10. Omar Valdimarsson, 2009, "Iceland Parliament Approves Debt Bill," *Reuters*, 28 August, accessed 25 January 2013, http://www.reuters.com/article/2009/08/28/ businesspro-us-iceland-debts-idUSTRE57R3B920090828.

11. Jackson, 2008.

12. Rowena Mason, 2009, "David Oddsson's Ascent to Iceland's Editor in Chief Splits Opinion as Bloggers Gain Ground," *Telegraph*, 29 September, accessed 1 February 2013, http://blogs.telegraph.co.uk/finance/rowenamason/100001134/ david-oddssons-ascent-to-icelands-editor-in-chief-splits-opinion-as-bloggers-gain -ground/.

13. Vincent Maraia, 2006, *The Build Master: Microsoft's Software Configuration Management Best Practices* (Upper Saddle River, NJ: Addison-Wesley).

14. Jenny Strasburg and Jacob Bunge, 2012, "Loss Swamps Trading Firm: Knight Capital Searches for Partner as Tab for Computer Glitch Hits $440 Million," *Wall Street Journal*, 2 August, accessed 21 January 2013, http://online.wsj.com/article/ SB10000872396390443866404577564772083961412.html.

15. Matthew Jarzemsky, 2012, "'Fat-Finger' Error Caused Oil-Stock Price Swings," *Wall Street Journal*, 19 September, accessed 21 January 2013, http://blogs .wsj.com/marketbeat/2012/09/19/fat-finger-error-caused-oil-stock-price -swings/?KEYWORDS=Oilwell+Varco.

16. Lawrence J. White, 1997, "Technological Change, Financial Innovation, and Financial Regulation in the U.S.: The Challenges for Public Policy," presentation at the Conference on Performance of Financial Institutions, Wharton Financial Institutions Center, University of Pennsylvania, Philadelphia, May 8–10, 24.

17. Ibid.

18. Charles Roxburgh, Susan Lund, and John Piotrowski, 2011, *Updated Research: Mapping Global Capital Markets* (New York: McKinsey), August, 2, accessed 21 January 2013, http://www.mckinsey.com/insights/mgi/research/financial_markets/ mapping_global_capital_markets_2011.

19. Charles Roxburgh et al., 2009, *Global Capital Markets: Entering a New Era* (New York: McKinsey), September, 21, accessed 21 January 2013, http://www .mckinsey.com/insights/mgi/research/financial_marketsglobal_capital_markets_ entering_a_new_era.

20. Prasanna Gai, Andrew Haldane, and Sujit Kapadia, 2011, "Complexity, Concentration, and Contagion," *Journal of Monetary Economics* 58 (5): 453–470.

21. See Charles Perrow, 2009, "Modeling Firms in the Global Economy: New Forms, New Concentrations," *Theory and Society* 38 (3): 217–243; William K. Tabb, 2004, *Economic Governance in the Age of Globalization* (New York: Columbia University Press); and Jeniffer Bair, 2008, *Frontiers of Commodity Chain Research* (Stanford, CA: Stanford University Press). Quote from Perrow, 2009, 217.

22. Ian Goldin, 2010, "Managing and Mitigating Global Risks," in *Global Redesign: Strengthening Cooperation in a More Interdependent World*, ed. Richard Samans, Klaus Schwab, and Mark Malloch-Brown (Geneva: World Economic Forum), 429–442, quote on 431.

23. Garry B. Gorton and Andrew Metrick, 2010b, "Securitized Banking and the Run on Repo," NBER Working Paper 15223, National Bureau of Economic Research, Cambridge, MA.

24. A tail risk is the risk that a relatively large loss will emerge toward the end of a transaction, when relatively few loans remain in the securitization pool.

25. Markus K. Brunnermeier, 2008, "Deciphering the Liquidity and Credit Crunch, 2007–08," NBER Working Paper 14612, National Bureau of Economic Research, Cambridge, MA, accessed 21 January 2013, http://www.nber.org/papers/w14612.

26. Nicola Gennaioli, Andrei Shleifer, and Robert W. Vishny, 2012, "Neglected Risks, Financial Innovation, and Financial Fragility," *Journal of Financial Economics* 104 (3): 452–468.

27. William A. Brock, Cars H. Hommes, and Florian O. O. Wagener, 2008, "More Hedging Instruments May Destabilize Markets," CeNDEF Working Paper 08-04, Center for Nonlinear Dynamics in Economics and Finance, University of Amsterdam, Amsterdam.

28. Alp Simsek, 2011, "Speculation and Risk Sharing with New Financial Assets," NBER Working Paper 17506, National Bureau of Economic Research, Cambridge, MA.

29. This is an aggregate figure for 2007 and 2008 based on data derived from figure 2.5 and Viral V. Acharya et al., 2011, "Dividends and Bank Capital in the Financial Crisis of 2007–2009," NBER Working Paper 16896, National Bureau of Economic Research, Cambridge, MA, table 3a, accessed 21 January 2013, http://www.nber.org/papers/w16896.

30. Among the recipients were JP Morgan ($25 billion), Wells Fargo ($25 billion), Citigroup ($45 billion), Morgan Stanley ($10 billion), Bank of America ($45 billion), and Goldman Sachs ($10 billion). Ibid.

31. Senate Banking Committee, 1999, "Gramm's Statement at Signing Ceremony for Gramm-Leach-Bliley Act," Senate Banking Committee Press Release, 12 November, accessed 21 January 2013, http://banking.senate.gov/prel99/1112gbl.htm.

32. William Keegan, 2012, "Bank Deregulation Leads to Disaster: Shout It from the Rooftops," *Observer*, 6 May, accessed 21 January 2013, http://www.guardian.co.uk/business/2012/may/06/shout-rooftops-bank-deregulation-leads-to-disaster.

33. See, for example, Raghuram G. Rajan, 2005, "The Greenspan Era: Lessons for the Future," speech delivered at Financial Markets, Financial Fragility, and Central Banking, a symposium sponsored by the Federal Reserve Bank of Kansas City, Jackson Hole, Wyoming, 27 August, accessed 21 January 2013, http://www.imf.org/external/np/speeches/2005/082705.htm. For Rajan's assessment of the deeper causes of the financial crisis and further warnings that a "potentially more devastating crisis" may follow, see Raghuram G. Rajan, 2011, *Fault Lines: How Hidden Fractures Still Threaten the World Economy* (Princeton, NJ: Princeton University Press).

34. Paul R. Krugman, 2009, *The Conscience of a Liberal* (New York: Penguin), xii.

35. George Kanatas and Jianping Qi, 2003, "Integration of Lending and Underwriting: Implications of Scope Economies," *Journal of Finance* 58 (3): 1167–1191; George Kanatas and Jianping Qi, 1998, "Underwriting by Commercial Banks: Incentive Conflicts, Scope Economies, and Project Quality," *Journal of Money, Credit, and Banking* 30: 119–133; and Xavier Freixas, Gyöngyi Lóránth, and Alan D. Morrison, 2007, "Regulating Financial Conglomerates," *Journal of Financial Intermediation* 16: 479–514.

36. Tom Foreman, 2008, "Culprits of the Collapse—#7 Phil Gramm," CNN website, 14 October, accessed 22 January 2013, http://ac360.blogs.cnn.com/2008/10/14/culprits-of-the-collapse-7-phil-gramm/; and Goldin and Vogel, 2010, 7. This follows a long-established pattern of a revolving door between Wall Street and the leadership of the U.S. Treasury, with Treasury secretaries often recruited following a period at the helm of one of the major U.S. banks and returning afterward to a chairmanship or other lucrative advisory position in the financial services industry. Treasury secretaries since 2001 with links to finance and industry include Paul O'Neill (Alcoa, Rand Corporation), John Snow (CSX Corporation, Cerberus Capital Management Group), and Henry Paulson (Goldman Sachs). In addition, U.S. authorities had substantially deregulated loan products by means of the Depository Institutions and Monetary Control Act of 1980 and the Alternative Mortgage Transaction Parity Act of 1982.

37. Shaun French, Andrew Leyshon, and Nigel Thrift, 2009, "A Very Geographical Crisis: The Making and Breaking of the 2007–2008 Financial Crisis," *Cambridge Journal of Regions, Economy, and Society* 2 (2): 287–302.

38. Simon Johnson, 2009, "The Quiet Coup," *Atlantic Magazine,* May, accessed 16 October 2012, http://www.theatlantic.com/magazine/archive/2009/05/the-quiet -coup/307364/.

39. Nestor A. Espenilla Jr., 2009, "Regulatory Factors That Contributed to the Global Financial Crisis," *Asia-Pacific Social Science Review* 9 (1) : 35–40.

40. James H. Stock and Mark W. Watson, 2002. "Has the Business Cycle Changed and Why?," in *NBER Macroeconomics Annual,* vol. 17, ed. Mark Gertler and Kenneth Rogoff (Cambridge, MA: MIT Press), 159–218.

41. Andrew G. Haldane, 2009, "Rethinking the Financial Network," speech delivered to the Amsterdam Student Association, April, accessed 21 January 2013, http://www.bankofengland.co.uk/archive/Documents/historicpubs/speeches/2009/speech386.pdf.

42. Authors' calculation based on data from Lucinda Maer and Nida Brough-ton, 2012, "Financial Services: Contribution to the UK Economy," SN/EP/06193, House of Commons Library (Economics, Politics, and Statistics Section), p. 3, table 1, accessed 22 January 2013, http://www.parliament.uk/briefing-papers/SN06193.pdf.

43. Maer and Broughton, 2012, 1.

44. Sebastian Schich and Sofia Lindh, 2012, "Implicit Guarantees for Bank Debt: Where Do We Stand?," *OECD Journal: Financial Market Trends* 2012 (1), accessed 22 January 2013, http://www.oecd.org/finance/financialmarkets/Implicit-Guarantees -for-bank-debt.pdf.

45. Federal Reserve Bank of St. Louis, 2012, "Debt Outstanding Domestic Finan-cial Sectors," Board of Governors of the Federal Reserve System, accessed 7 Decem-ber, http://research.stlouisfed.org/fred2/data/DODFS.txt.

46. Mathias Dewatripont and Jean-Charles Rochet, 2010, "The Treatment of Dis-tressed Banks," in *Balancing the Banks: Global Lessons from the Financial Crisis*, ed. Mathias Dewatripont, Jean-Charles Rochet, and Jean Tirole (Princeton, NJ: Princeton University Press), 107–130, esp. 113.

47. Andrew G. Haldane and Robert M. May, 2011, "Systemic Risk in Banking Ecosystems," *Nature* 469: 351–355, quotes on 351.

48. Franklin Allen and Douglas Gale, 2000, "Financial Contagion," *Journal of Political Economy* 108 (1): 1–33; and Prasanna Gai and Sujit Kapadia, 2010, "Conta-gion in Financial Networks," Bank of England Working Paper 383, Bank of England, London.

49. Ricardo J. Caballero and Alp Simsek, 2009, "Fire-Sales in a Model of Com-plexity," MIT Department of Economics Working Paper 09-28, Massachusetts Insti-tute of Technology, Cambridge, MA, abstract.

50. See Andrew G. Haldane, 2012, "The Dog and the Frisbee," speech delivered at the Federal Reserve Bank of Kansas City's 36th Economic Policy Symposium, The Changing Policy Landscape, Jackson Hole, Wyoming, 31 August, accessed 31 January 2013, http://www.bankofengland.co.uk/publications/Documents/speeches/2012/ speech596.pdf.

51. One approach that might be adapted to provide a set of simple rules to help manage growing financial complexity has been suggested by Gerd Gigerenzer, 2010, *Rationality for Mortals: How People Cope with Uncertainty* (New York: Oxford University Press).

52. Philipp Hartmann, Oliver De Bandt, and José Luis Peydró-Alcalde, 2009, "Systemic Risk in Banking: An Update," in *The Oxford Handbook of Banking*, ed. Allen N. Berger, Philip Molyneux, and John O. S. Wilson (Oxford, UK: Oxford Uni-versity Press).

53. IMF (International Monetary Fund) Staff, 2009, "Guidance to Assess the Sys-temic Importance of Financial Institutions, Markets, and Instruments," Report to G20 Finance Ministers and Governors, International Monetary Fund, Bank for Interna-tional Settlements, and Financial Stability Board, October, 2, accessed 1 February 2013, http://www.financialstabilityboard.org/publications/r_091107c.pdf; see also IMF Staff,

2010, "The Financial Crisis and Information Gaps," Progress Report, International Monetary Fund Bank for International Settlements and Financial Stability Board, May, accessed 1 February 2013, http://www.imf.org/external/np/g20/pdf/053110.pdf.

54. ECB (European Central Bank), 2009, "The Concept of Systemic Risk," *Financial Stability Review*, December, European Central Bank, Frankfurt, 134–142.

55. An extensive review of the literature of financial networks is provided by Franklin Allen, Anna Babus, and Elena Carletti, 2010, "Financial Connections and Systemic Risk," EUI Working Paper ECO 2010/30, Department of Economics, European University Institute, Badia Fiesolana, Italy.

56. Allen and Gale, 2000.

57. Gai and Kapadia, 2010.

58. Haldane, 2009.

59. Giulia Iori, Saqib Jafarey, and Francisco G. Padilla, 2006, "Systemic Risk on the Interbank Market," *Journal of Economic Behavior and Organization* 61: 525–542.

60. Co-Pierre Georg and Jenny Poschmann, 2010, "Systemic Risk in a Network Model of Interbank Markets with Central Bank Activity," Jena Economic Research Paper 2010-33, Friedrich Schiller University and the Max Planck Institute of Economics, Jena, Germany, accessed 1 February 2013, http://pubdb.wiwi.uni-jena.de/pdf/wp_2010_033.pdf; and Co-Pierre Georg, 2011, "The Effect of the Interbank Network Structure on Contagion and Financial Stability," Discussion Paper Series 2: Banking and Financial Studies 12/2011, Deutsche Bundesbank, Frankfurt, accessed 1 February 2013, http://econstor.eu/bitstream/10419/52134/1/671536869.pdf.

61. Haldane, 2009.

62. Erlend Nier et al., 2007, "Network Models and Financial Stability," *Journal of Economic Dynamics and Control* 31 (6): 2033–2060.

63. Viral V. Acharya and Tanju Yorulmazer, 2008, "Cash-in-the-Market Pricing and Optimal Resolution of Bank Failures," *Review of Financial Studies* 21 (6): 2705–2742.

64. Viral V. Acharya, 2009, "A Theory of Systemic Risk and Design of Prudential Bank Regulation," *Journal of Financial Stability* 5 (3): 224–255.

65. Georg and Poschmann, 2010.

66. Gianni De Nicolo and Myron L. Kwast, 2002, "Systemic Risk and Financial Consolidation: Are They Related?," *Journal of Banking and Finance* 26 (5): 861–880.

67. Alfred Lehar, 2005, "Measuring Systemic Risk: A Risk Management Approach," *Journal of Banking and Finance* 29 (10): 2577–2603.

68. See Viral V. Acharya and Tanju Yorulmazer, 2003, "Information Contagion and Inter-Bank Correlation in a Theory of Systemic Risk," CEPR Discussion Paper 3473, Centre for Economic Policy Research, London; and Nier et al., 2007.

69. Hartmann, De Bandt, and Peydró-Alcalde, 2009.

70. Acharya and Yorulmazer, 2003.

71. For an overview of the literature on bank herding as a source of systemic risk, see Hartmann, De Bandt, and Peydró-Alcalde, 2009.

72. Acharya and Yorulmazer, 2003.

73. Claudio Borio, 2010, "Implementing a Macroprudential Framework: Blending Boldness and Realism," keynote speech at the Hong Kong Institute for Monetary Research and the Bank for International Settlements conference "Financial Stability: Towards a Macroprudential Approach," Hong Kong, 5–6 July, accessed 1 February 2013, http://www.bis.org/repofficepubl/hkimr201007.12c.pdf.

74. ECB (European Central Bank), 2010, "Analytical Models and Tools for the Identification and Assessment of Systemic Risks," *Financial Stability Review,* June, European Central Bank, Frankfurt, 138–146.

75. Helga Kristin Einarsdottir and Tasneem Brogger, 2008, "Icelanders Take to Streets to Protest Policy Makers' Failures," *Bloomberg,* 15 November, accessed 5 February 2013, http://www.bloomberg.com/apps/news?pid=newsarchive&sid=a0r9Lfo 7mSUw&refer=europe.

76. Goldin and Vogel, 2010, 6.

77. Mike Mariathasan, and Ouarda Merrouche, 2013, "The Manipulation of Basel Risk-Weights," CEPR Discussion Paper 9494, Centre for Economic Policy Research, London, May.

78. Goldin and Vogel, 2010, 4–15.

79. See Daniel K. Tarullo, 2008, *Banking on Basel: The Future of International Financial Regulation* (Washington, DC: Peterson Institute for International Economics); or Jean-Charles Rochet, 2010, "The Future of Banking Regulation," in *Balancing the Banks: Global Lessons from the Financial Crisis,* ed. Mathias Dewatripont, Jean-Charles Rochet, and Jean Tirole (Princeton, NJ: Princeton University Press), 78–103.

80. The failure regarding Fortis Bank is discussed in Dewatripont and Rochet, 2010, 108.

81. Ibid.

82. Haldane, 2009.

83. White, 1997.

84. For a more extensive discussion of lessons from the crisis, see, for example, Viral V. Acharya et al., eds., 2010, *Regulating Wall Street: The Dodd-Frank Act and the New Architecture of Global Finance* (Hoboken, NJ: John Wiley and Sons); Financial Crisis Inquiry Commission, 2011, *Financial Crisis Inquiry Report: Final Report of the National Commission on the Causes of the Financial and Economic Crisis in the United States* (Washington, DC: U.S. Public Affairs); or Jean Tirole, 2010, "Lessons from the Crisis," in *Balancing the Banks: Global Lessons from the Financial Crisis,* ed. Mathias Dewatripont, Jean-Charles Rochet, and Jean Tirole (Princeton, NJ: Princeton University Press), 10–77.

85. Dieter Kerwer, 2005, "Rules That Many Use: Standards and Global Regulation," *Governance* 18 (4): 611–632.

86. Robert M. May, Simon A. Levin, and George Sugihara, 2008, "Complex Systems: Ecology for Bankers," *Nature* 451 (21 February): 893–895, quote on 893.

87. For example, the simple 1/N investment rule that Markowitz followed empirically outperforms the more complex models of portfolio theory he developed. See Harry M. Markowitz, 1952, "Portfolio Selection," *Journal of Finance* 7: 77–91.

88. Gordon L. Clark, Adam D. Dixon, and Ashby H. B. Monk, eds., 2009, *Managing Financial Risks: From Global to Local* (Oxford, UK: Oxford University Press), 2.

89. Ibid., xv.

90. See Haldane, 2012. Haldane drew on Gerd Gigerenzer, Ralph Hertwig, and Thorsten Pachur, eds., 2011, *Heuristics: The Foundations of Adaptive Behavior* (Oxford, UK: Oxford University Press).

CHAPTER 3: SUPPLY CHAIN RISKS

1. See Anna Nagurney, 2006, *Supply Chain Network Economics: Dynamics of Prices, Flows, and Profits* (Cheltenham, UK: Edward Elgar).

2. See the discussion in Randy Starr, Jim Newfrock, and Michael Delurey, 2003, "Enterprise Resilience: Managing Risk in the Networked Economy," *Booz Allen Hamilton Strategy and Business Magazine* (30): 1–10, accessed 23 January 2013, http://www.boozallen.com/media/file/139766.pdf.

3. See, for example, Leslie Hook, 2012, "China's Rare Earth Stranglehold in Spotlight," *Financial Times*, 13 March, accessed 23 January 2013, http://www.ft.com/cms/s/0/b3332e0a-348c-11e2-8986-00144feabdc0.html#axzz2DVY78Spi.

4. Ibid.

5. Paul Markillie, 2006, "The Physical Internet," *Economist*, 15 June, accessed 1 February 2013, http://www.economist.com/node/7032165.

6. Ian Goldin, 2011, "Globalisation and Risks for Business: Implications for an Increasingly Connected World," *Lloyd's 360° Risk Insight* (London: Lloyds, and Oxford, UK: James Martin 21st Century School), 8, accessed 9 January 2013, http://www.lloyds.com/~/media/Lloyds/Reports/360/360%20Globalisation/Lloyds_360_Globalisaton.pdf.

7. Carol McAusland, 2008, "Globalisation's Direct and Indirect Effects on the Environment," paper presented at the Organization for Economic Co-operation and Develpment's Global Forum on Transport and Environment in a Globalising World, Guadalajara, Mexico, 10–12 November, 6, accessed 21 January 2013, http://www.oecd.org/env/transportandenvironment/41380703.pdf.

8. McAusland, 2008, 5.

9. See, for example, Loren Brandt and Thomas G. Rawski, 2008, *China's Great Economic Transformation* (Cambridge, UK: Cambridge University Press).

10. David Hummels, 2007, "Transportation Costs and International Trade in the Second Era of Globalization," *Journal of Economic Perspectives* 21 (3): 131–154, esp. 132.

11. Ibid., 134.

12. China is now the world's largest exporter of electronic products, which totaled well over US$450 billion in 2009. The foreign content value of these exports stood at around the US$180 billion mark. See WTO (World Trade Organization), 2013a, "OECD–WTO Database on Trade in Value-Added: Preliminary

Results," *OECD–WTO Brochure*, World Trade Organization, 17 January, p. 2 and figure 4, accessed 23 January, http://www.wto.org/english/res_e/statis_e/miwi_e/tradedataday13_e/oecdbrochurejanv13_e.pdf.

13. One strand of research attempts to analyze the economic transformation of China and other countries using the product space methodology. The basic idea is that if a country already possesses a broad set of capabilities, it will be easier to develop additional products for export and to specialize further ("perpetual novelty") once supply chains have become sufficiently complex and diverse. See Cesar Hidalgo et al., 2007, "The Product Space Conditions the Development of Nations," *Science* 317 (5837): 482–487. Using powerful tools such as the Observatory of Economic Complexity's "product space app" (http://atlas.media.mit.edu/), it is possible to explore how the product space of China's exports has become increasingly dynamic and densely populated over the past 20 years.

14. Goldin, 2011, 11.

15. Thomas F. Golob and Amelia C. Regan, 2001, "Impacts of Information Technology on Personal Travel and Commercial Vehicle Operations: Research Challenges and Opportunities," *Transportation Research Part C* 9: 87–121, quote on 88.

16. See, for example, Thomas A. Kochan, Russell D. Lansbury, and John P. MacDuffie, eds., 1997, *After Lean Production: Evolving Employment Practices in the World Auto Industry* (Ithaca, NY: Cornell University Press).

17. Taiichi Ohno, 1988, *Toyota Production System: Beyond Large-Scale Production* (Portland, OR: Productivity Press).

18. Goldin, 2011, 30–31; see also David Magee, 2008, *How Toyota Became #1: Leadership Lessons from the World's Greatest Car Company* (New York: Portfolio).

19. For a more detailed discussion of Toyota's economic system, see Michael L. George, David T. Rowlands, and Bill Kastle, 2003, *What Is Lean Six Sigma?* (New York: McGraw-Hill Professional); Jeffrey Liker, 2004, *The Toyota Way: 14 Management Principles from the World's Greatest Manufacturer* (New York: McGraw-Hill Professional); Magee, 2008; or Goldin, 2011, among others.

20. Markillie, 2006.

21. One estimate puts the total economic losses attributed to the floods by 1 December 2011 at US$45.7 billion and the damage to manufacturing at US$32 billion. See Cristophe Courbage and Walter R. Stahel, eds., 2012, "Extreme Events and Insurance: 2011 Annus Horribilis," *Geneva Reports* 5 (May): 121–132, esp. 122–123.

22. WEF (World Economic Forum), 2012a, "Impact of Thailand Floods 2011 on Supply Chain," mimeo, World Economic Forum.

23. Ibid.

24. Ibid.

25. WEF (World Economic Forum), 2012b, *Global Risks 2012* (Geneva: World Economic Forum), 32.

26. Korea Net, 2013, "Overview," accessed 2 February, http://www.korea.net/AboutKorea/Economy/Overview.

27. Paul Withers, 2012, "iPhone 5 Production Delayed as Foxconn Staff Walk Out," *Mobile News,* 8 October, accessed 16 October, http://www.mobilenewscwp .co.uk/2012/10/08/iphone-5-production-delayed-as-foxconn-staff-walk-out/.

28. *Economist,* 2006, "When the Chain Breaks: Being Too Lean and Mean Is a Dangerous Thing," 15 June, accessed 23 January 2013, http://www.economist.com/ node/7032258.

29. Ohno, 1988.

30. All citations in the following two paragraphs are from Goldin, 2011, 30–31.

31. A word search for the phrase "management literature" on Google Scholar yields "around 4,570,000 results" (as of 24 January 2013). If the same search is narrowed to the years 1990–2000, the number of hits falls to "around 872,000."

32. Morgen Witzel, 2011, *A History of Management Thought* (New York: Routledge), back cover.

33. Goldin, 2011, 11.

34. For a comprehensive description of the history of management education in the United Kingdom, see Alan P. O. Williams, 2010, *The History of UK Business and Management Education* (Bingley, UK: Emerald Group).

35. Kai Peters and Narendra Laljani, 2009, "The Evolving MBA," *Global Study Magazine* 4 (3): 36–49, esp. 37.

36. Gai Changxin, 2011, "CEIBS Calls for More MBA Programs," *China Daily,* 11 April, accessed 7 July 2012, http://www.chinadaily.com.cn/business/2011-04/11/ content_12305897.htm.

37. Peters and Laljani, 2009, 37.

38. Hubert Escaith and Fabian Gonguet, 2009, "International Trade and Real Transmission Channels of Financial Shocks in Globalized Production Networks," Staff Working Paper ERSD-2009-06, Economics and Statistics Division, World Trade Organization, accessed 1 February 2013, http://www.wto.org/english/res_e/reser_e/ ersd200906_e.pdf.

39. Hubert Escaith, Nannette Lindenberg, and Sébastien Miroudot, 2010, "International Supply Chains and Trade Elasticity in Times of Global Crisis," Staff Working Paper ESRD-2010-08, Economics and Statistics Division, World Trade Organization, accessed 1 February 2013, http://www.wto.org/english/res_e/reser_e/ersd201008_e .pdf.

40. EEF (The Manufacturers' Organisation, UK), 2011, "Industry Looks to Reshore Production in Response to Supply Risks," The Manufacturers' Organization, accessed 31 January 2013, http://www.eef.org.uk/releases/uk/2011/Industry-looks -to-re-shore-production-in-response-to-supply-risks-.htm. The EEF was formerly known as the Engineering Employers' Federation and is still referred to as EEF in spite of the name change.

41. Charles K. Fine, 2005, "Are You Modular or Integral? Be Sure Your Supply Chain Knows," *Strategy+Business* 39 (23 May), accessed 1 February 2013, http:// www.strategy-business.com/article/05205?pg=all.

42. White House, 2012, "National Strategy for Global Supply Chain Security," White House, Washington, DC, ii.

43. Ibid.

44. The layers of complexity in global manufacuring have been geographically mapped in Alexandra Brintrup et al., 2011, "Mapping the Toyota Supply Network: Emergence of Resilience," Saïd Business School Working Paper 2011-05-012, University of Oxford, Oxford, UK.

45. Andreas Maurer and Christophe Degain, 2010, "Globalization and Trade Flows: What You See Is Not What You Get!," Staff Working Paper ERSD-2010-12, Economics and Statistics Division, World Trade Organization, 1, accessed 2 February 2013, http://www.wto.org/english/res_e/reser_e/ersd201012_e.pdf.

46. The fact that "trade finance" constitutes an entire subfield of research within the area of trade illustrates the relevance and complexity of this issue.

47. Stefano Battiston et al., 2007, "Credit Chains and Bankruptcy Propagation in Production Networks," *Journal of Economic Dynamics and Control* 31 (6): 2061–2084.

48. McKinsey, 2008, "McKinsey Global Survey Results: Managing Global Supply Chains," *McKinsey Quarterly*, August, accessed 28 January 2013, http://www.mckinseyquarterly.com/McKinsey_Global_Survey_Results_Managing_global_supply_chains_2179.

49. Pittiglio, Rabin, Todd, and McGrath (generally known as PRTM).

50. Reinhard Geissbauer and Shoshanah Cohen, 2008, "Globalization in Uncertain Times: How Leading Companies Are Building Adaptable Supply Chains to Reap Benefits and Manage Risk," reprinted from *PRTM Insight* 4: 2, accessed 2 February 2013, http://www.gsb.stanford.edu/sites/default/files/documents/PRTM_Globalization_In_Uncertain_Times.pdf.

51. Hau L. Lee, 2004, "Triple-A Supply Chains," *Harvard Business Review*, 1 October, 102.

52. Marsh and McLennan, 2012, "Supply Chain," Marsh USA website, accessed 1 August, http://usa.marsh.com/RiskIssues/SupplyChain/lapg-5776/2.aspx.

53. For a more detailed discussion of this distinction, particularly in the field of evolutionary biology, see Simon A. Levin and Jane Lubchenco, 2008, "Resilience, Robustness, and Marine Ecosystem–Based Management," *Bio Science* 58 (1): 27–32. Ross A. Hammond, 2009, "Systemic Risk in the Financial System: Insights from Network Science," Insights from Network Science Briefing Paper 12 (Washington, DC: Pew Charitable Trust) characterizes the distinction between the resilience and robustness of networks in the context of the financial sector. For a survey of different concepts and forms of adaptation, see David A. Clark, ed., 2012, *Adaptation, Poverty, and Development: The Dynamics of Subjective Well-being* (Basingstoke, UK: Palgrave Macmillan).

54. For a similar recommendation with reference to the financial sector, see Hammond, 2009, 6.

CHAPTER 4: INFRASTRUCTURE RISKS

1. USGS (U.S. Geological Survey), 2000, "Volcanic Ash Fall—A 'Hard Rain' of Abrasive Particles," Fact Sheet 0027-00, U.S. Geological Survey, accessed 15 July 2013, http://pubs.usgs.gov/fs/fs027-00/fs027-00.pdf.

2. UNEP (United Nations Environment Programme), 2011, *UNEP Year Book 2011: Emerging Issues in Our Global Environment* (Nairobi: United Nations Environment Programme), 2, accessed 25 January 2013, http://www.unep.org/yearbook/2011/pdfs/UNEP_YEARBOOK_Fullreport.pdf.

3. Oxford Economics, 2010, *The Economic Impacts of Air Travel Restrictions Due to Volcanic Ash*, report prepared for Airbus (Oxford, UK: Oxford Economics), 4.

4. Luis G. Aranda, n.d., "Economic and Social Impact of Volcanic Eruptions," mimeo, 2; see also the published version, Ono Yuichi and Luis G. Aranda, 2011, *Economic and Social Impact of Volcanic Eruptions*, World Economic Forum Report, December (Geneva: World Economic Forum).

5. Compass Worldwide Logistics, 2012, "Weather Closes All Italian Motorways," 10 September, accessed 25 January 2013, http://www.cwwl.co.uk/2012/02/weather-closes-all-italian-motorways/.

6. Ibid.

7. BBC, 2010, "Snow and Ice Leads to Travel Delays and School Closures," *BBC News*, 5 January, accessed 25 January 2013, http://news.bbc.co.uk/1/hi/8440601.stm.

8. Arun Janardhanan, 2011, "Air Cargo Piles Up Due to Administrative Problems," *Times of India*, 29 April, accessed 25 January 2013, http://articles.timesofindia.indiatimes.com/2011-04-29/chennai/29487072_1_cargo-handling-chennai-air-cargo-cargo-operations.

9. Genesis Forwarding News, 2010, "Guarulhos Airport Congestion Chaos," accessed circa 2010 (article no longer available on website), http://www.genesis-forwarding.com/News/Guarulhos-Airport-Congestion-Chaos.aspx.

10. Ruaidhri Horan, 2012, "Frankfurt Airport Strike Causes Air Freight Chaos," *Emerald Freight Express*, 17 February, http://www.emeraldfreight.com/news/frankfurt-airport-strike-causes-air-freight-chaos.

11. See, for example, Laura Donnelly, 2013, "British Airways and Heathrow in Blame Game over Snow Chaos," *Telegraph*, 19 January, accessed 6 February, http://www.telegraph.co.uk/topics/weather/9813427/British-Airways-and-Heathrow-in-blame-game-over-snow-chaos.html.

12. Joseph DiJohn and Karen Allen, 2009, "The Burnham Transportation Plan of Chicago: 100 Years Later," Transport Research Forum, 16–18 March, accessed 25 January 2013, http://www.trforum.org/forum/downloads/2009_32_BurnhamTransportation_paper.pdf.

13. Clifford Krauss, 2012, "Shippers Concerned over Possible Suez Canal Disruptions," *New York Times*, 2 February, accessed 1 February 2013, http://www.nytimes.com/2011/02/03/world/middleeast/03suez.html.

14. In 2011, 17,799 vessels passed through the canal (a daily average of 48.8), transporting 928.9 million in annual net tonnage. Although the number of vessels has remained about the same since at least 1976, these numbers mean that the tonnage carried has about doubled since the beginning of the century. See Suez Canal Authority, 2011, *Yearly Report* (Ismailia, Egypt: Suez Canal Authority).

15. Benoit Montreuil, 2011, "Towards a Physical Internet: Meeting the Global Logistics Sustainability Grand Challenge," CIRRELT Working Paper 2011-03, Interuniversity Research Centre on Enterprise Networks, Logistics, and Transportation, University of Montreal, Montreal, Canada, 2.

16. Ibid.

17. UCPSOTF (U.S.–Canada Power System Outage Task Force), 2004, *Final Report on the August 14, 2003, Blackout in the United States and Canada: Causes and Recommendations*, US–Canada Power System Outage Task Force, April, accessed 16 July 2013, http://energy.gov/sites/prod/files/oeprod/DocumentsandMedia/BlackoutFinal-Web.pdf.

18. Eric Lerner, 2003, "What's Wrong with the Electric Grid?," *Industrial Physicist* 9: 8–13.

19. See, for example, Ken Belson, 2008, "'03 Blackout Is Recalled, amid Lessons Learned," *New York Times*, 13 August, accessed 1 February 2013, http://www.nytimes.com/2008/08/14/nyregion/14blackout.html?_r=0.

20. Eben Kaplan, 2007, "America's Vulnerable Energy Grid," *Council on Foreign Relations Backgrounders*, 17 April, accessed 20 March 2012, http://www.cfr.org/energy-security/americas-vulnerable-energy-grid/p13153.

21. Ibid.

22. Cro Forum, 2011, "Power Blackout Risks: Risk Management Options," Emerging Risk Initiative Position Paper, November, 9, accessed 25 January 2013, http://www.agcs.allianz.com/assets/PDFs/Special%20and%20stand-alone%20articles/Power_Blackout_Risks.pdf.

23. BBC, 1999, "Lightning Knocked Out Brazil Power," *BBC World Service*, 13 March, accessed 25 January 2013, http://news.bbc.co.uk/1/hi/world/americas/296038.stm.

24. Cro Forum, 2011, 8.

25. *The New York Times*, 1999, "Wide Power Failure Strikes Southern Brazil," 12 March, accessed 17 October 2012, http://www.nytimes.com/1999/03/12/world/wide-power-failure-strikes-southern-brazil.html?n=Top/Reference/Times%20Topics/Subjects/B/Blackouts%20and%20Brownouts%20.

26. Kaplan, 2007.

27. McIlvaine Company, 2006, "Storm Halts Refining at ConocoPhillips in Hartford, IL," refinery update, August, accessed 26 January 2013, http://www.mcilvainecompany.com/industryforecast/refineries/Updates/2006%20updates/aug%2006%20update.htm.

28. Christophe-Alexandre Paillard, 2010, "Russia and Europe's Mutual Energy Dependence," *Journal of International Affairs* 63 (2): 65–84.

29. Authors' calculations based on global estimates of "Internet users per 100 people" and "total population" from World Bank, 2013, *World Development Indicators*, World DataBank, accessed 26 January, http://databank.worldbank.org/.

30. These predictions and comparisons come from Cisco, 2012, "The Zettabyte Era," white paper, May, accessed 4 February 2013, http://www.cisco.com/en/US/solutions/collateral/ns341/ns525/ns537/ns705/ns827/VNI_Hyper connectivity_WP.html.

31. The following discussion draws on Ian Goldin, 2013, *Divided Nations: Why Global Governance Is Failing, and What We Can Do about It* (Oxford, UK: Oxford University Press), 27–34.

32. Joshua Davis, 2007, "Hackers Take Down the Most Wired Country in Europe," *Wired Magazine* 15 (9), accessed 25 January 2013, http://www.wired.com/politics/security/magazine/15-09/ff_estonia?currentPage=all.

33. Lance Whitney, 2010, "With Legal Nod, Microsoft Ambushes Waledac Botnet," *CNET News*, 26 February, accessed 17 July 2013, http://news.cnet.com/8301-1009_3-10459558-83.html.

34. Apple has placed clear restrictions on the programs and code that can be run on the iPad.

35. Alexandra Topping, 2013, "Hannah Smith Suicide: MPs Call for Education in Social-Media Awareness," *Guardian*, 7 August, accessed 5 September, http://www.theguardian.com/society/2013/aug/07/hannah-smith-suicide-cyberbullying-ask-fm-twitter; BBC, 2013b, "Teenager's Death Sparks Cyber-Blackmailing Probe," *BBC News*, 16 August, accessed 5 September, http://www.bbc.co.uk/news/uk-scotland-edinburgh-east-fife-23712000; and Andrew Bounds, 2013, "Two Arrested after Cyber Attack on Manchester Internet Company," *Financial Times*, 8 August, accessed 29 October, http://www.ft.com/cms/s/0/47878080-0050-11e3-9c40-00144feab7de.html#axzz2j7yEXNAT.

36. Several prominent cases leading to suicide or self-harming have been investigated as crimes in recent times. See also the Cyberbullying Research Center website (http://cyberbullying.us/) and Sameer Hinduja and Justin W. Patchin, 2013, "Social Influences on Cyberbullying Behaviors among Middle and High School Students," *Journal of Youth and Adolescence*, 42 (5): 711–722.

37. Alastair Jamieson, 2009, "Google: 'Human Error' Brings Internet Chaos for Millions," *Telegraph*, 31 January, accessed 26 January 2013, http://www.telegraph.co.uk/technology/google/4414452/Google-Human-error-brings-internet-chaos-for-millions.html.

38. Emma Barnett, 2009, "How Did Michael Jackson's Death Affect the Internet's Performance?," *Telegraph*, 26 June, accessed 17 July 2013, http://www.telegraph.co.uk/technology/5649500/How-did-Michael-Jacksons-death-affect-the-internets-performance.html.

39. Google, 2013, "The 1,000 Most-Visited Sites on the Web" (as of July 2011), accessed 26 January, http://www.google.com/adplanner/static/top1000/.

40. Rich Miller, 2010, "How Many Servers Does Facebook Have?" *Data Center Knowledge,* 27 September, accessed 26 January 2013, www.datacenterknowledge .com/the-facebook-data-center-faq-page-2.

41. Rich Miller, 2011 [2009], "Who Has the Most Servers?" *Data Center Knowledge,* 14 May 2009, updated April 2011, accessed 26 January 2013, www .datacenterknowledge.com/archives/2009/05/14/whos-got-the-most-web-servers.

42. Roland Gribben, 2011, "BT Power Breakdown Leaves 275,000 Customers without Internet," *Telegraph,* 4 October, accessed 26 January 2013, http://www.telegraph .co.uk/finance/newsbysector/mediatechnologyandtelecoms/telecoms/8804971/ BT-power-breakdown-leaves-275000-customers-without-internet.html.

43. Ross A. Hammond and Laurette Dubé, 2012, "A Systems Science Perspective and Transdisciplinary Models for Food and Nutrition Security," *Proceedings of the National Academy of Sciences (PNAS)* 109 (31): 12356–12363, 12361.

44. Ibid.

45. See, for example, Jonathan Zittrain, 2009, *The Future of the Internet—And How to Stop It* (London: Penguin).

CHAPTER 5: ECOLOGICAL RISKS

1. Brent Marshall, 1999, "Globalisation, Environmental Degradation, and Ulrich Beck's Risk Society," *Environmental Values* 8: 253–275, quotes on 253, italics ours.

2. For examples of monetary benefits provided by a functioning ecosystem, see Pushpam Kumar, ed., 2012, *The Economics of Ecosystems and Biodiversity: Ecological and Economic Foundations* (London: Routledge); see also The Economics of Ecosystems and Biodiversity's website (www.teebweb.org).

3. Daniel C. Esty, 2001, "Bridging the Trade–Environment Divide," *Journal of Economic Perspectives* 15 (3): 113–130, esp. 120.

4. Stéphane Hallegatte, 2011, "How Economic Growth and Rational Decisions Can Make Disaster Losses Grow Faster Than Wealth," Policy Research Working Paper 5617, March, Office of the Chief Economist, World Bank, Washington, DC.

5. Climate change is not the central remit of this book, and its likely costs have been explored elsewhere. For a more detailed discussion of these hazards, see William D. Nordhaus, 1994, *Managing the Global Commons: The Economics of Climate Change* (Cambridge, MA: MIT Press); William D. Nordhaus, 2008, *A Question of Balance: Weighing the Options on Global Warming Policies* (New Haven, CT, and London: Yale University Press); and Nicholas H. Stern, 2010, *A Blueprint for a Safer Planet: How We Can Save the World and Create Prosperity* (London: Vintage).

6. WHO, 2012a, "10 Facts on Climate Change and Health," *Fact File,* accessed 30 August, http://www.who.int/features/factfiles/climate_change/facts/en/index.html.

7. Ibid.

8. This paragrah draws on WHO, 2012a, unless otherwise stated.

9. Gregg Greenough et al., 2001, "The Potential Impacts of Climate Variability and Change on Health Impacts of Extreme Weather Events in the United States," *Environmental Health Perspectives* 109 (2): 191–198, quote on 192.

10. For a recent discussion of the Darfur conflict in the context of ecological risks and environmental policies, see Harry Verhoeven, 2011, "Climate Change, Conflict, and Development in Sudan: Global Neo-Malthusian Narratives and Local Power Struggles," *Development and Change* 42 (3): 679–707.

11. OECD (Organisation for Economic Co-operation and Development), 2003, *Emerging Risks in the 21st Century: An Agenda for Action* (Paris: Organisation for Economic Cooperation and Development), 45, accessed 26 January 2013, http://www .oecd.org/futures/globalprospects/37944611.pdf.

12. Swiss Re, 2002, *Opportunities and Risks of Climate Change* (Zurich: Swiss Re Publications), 12, accessed 26 January 2013, http://stephenschneider.stanford .edu/Publications/PDF_Papers/SwissReClimateChange.pdf.

13. OECD, 2003a, 45.

14. Christopher B. Barrett et al., 2002, "Poverty Traps and Resource Degradation," *Basis Brief 6*, January, accessed 26 January 2013, http://pdf.usaid.gov/pdf_ docs/PNACP283.pdf.

15. Daniel Reader and John All, 2008, "Sustainability with Globalization: A Chilean Case Study," paper presented at the Association of American Geographers (AAG) Conference, Boston, 15–19 April, 17. The authors ultimately argue that "globalization has a negative impact upon the potential for sustainability in Chile" (19).

16. James Stafford, 2012, "Tom Murphy Interview: Resource Depletion Is a Bigger Threat Than Climate Change," *Oilprice.com*, 22 March, accessed 18 August, http://oilprice.com/Interviews/Tom-Murphy-Interview-Resource-Depletion-is-a -Bigger-Threat-than-Climate-Change.html.

17. See, for example, Ian Goldin, ed., forthcoming, *Is the Planet Full?* (Oxford, UK: Oxford University Press).

18. OECD, 2003a, 42.

19. Monitira J. Pongsiri et al., 2009, "Biodiversity Loss Affects Global Disease Ecology," *BioScience* 59 (11): 945–954, quote on 945.

20. Nick Nuttall, 2004, "Overfishing: A Threat to Marine Biodiversity," *Ten Stories*, United Nations website, accessed 14 April 2012, http://www.un.org/events/ tenstories/06/story.asp?storyID=800.

21. OECD, 2003a, 42.

22. Ibid.

23. TEEB (The Economics of Ecosystems and Biodiversity), 2010, *The Economics of Ecosystems and Biodiversity: Mainstreaming the Economics of Nature; A Synthesis of the Approach, Conclusions, and Recommendations of TEEB*, United Nations Environment Programme (Malta: Progress Press), 8.

24. Pongsiri et al., 2009, 945.

25. Stern, 2010.

26. McKinsey, 2008, "McKinsey Global Survey Results: Managing Global Supply Chains," *McKinsey Quarterly*, August, 3, accessed 28 January 2013,

http://www.mckinseyquarterly.com/McKinsey_Global_Survey_Results_Managing_global_supply_chains_2179.

27. Ian Goldin and L. Alan Winters, eds., 1992, *The Economics of Sustainable Development* (Cambridge, UK: Cambridge University Press).

28. Werner Antweiler, Brian R. Copeland, and M. Scott Taylor, 2001, "Is Free Trade Good for the Environment?," *American Economic Review* 91 (4): 877–908, esp. 877.

29. Ibid., 878.

30. Matthew A. Cole and Robert J. R. Elliott, 2003, "Determining the Trade–Environment Composition Effect: The Role of Capital, Labor, and Environmental Regulations," *Journal of Environmental Economics and Management* 46: 363–383. Note that "the 'scale' effect refers to the impact on greenhouse gas emissions from the increased output or economic activity resulting from freer trade. The general presumption is that trade opening will increase economic activity and hence energy use. Everything else being equal, this increase in the scale of economic activity and energy use will lead to higher levels of greenhouse gas emissions." See WTO, 2013c, "The Multilateral Trading System and Climate Change," World Trade Organization, accessed 1 December 2013, http://www.wto.org/english/tratop_e/envir_e/climate_change_e.pdf.

31. Junyi Shen, 2008, "Trade Liberalization and Environmental Degradation in China," *Applied Economics* 40: 997–1004, quote on 997.

32. Pongsiri et al., 2009, 945.

33. Ibid.

34. L. Philip Lounibos, 2001, "Invasions by Insect: Vectors of Human Disease," *Annual Review of Entomology* 47: 233–266, quote on 233.

35. Ibid.

36. Authors' calculation using producer support estimates for OECD countries relating to 2007–11. See OECD, 2013, "2012 Producer Support Estimates by Country," *OECD.Stat Extracts*, accessed 6 February, http://stats.oecd.org/.

37. Antweiler, Copeland, and Taylor, 2001, 878, italics ours.

38. Ibid., 877.

39. Cole and Elliott, 2003, 372, and Goldin and Winters, 1992.

40. Cole and Elliott, 2003, 372–373.

41. Shen, 2008, 997.

42. Jeffrey A. Frankel and Andrew K. Rose, 2005, "Is Trade Good or Bad for the Environment? Sorting out the Causality," *Review of Economics and Statistics* 87 (1): 85–91, quote on 85.

43. Ibid.

44. André Dua and Daniel C. Esty, 1997, *Sustaining the Asia Pacific Miracle: Environmental Protection and Economic Integration* (Washington, DC: Peterson Institute), 1.

45. Esty, 2001, 115.

46. Such practices lead to what has been termed "ecologically unequal exchange." See Andrew K. Jorgenson, J. Kelly Austin, and Christopher Dick, 2009, "Ecologically Unequal Exchange and the Resource Consumption / Environmental Degradation Paradox: A Panel Study of Less-Developed Countries, 1970–2000," *International Journal of Comparative Sociology* 50 (3–4): 263–284.

47. Carol McAusland, 2008, "Globalisation's Direct and Indirect Effects on the Environment," paper presented at the Organization for Economic Co-operation and Development's Global Forum on Transport and Environment in a Globalising World, Guadalajara, Mexico, 10–12 November, 6.

48. Ibid.

49. See, for example, Brian R. Copeland and M. Scott Taylor, 2004, "Trade, Growth, and the Environment," *Journal of Economic Literature* 42 (1): 7–71, or McAusland, 2008.

50. Jana Milford et al., 2005, *Clearing California's Coal Shadow from the American West*, Environmental Defense, iv–v, accessed 18 July 2013, http://www.westernresourceadvocates.org/energy/pdf/CA%20Coal%20Shadow.pdf.

51. Nick Mabey and Richard McNally, 1998, *Foreign Direct Investment and the Environment: From Pollution Havens to Sustainable Development*, WWF-UK report, July, 19, World Wide Fund for Nature, accessed 27 January 2013, http://www.wwf.org.uk/filelibrary/pdf/fdi.pdf.

52. Laurens M. Bouwer et al., 2007, "Confronting Disaster Losses," *Science* 318 (5851): 753.

53. The loss potentials reflect the percentage increase in a city's real GDP over the relevant time frame. The corresponding estimates for the seven remaining megacities (in alphabetical order) are as follows: Delhi (82 percent), Dhaka (81 percent), Kolkata (77 percent), Mexico City (55 percent), Mumbai (79 percent), New York (24 percent), and São Paulo (49 percent). Ibid., 753, and table S1 in the online supporting material for this article, available at www.sciencemag.org/cgi/content/full/318/5851/753/DC1.

54. Perro de Jong, 2006, "Louisiana Studies Dutch Dams," *BBC News*, 13 January, accessed 30 October 2013, http://news.bbc.co.uk/1/hi/world/europe/4607452.stm.

55. Bouwer et al., 2007, 753.

56. Esty, 2001, 118.

57. Copeland and Taylor, 2004, 67.

CHAPTER 6: PANDEMICS AND HEALTH RISKS

1. This paragraph draws on Fiona Fleck, 2003, "How SARS Changed the World in Less than Six Months," *Bulletin of the World Health Organization* 81 (8): 625–626.

2. Larry Brilliant, 2006, "Larry Brilliant Wants to Stop Pandemics," *TED Talks*, February, accessed 27 January 2013, http://www.ted.com/talks/larry_brilliant_wants_to_stop_pandemics.html.

3. WHO (World Health Organization), 2004a, "China's Latest SARS Outbreak Has Been Contained, but Biosafety Concerns Remain—Update 7," Global Alert and Response, World Health Organization, 18 May, accessed 28 January 2013, http://www.who.int/csr/don/2004_05_18a/en/index.html.

4. Jeffrey L. Arnold, 2002, "Disaster Medicine in the 21st Century: Future Hazards, Vulnerabilities, and Risk," *Prehospital and Disaster Medicine* 17 (1): 3–11.

5. Peter Doshi, 2011, "The Elusive Definition of Pandemic Influenza," *Bulletin of the World Health Organization* 89 (7): 532–538, quote on 533.

6. WHO (World Health Organization), 2012b, "Current WHO Phase of Pandemic Alert (Avian Influenza H5N1)," accessed 21 August, http://www.who.int/influenza/preparedness/pandemic/h5n1phase/en/.

7. David M. Morens, Gregory K. Folkers, and Anthony S. Fauci, 2009, "What Is a Pandemic?," *Journal of Infectious Diseases* 200 (7): 1018–1021.

8. USDHHS (U.S. Department of Health and Human Services), 2012a, "About Pandemics," U.S. Department of Health and Human Services, accessed 21 August, http://www.flu.gov/pandemic/about/index.html.

9. Doshi, 2011, 532–533.

10. Merriam-Webster Inc., 2004, *The Merriam-Webster Dictionary*, new. ed. Merriam-Webster Mass Market Paperbacks. For a detailed examination of the term *epidemic,* see Manfred S. Green et al. 2002., "When Is an Epidemic an Epidemic?," *Israel Medical Association Journal* 4: 3–6.

11. Donald R. Hopkins, *Smallpox: The Greatest Killer in History* (London: University of Chicago Press), esp. 313 ff.

12. *Economist,* 2012a, "Six Degrees of Mobilisation," 1 September, accessed 28 January 2013, http://www.economist.com/node/21560977.

13. Ibid.

14. David M. Bell et al., 2009, "Pandemic Influenza as 21st Century Urban Public Health Crisis," *Emerging Infectious Diseases* 15 (12): 1963–1969, esp. 1963. The proportion of people living in cities was 50 percent at the time of their study, in 2009.

15. Ibid. A megacity is a metropolitan area with a population of over 10 million.

16. Ross A. Hammond, 2009, "Systemic Risk in the Financial System: Insights from Network Science," Insights from Network Science Briefing Paper 12, Pew Charitable Trust, Washington, DC, 5. The citation from Hammond refers to Duncan J. Watts, 2002, "A Simple Model of Global Cascades on Random Networks," *Proceedings of the National Academy of Science (PNAS)* 99 (9): 5766–5771.

17. Hammond, 2009, 4–5.

18. Catherine Paddock, 2012, "H5N1 Bird Flu Pandemic Potential Revealed," *Medical News Today,* 24 June, accessed 24 August, http://www.medicalnewstoday.com/articles/246964.php.

19. David Rosner, 2010, "'Spanish Flu, or Whatever It Is . . .': The Paradox of Public Health in a Time of Crisis," *Public Health Reports* 125 (3): 38–47, quotes on 46.

20. Marguerite Pappaioanou, 2009, "Highly Pathogenic H5N1 Avian Influenza Virus: Cause of the Next Pandemic?," *Comparative Immunology, Microbiology, and Infectious Diseases* 32 (4): 287–300.

21. Lincoln C. Chen, Tim G. Evans, and Richard A. Cash, 1999, "Health as a Global Public Good," in *Global Public Goods: International Cooperation in the 21st Century,* ed. Inge Kaul, Isabelle Grunberg, and Marc A. Stern (New York: Oxford University Press for the United Nations Development Programme), 284–304.

22. In the absence of a unique definition of the term *pandemic,* Morens, Folkers, and Fauci (2009) state that most definitions characterize a pandemic as an "extensive epidemic" (1018).

23. Chen, Evans, and Cash, 1999.

24. Ibid. See also Jared Diamond, 2005, *Guns, Germs and Steel: The Fate of Human Societies* (London: Vintage).

25. Edwin D. Kilbourne, 2006, "Influenza Pandemics of the 20th Century," *Emerging Infectious Diseases* 12 (1): 9–14; and David M. Morens and Anthony S. Fauci, 2007, "The 1918 Influenza Pandemic: Insights for the 21st Century," *Journal of Infectious Diseases* 195: 1018–1028.

26. Susan Mayor, 2000, "Flu Experts Warn of Need for Pandemics Plan," *British Medical Journal,* 321 (7265): 852, and Morens and Fauci, 2007, 1018.

27. Morens and Fauci, 2007, 1022.

28. Ibid., 1019.

29. Ibid., 1025.

30. Carol R. Byerly, 2010, "The U.S. Military and the Influenza Pandemic of 1918–1919," *Public Health Reports* 125 (3): 82–91.

31. Morens and Fauci, 2007.

32. USDHHS (U.S. Department of Health and Human Services), 2012b, "Pandemic Flu History," U.S. Department of Health and Human Services, accessed 21 August, http://www.flu.gov/pandemic/history/#. Morens and Fauci (2007), however, report that the Asian and the Hong Kong pandemics did not exhibit recurrent waves.

33. All information reported in this paragraph is taken from USDHHS, 2012b.

34. USDHHS, 2012b.

35. Kilbourne, 2006.

36. Christian Nordqvist, 2009, "What Is a Pandemic? What Is an Epidemic?," *Medical News Today,* 5 May, accessed 25 August 2012, http://www.medicalnews today.com/articles/148945.php, and Green et al., 2002.

37. AIDS.gov, 2012, "Global Statistics—The Global HIV/AIDS Crisis Today," 6 June, accessed 2 February 2013, http://aids.gov/hiv-aids-basics/hiv-aids-101/global -statistics/index.html.

38. WHO (World Health Organization), 2011b, "Annex 8—HIV and AIDS Statistics, by WHO and UNICEF Regions, 2010," in *Global HIV/AIDS Response: Epidemic Update and Health Sector Progress Towards Universal Access,* progress report (Geneva: WHO, UNAIDS, and UNICEF, accessed 2 February 2013), http://www.who .int/hiv/data/tuapr2011_annex8_web.xls.

39. Ibid.

40. Dyna Arhin-Tenkorang and Pedro Conceição, 2003, "Beyond Communicable Disease Control: Health in the Age of Globalization," in *Providing Global Public Goods,* ed. Inge Kaul (Oxford, UK: Oxford University Press), 484–515, quote on 493.

41. Ibid.

42. WHO (World Health Organization), 2011a, "Annex 5—Reported Number of People Receiving Antiretroviral Therapy in Low- and Middle-Income Countries by

Sex and by Age, and Estimated Number of Children Receiving and Needing Antiretroviral Therapy and Coverage Percentages, 2010," in *Global HIV/AIDS Response: Epidemic Update and Health Sector Progress Towards Universal Access*, progress report (Geneva: WHO, UNAIDS, and UNICEF), accessed 2 February 2013, http://www.who.int/hiv/data/tuapr2011_annex5_web.xls.

43. World Health Assembly, 2003, "Severe Acute Respiratory Syndrome (SARS)," *Fifty-Sixth World Health Assembly Resolution WHA56.29*, 26 May, 1, accessed 2 February 2013, http://www.who.int/csr/sars/en/ea56r29.pdf.

44. Michael Small and Chi K. Tse, 2005, "Small World and Scale Free Model of Transmission of SARS," *International Journal of Bifurcation and Chaos* 15 (5): 1745–1755, esp. 1746.

45. WHO (World Health Organization), 2004b, "WHO Guidelines for the Global Surveillance of Severe Acute Respiratory Syndrome: Updated Recommendations," WHO/CDS/CSR/ARO/2004.1, October, 6, accessed 3 February 2013, http://www.who.int/csr/resources/publications/WHO_CDS_CSR_ARO_2004_1.pdf.

46. WHO (World Health Organization), 2003, "WHO Scientific Research Advisory Committee on Severe Acute Respiratory Syndrome," Report of the First Meeting, Geneva, Switzerland, WHO/CDS/CSR/GAR/2004.16, 20–21 October, 2, accessed 3 February 2013, http://www.who.int/csr/resources/publications/SRAC-CDSCSRGAR2004_16.pdf.

47. WHO (World Health Organization), 2013, "Global Outbreak Alert and Response Network," accessed 3 February 2013, http://www.who.int/csr/outbreaknetwork/en/.

48. Ibid.

49. WHO (World Health Organization), 2011c, "Avian Influenza," *WHO Factsheet*, April, accessed 3 February 2013, http://www.who.int/mediacentre/factsheets/avian_influenza/en/index.html.

50. Pappaioanou, 2009, 288.

51. Ibid., 291.

52. Nicolas Gaidet et al., 2010, "Potential Spread of Highly Pathogenic Avian Influenza H5N1 by Wildfowl: Dispersal Ranges and Rates Determined from Large-Scale Satellite Telemetry," *Journal of Applied Ecology* 47 (5): 1147–1157, quotes on 1147.

53. Doshi, 2011.

54. Gavin J. D. Smith et al., 2009, "Origins and Evolutionary Genomics of the 2009 Swine-Origin H1N1 Influenza A Epidemic," *Nature* 459: 1122–1126, esp. 1122.

55. Jonathan Lynn, 2010, "WHO to Review Its Handling of H1N1 Flu Pandemic," *Reuters*, 12 January, accessed 25 August 2012, http://www.reuters.com/article/2010/01/12/us-flu-who-idUSTRE5BL2ZT20100112; and Fatimah S. Dawood et al., 2012, "Estimated Global Mortality Associated with the First 12 Months of 2009 Pandemic Influenza A H1N1 Virus Circulation: A Modelling Study," *Lancet Infectious Diseases* 12 (9): 687–695. The higher estimate is from Dawood et al., 2012.

56. A. Marm Kilpatrick, 2011, "Globalization, Land Use, and the Invasion of West Nile Virus," *Science* 334 (6054): 323–327, quote on 323.

57. Ibid.

58. CDC (Centers for Disease Control and Prevention), 2013, "Final Maps and Data for 1999–2012," Centers for Disease Control and Prevention, accessed 19 July, http://www.cdc.gov/westnile/statsMaps/final.html.

59. Kilpatrick, 2011, 326, and Bell et al., 2009. Bell et al. also report that the H1N1 virus appeared first in 2009 in Mexico City and New York, that is, in metropolitan areas with populations of about 20 million.

60. Kilpatrick, 2011, 323.

61. Ibid.

62. Ibid., 324.

63. Ibid., 327.

64. According to Chen, Evans, and Cash, 1999, smoking increases by 2.5 percent in developing countries for every 0.5 percent decrease in developed countries.

65. WHO (World Health Organization), 2011d, *Global Status Report on Non-communicable Diseases 2010* (Geneva: World Health Organization), 9, accessed 3 February 2013, http://whqlibdoc.who.int/publications/2011/9789240686458_eng .pdf.

66. Ibid., v, 2, 33–36, and 86–87.

67. Arhin-Tenkorang and Conceição, 2003.

68. Ibid., 484.

69. Unless noted otherwise, all background information in this section is from Arhin-Tenkorang and Conceição, 2003.

70. Ibid., 487.

71. Brilliant, 2006.

72. Ibid. See also Frank Fenner et al., 1988, *Smallpox and Its Eradication* (Geneva: World Health Organization).

73. Joshua Lederberg, 1997, "Infectious Disease as an Evolutionary Paradigm," *Emerging Infectious Diseases* 3 (4): 417–423, quote on 418.

74. Ibid.

75. Kilpatrick, 2011, 323.

76. Lederberg, 1997.

77. Ibid., 423.

78. Chen, Evans, and Cash, 1999, 285.

79. Ibid.

80. Ibid., 288.

81. Bell et al., 2009, 1965.

82. Ibid.

83. Pappaioanou, 2009, 293–294.

84. Ibid., 295.

85. Ibid., 296.

86. Brilliant, 2006, italics ours.

87. Ibid.

88. Jie Zhao, Peiquan Jin, and Guorui Huang, 2011, "A Survey on Detecting Public Emergencies from Web Pages," *Advances on Information Sciences and Service Sciences* 3 (3): 56–63.

89. Brilliant, 2006.

CHAPTER 7: INEQUALITY AND SOCIAL RISKS

1. Lant Pritchett, 1997, "Convergence, Big Time," *Journal of Economic Perspectives* 11 (3): 3–17.

2. Ian Goldin and Kenneth Reinert, 2012, *Globalization for Development: Meeting New Challenges*, new ed. (Oxford, UK: Oxford University Press).

3. Dani Rodrik, 2002, "Globalization for Whom?," *Harvard Magazine*, July–August: 29–31, and Dani Rodrik, 2011, *The Globalization Paradox: Democracy and the Future of the World Economy* (New York and London: W. W. Norton).

4. See, for example, Rodrik, 2011; Joseph E. Stiglitz, 2006, *Making Globalization Work* (London: W. W. Norton); or François Bourguignon, 2012, *La Mondialisation de l'inégalité* (Paris: Editions du Seuil et La Republique des Idees).

5. World Bank, 2012b, "Poverty and Equity Data," accessed circa late 2012, http://povertydata.worldbank.org/poverty/home. The poverty headcount ratio is defined as the number of individuals living below the poverty threshold over the total population in the group of developing countries.

6. Dominic Wilson and Raluca Dragusanu, 2008, "The Expanding Middle: The Exploding World Middle Class and Falling Global Inequality," Global Economic Papers 170, Goldman Sachs, New York, 10.

7. OECD (Organisation for Economic Co-operation and Development), 2011b, *Growing Income Inequality in OECD Countries: What Drives It and How Can Policy Tackle It?*, OECD Forum on Tackling Inequality, Paris, 2 May, 5, accessed 3 February 2013, http://www.oecd.org/els/socialpoliciesanddata/47723414.pdf.

8. Causal relationships in this context are hard to establish, and economists are aware that factors such as "social, political, cultural, coercive and environmental capital" may confound the corresponding analysis. See Paul Shaffer, 2008, "New Thinking on Poverty: Implications for Globalisation and Poverty Reduction Strategies," DESA Working Paper 65, United Nations Department of Economic and Social Affairs, New York, 2. Nonetheless, other studies are able to detect evidence of a truly causal relationship. See, for example, Almas Heshmati, 2004, "The Relationship between Income Inequality, Poverty, and Globalisation," IZA Discussion Paper 1277, Institute for the Study of Labour, Bonn, accessed 3 February 2013, http://ftp.iza.org/dp1277.pdf.

9. See, for example, Robert M. Solow, 1956, "A Contribution to the Theory of Economic Growth," *Quarterly Journal of Economics* 70 (1): 65–94, or Robert J. Barro and Xavier Sala-i-Martín, 1992, "Convergence," *Journal of Political Economy* 100 (2): 223–251.

10. OECD, 2011b, 5. Note that across countries the view of conditional convergence is not undisputed. Matthew Slaughter, for example, finds that trade liberalization does not trigger income convergence, whereas Gilles Dufrénot and associates find slow or no convergence among developing countries. Branko Milanović also suggests that the gap between rich and poor countries has been widening since the 1850s, even in comparison to successful cases of developing economies, such as China or India. See Matthew J. Slaughter, 1998, "International Trade and Per Capita Income Convergence: A Difference-in-Differences Analysis," NBER Working Paper 6557, National Bureau of Economic Research, Cambridge, MA, accessed 3 February 2013, http://www.nber.org/papers/w6557.pdf; Gilles Dufrénot, Valérie Mignon, and Théo Naccache, 2009, "The Slow Convergence of Per Capita Income between the Developing Countries: Growth Resistance and Sometimes Growth Tragedy," CREDIT Research Paper 09/03, Centre for Research in Economic Development and International Trade, Nottingham, UK; and Branko Milanović, 2011, "Global Inequality from Class to Location, from Proletarians to Migrants," Policy Research Working Paper 5820, World Bank, Washington, DC.

11. Quote from OECD, 2011b, 6.

12. The OECD finds that "the highest 10% of earners have been leaving the middle earners behind more rapidly than the lowest earners have been drifting away from the middle." Ibid., 6.

13. See chapter 3 on global supply chains.

14. OECD, 2011b, 8. Other important factors include "changes in family formation and household structures" and changes in the redistributive focus of tax and benefit systems (ibid.).

15. OECD, 2011b, 9.

16. OECD (Organisation for Economic Co-operation and Development), 2011a, *Divided We Stand: Why Inequality Keeps Rising* (Paris: OECD Publishing), 110.

17. Martin Rama, 2003, "Globalization and Workers in Developing Countries," Policy Research Working Paper 2958, World Bank, Washington, DC, 32–33, accessed 3 February 2013, http://www-wds.worldbank.org/external/default/WDSContentServer/WDSP/IB/2003/02/07/000094946_03013004074424/Rendered/PDF/multi0page.pdf.

18. Florence Jaumotte, Subir Lall, and Chris Papageorgiou, 2008, "Rising Income Inequality: Technology, or Trade and Financial Globalization?," IMF Working Paper 185, International Monetary Fund, Washington, DC, accessed 3 February 2013, http://www.imf.org/external/pubs/ft/wp/2008/wp08185.pdf.

19. China's Gini index increased from 27.9 in 1988 to 42.6 in 2002 and then stabilized in the mid- to late 2000s. World Bank, 2013, *World Development Indicators,* World DataBank, accessed 19 July 2013, http://databank.worldbank.org/data/home.aspx.

20. India's Gini index reached 33.9 in 2010. World Bank, 2013. Limited data points are available for India and China.

21. OECD, 2011b, 9.

22. Defined by a GDP of less than US$9,000 (at 1995 international prices) per capita according to Branko Milanović and Lynn Squire, 2007, "Does Tariff Liberalization Increase Wage Inequality? Some Empirical Evidence," in *Globalization and Poverty*, ed. Ann Harrison (London: University of Chicago Press), 143–181, esp. 160.

23. Milanović and Squire, 2007.

24. OECD, 2011b, 9.

25. See Jaumotte, Lall, and Papageorgiou, 2008, for evidence of such effects.

26. Milanović, 2011, 12.

27. See, for example, Branko Milanović, 2009, "Global Inequality Recalculated: The Effect of New 2005 PPP Estimates on Global Inequality," Policy Research Working Paper 5061, World Bank, Washington, DC, accessed 19 July 2013, http://www-wds.worldbank.org/external/default/WDSContentServer/WDSP/IB/2009/09/22/000158349_20090922160230/Rendered/PDF/WPS5061.pdf.

28. The middle class is defined by income levels of between $6,000 and $30,000 in PPP. Wilson and Dragusanu, 2008, 3.

29. Wilson and Dragusanu, 2008, 10.

30. Ibid., 6. Wilson and Dragusanu provide further evidence of the (predicted) absolute decline in poverty.

31. Note that although the conclusions of Wilson and Dragusanu (2008) are different from those of Milanović (2011), the results of the two studies are not necessarily contradictory. It might well be that the overall distribution is narrowing, even though the distance between the lower and upper limits is increasing. The fact that the former authors expect some African countries to remain poor and the observation that changes are not structural are consistent with this interpretation.

32. See Goldin and Reinert, 2012.

33. See Rama, 2003, 32; OECD, 2011a, 113; and Amartya K. Sen, 1999, *Development as Freedom* (Oxford, UK: Oxford University Press).

34. OECD, 2011a,b.

35. BBC, 2012a, "Apple Paid Only 2% Corporation Tax Outside US," *BBC News*, 4 November, accessed 6 February 2013, http://www.bbc.co.uk/news/business-20197710; BBC, 2012b, "Starbucks, Google, and Amazon Grilled over Tax Avoidance," *BBC News*, 12 November, accessed 6 February 2013, http://www.bbc.co.uk/news/business-20288077; and BBC, 2012c, "Starbucks 'Paid Just £8.6m UK Tax in 14 Years,'" *BBC News*, 16 October, accessed 6 February 2013, http://www.bbc.co.uk/news/business-19967397.

36. G8 (Group of Eight), 2013, "Lough Erne Declaration," 18 June, Lough Erne Summit, Northern Ireland, accessed 23 July 2013, http://www.g8.utoronto.ca/summit/2013lougherne/Lough_Erne_Declaration_130618.pdf.

37. G20 (Group of Twenty), 2013, "OECD Presents Its Action Plan on Base Erosion and Profit Shifting," 19 July, accessed 23 July, http://www.g20.org/news/20130719/781655012.html.

38. The question of whether a growing and increasingly complex global society is sustainable is taken up in Anthony B. Atkinson, forthcoming, "Optimum Population,

Welfare Economics, and Inequality," in *Is the Planet Full?*, ed. Ian Goldin (Oxford, UK: Oxford University Press).

39. Luke Martell, 2010, *The Sociology of Globalization* (Cambridge, UK: Polity Press), 1.

40. Wilson and Dragusanu, 2008, 15.

41. Rodrik, 2011.

42. Wilson and Dragusanu, 2008, 3.

43. See Rodrik, 2002 or 2011.

44. Wilson and Dragusanu, 2008, 15.

45. Quote in ibid., 17.

46. Quote in ibid., 5.

47. François Bourguignon and Christian Morrisson, 2002, "Inequality among World Citizens: 1820–1992," *American Economic Review* 39 (4): 727–744.

48. Milanović, 2011, 7. For further evidence of the relevance of the country of employment, see also table 7.1 and figure 7.3.

49. For example, with reference to the late twentieth century he observes, "Globally, the issue [of a conflict between capital and labour] has receded in importance as the objective conditions that gave rise to it have changed." Milanović, 2011, 16.

50. EUI (European University Institute), 2011, "Indignados / Occupy Movement: A Global Phenomenon—A Round Table," European University Institute, 22 November, accessed 1 June 2012, http://www.eui.eu/SeminarsAndEvents/Live.aspx.

51. OECD, 2011a, 17.

52. Ibid., 40.

53. This view, however, is not undisputed. American journalist Christian Cadwell, for instance, argues that the current generation of 15- to 30-year-olds is "tiny" and therefore unable to "make trouble." See CSIS (Center for Strategic and International Studies), 2012, "Europe Economic Crisis and the Rise of Populism, Nationalism, and Extremism," CSIS Global Security Forum 2012, Washington, DC, Federal News Service transcript, 21, accessed 3 February 2013, http://csis.org/files/attachments/120413_EuropeEconomicCrisis_GSF_Transcript_0.pdf.

54. Milanović, 2011, i and 21.

55. Ibid., 21. See also Ian Goldin, Geoffrey Cameron, and Meera Balarajan, 2011, *Exceptional People: How Migration Shaped Our World and Will Define Our Future* (Princeton, NJ: Princeton University Press), and Goldin and Reinert, 2012.

56. Keno Verseck, 2012, "Eastern Europe Swings Right," *Spiegel Online*, 18 January, accessed 1 June, http://www.spiegel.de/international/europe/poor-and-prejudiced-eastern-europe-swings-right-a-809827-druck.html.

57. Guy Sorman, 2012, "Back to Utopia?," *Project Syndicate*, 14 May, accessed 1 June, http://www.project-syndicate.org/commentary/back-to-utopia.

58. CSIS, 2012, 13.

59. Co-Pierre Georg and Manjana Milkoreit, 2013, "Similarities in Complexity—Lessons from Finance and Climate Change," mimeo, Oxford and Waterloo, UK.

60. Ibid.

61. Ibid.

62. Ibid. See also *Economist*, 2012c, "The Greek Election: Democracy in Action," 2 June, accessed 28 January 2013, http://www.economist.com/node/21556302, and Emmanuel Guerin and Laurence Tubiana, 2012, "Preparing for the Green Exit," *Project Syndicate*, 30 May, accessed 1 June, http://www.project-syndicate.org/print/preparing-for-the-green-exit.

63. Unnamed finance official quoted in Ulrike Guérot and Thomas Klau, 2012, "After Merkozy: How France and Germany Can Make Europe Work," Policy Brief ECFR56, May, European Council on Foreign Relations, London, 8, accessed 3 February 2013, http://ecfr.eu/page/-/ECFR56_FRANCE_GERMANY_BRIEF_AW.pdf.

64. The French official is quoted in Guérot and Klau, 2012, 2. For a telling analysis of public dissatisfaction with the functioning of national democracy in EU countries, see Matthew Goodwin, 2011, "Right Response: Understanding and Countering Populism and Extremism in Europe," a Chatham House report, September, Chatham House, London, 21–22, accessed 5 February 2103, http://www.chathamhouse.org/sites/default/files/r0911_goodwin.pdf.

65. Guérot and Klau, 2012, 4.

66. CSIS, 2012, 9.

67. Jirí Pehe, 2005, "Populism's Short March in Central Europe," *Project Syndicate*, 10 November, accessed 1 June 2012, http://www.project-syndicate.org/print/populism-s-short-march-in-central-europe.

68. Verseck, 2012.

69. Daniel Oesch, 2008, "Explaining Workers' Support for Right-Wing Populist Parties in Western Europe: Evidence from Austria, Belgium, France, Norway, and Switzerland," *International Political Science Review* 29 (3): 349–373, quote on 349.

70. Armin Falk, Andreas Kuhn, and Josef Zweimüller, 2011, "Unemployment and Right-Wing Extremist Crime," *Scandinavian Journal of Economics* 113 (2): 260–285, quote on 263.

71. Ibid.

72. Christian Dustmann, Francesca Fabbri, and Ian Peter Preston, 2011, "Racial Harassment, Ethnic Concentration, and Economic Conditions," *Scandinavian Journal of Economics* 113 (3): 689–711, quote on 691.

73. Jens Rydgren, 2008, "Immigration Sceptics, Xenophobes or Racists? Radical Right-Wing Voting in Six West European Countries," *European Journal of Political Research* 47: 737–765.

74. See also Goodwin, 2011.

75. Harry D. Raduege Jr., 2010, "The View from the United States: Fighting Weapons of Mass Disruption; Why America Needs a 'Cyber Triad,'" in *Global Cyber Deterrence: Views from China, the US, Russia, India, and Norway*, ed. Andrew Nagorski (New York: EastWest Institute), 3–5, quote on 3.

76. Tang Lan and Zhang Xin, 2010, "Can Cyber Deterrence Work?," in *Global Cyber Deterrence: Views from China, the US, Russia, India, and Norway*, ed. Andrew Nagorski (New York: EastWest Institute), 1–3, quote on 1.

77. Raduege, 2010, 4–5.

78. Jeffrey L. Arnold, 2002, "Disaster Medicine in the 21st Century: Future Hazards, Vulnerabilities, and Risk," *Prehospital and Disaster Medicine* 17 (1): 3–11.

79. Ibid., 5.

80. In June of 2013, a White House press statement reported that the Central Intelligence Agency had obtained credible evidence confirming that the Syrian regime had deployed chemical weapons (including the nerve agent sarin) against opposition forces, resulting in at least 100–150 deaths. White House, 2013, "Statement by Deputy National Security Advisor for Strategic Communications Ben Rhodes on Syrian Chemical Weapons Use," Office of the Press Secretary, White House, Washington, DC, 13 June, accessed 21 July, http://www.whitehouse.gov/the-press-office/2013/06/13/statement-deputy-national-security-advisor-strategic-communications-ben-.

81. Arnold, 2002.

82. Technology and events move quickly in a globalizing world. As this book is going through a final edit, reports have emerged of the world's first 3D gun being successfully test-fired in the United States. Rebecca Morelle, 2013, "Working Gun Made with 3D Printer," *BBC News,* 6 May, accessed 21 July, http://www.bbc.co.uk/news/science-environment-22421185. This is illustrative of how widespread access to potentially lethal information in combination with new technologies creates the opportunity for the development and manufacture of potent new threats.

83. Arnold, 2002.

84. Joseph E. Stiglitz, 2012, *The Price of Inequality* (London: Allen Lane), xiii.

85. Jaumotte, Lall, and Papageorgiou, 2008, 1.

86. OECD, 2011a.

87. Goldin and Reinert, 2012.

88. Ibid., 150–151.

89. The 0.7 percent target was officially recognized in October 1970 following a United Nations Resolution. See OECD (Organisation for Economic Co-operation and Development), 2003b, "History of the 0.7% ODA Target," *OECD Journal on Development* 3 (4): III-9–III-11.

90. Goldin, Cameron, and Balarajan, 2011.

CHAPTER 8: MANAGING SYSTEMIC RISK

1. BBC, 2013a, "Local Elections: Nigel Farage Hails Results as a 'Game Changer,'" *BBC News,* 3 May, accessed 24 July, http://www.bbc.co.uk/news/uk-politics-22382098.

2. Ian Goldin and Kenneth Reinert, 2012, *Globalization for Development: Meeting New Challenges,* new ed. (Oxford, UK: Oxford University Press); Ian Goldin, 2013, *Divided Nations: Why Global Governance Is Failing, and What We Can Do About It* (Oxford, UK: Oxford University Press); and Ian Goldin, Geoffrey Cameron, and Meera Balarajan, 2011, *Exceptional People: How Migration Shaped Our World and Will Define Our Future* (Princeton, NJ: Princeton University Press).

3. Robert O. Keohane and Joseph S. Nye Jr., 1977, *Power and Independence: World Politics in Transition* (Boston: Little, Brown).

4. Barack Obama, 2009, "Remarks by the President on a New Beginning," White House website, 4 June, accessed 12 August 2012, http://www.whitehouse.gov/the-press-office/remarks-president-cairo-university-6-04-09.

5. These principles that Ian Goldin developed with his Oxford colleague Ngaire Woods are explored more fully in Goldin, 2013, 174–176.

6. John Maynard Keynes, quoted in John Braithwaite and Peter Drahos, 2000, *Global Business Regulation* (Cambridge, UK: Cambridge University Press), 98.

7. G30 (Group of Thirty) Working Group, 1997, *Global Institutions, National Supervision, and Systemic Risk*, report (Washington, DC: Group of Thirty), 27.

8. We refer readers who are interested in the reform of global governance systems to Goldin, 2013.

9. See, for example, Patrick Duplat and Emile Pare, 2010, "Haiti from the Ground Up," *Refugees International Field Report*, March, accessed 30 January 2013, http://www.refugeesinternational.org/sites/default/files/030210_haiti_groundup.pdf.

10. For a possible reason for the slow coordination, see early reports on strategic disagreements between the Malian army and ECOWAS, for example, Anne Look, 2012, "Mali, ECOWAS Not on Same Page on Military Intervention," *Voice of America*, 18 September, accessed 1 February 2013, http://www.voanews.com/content/mali-ecowas-military-intervention/1510417.html.

11. Howard Kunreuther and Michael Useem, 2010a, "Preface," in *Learning from Catastrophes: Strategies for Reaction and Response*, ed. Howard Kunreuther and Michael Useem (Upper Saddle River, NJ: Prentice Hall), xv–xvii and xvi, italics in original.

12. A notable example is the speech given by Andrew Haldane, which we mentioned in chapter 2. Andrew G. Haldane, 2012, "The Dog and the Frisbee," speech delivered at the Federal Reserve Bank of Kansas City's 36th Economic Policy Symposium, The Changing Policy Landscape, Jackson Hole, WY, accessed 31 January 2013, http://www.bankofengland.co.uk/publications/Documents/speeches/2012/speech596.pdf.

13. A simple approach to managing complexity in an uncertain world is proposed by Gerd Gigerenzer, 2010, *Rationality for Mortals: How People Cope with Uncertainty* (New York: Oxford University Press). See also Dirk Helbing, 2013, "Globally Networked Risks and How to Respond," *Nature* 497: 51–59.

14. See, for example, Helen Carter, 2010, "Sub-zero Spell to Continue as Grit Supplies Reach the End of the Road," *Guardian*, 10 January, accessed 28 January 2013, http://www.guardian.co.uk/uk/2010/jan/10/sub-zero-grit-supplies-snow?INTCMP=SRCH.

15. Howard Kunreuther and Michael Useem, 2010b, "Principles and Challenges for Reducing Risks from Disasters," in *Learning from Catastrophes: Strategies for Reaction and Response*, ed. Howard Kunreuther and Michael Useem (Upper Saddle River, NJ: Prentice Hall), pp. 1–17, esp. 8–11.

16. That is, to "know the unknowns," as Donald Rumsfeld famously put it.

17. OECD (Organisation for Economic Co-operation and Development), 2003a, *Emerging Risks in the 21st Century: An Agenda for Action* (Paris: Organisation for Economic Cooperation and Development), 5, accessed 26 January 2013, http://www.oecd.org/futures/globalprospects/37944611.pdf.

18. OECD, 2003a, 5.

19. Ibid., 25–27.

20. All citations in this paragraph are from G30 Working Group, 1999, 28.

21. Robert Axelrod and Robert O. Keohane, 1985, "Achieving Cooperation under Anarchy: Strategies and Institutions," *World Politics* 38 (1): 226–254.

22. See also Goldin, 2013.

23. See, for example, Hans Morgenthau, 1948, *Politics among Nations: The Struggle for Power and Peace* (New York: Knopf), and Kenneth Waltz, 1979, *The Theory of International Politics* (Boston: McGraw–Hill).

24. The estimates for pandemics are our own and are derived from conversations with experts. The estimates for military expenditures are taken from the World Bank and relate to the period 2008–2012. See World Bank, 2013, *World Development Indicators,* World DataBank, accessed 31 January, http://databank.worldbank.org/.

25. Among the groups that are seeking to do such interdisciplinary modeling is the ETH Risk Center of the Swiss Federal Institute of Technology in Zurich and the Oxford Martin School at Oxford University.

26. We are grateful to Tim Palmer for this point. For further details, see Tim Palmer, 2011, "A CERN for Climate Change," *Physics World*, March, 14–15, accessed 24 July 2013, http://www.oxfordmartin.ox.ac.uk/downloads/press/climate-Palmer.pdf.

27. The recently created Institute for New Economic Thinking is a good example of this renewal.

28. Oxford Martin Commission for Future Generations, 2013, *Now for the Long Term: The Report of the Oxford Martin Commission for Future Generations* (Oxford, UK: Oxford Martin School, University of Oxford), October, accessed 29 October, http://www.oxfordmartin.ox.ac.uk/downloads/commission/Oxford_Martin_Now_for_the_Long_Term.pdf.

29. We are indebted to Peter Dougherty for offering the points in this paragraph for framing the arguments.

References

Acharya, Viral V. 2009. "A Theory of Systemic Risk and Design of Prudential Bank Regulation." *Journal of Financial Stability* 5 (3): 224–255.

Acharya, Viral V., and Tanju Yorulmazer. 2003. "Information Contagion and Inter-Bank Correlation in a Theory of Systemic Risk." CEPR Discussion Paper 3473. Centre for Economic Policy Research, London.

———. 2008. "Cash-in-the-Market Pricing and Optimal Resolution of Bank Failures." *Review of Financial Studies* 21 (6): 2705–2742.

Acharya, Viral V., Thomas F. Cooley, Matthew P. Richardson, and Ingo Walter, eds. 2010. *Regulating Wall Street: The Dodd-Frank Act and the New Architecture of Global Finance.* Hoboken, NJ: John Wiley & Sons.

Acharya, Viral V., Irvind Gujral, Nirupama Kulkarni, and Hyun Song Shin. 2011. "Dividends and Bank Capital in the Financial Crisis of 2007–2009." NBER Working Paper 16896. National Bureau of Economic Research, Cambridge, MA. Accessed 21 January 2013. http://www.nber.org/papers/w16896.

AIDS.gov. 2012. "Global Statistics—The Global HIV/AIDS Crisis Today." 6 June. Accessed 2 February 2013. http://aids.gov/hiv-aids-basics/hiv-aids-101/global-statistics/index.html.

Allen, Franklin, and Douglas Gale. 2000. "Financial Contagion." *Journal of Political Economy* 108 (1): 1–33.

Allen, Franklin, Anna Babus, and Elena Carletti. 2010. "Financial Connections and Systemic Risk." EUI Working Paper ECO 2010/30. Department of Economics, European University Institute, Badia Fiesolana, Italy.

Antweiler, Werner, Brian R. Copeland, and M. Scott Taylor. 2001. "Is Free Trade Good for the Environment?" *American Economic Review* 91 (4): 877–908.

Apple. 2011. "Apple Suppliers 2011." Accessed 16 October 2012. http://images.apple.com/supplierresponsibility/pdf/Apple_Supplier_List_2011.pdf.

Aranda, Luis G. n.d. "Economic and Social Impact of Volcanic Eruptions." Mimeo.

Arhin-Tenkorang, Dyna, and Pedro Conceição. 2003. "Beyond Communicable Disease Control: Health in the Age of Globalization." In *Providing Global Public Goods,* ed. Inge Kaul. Oxford: Oxford University Press, 484–515.

Arnold, Jeffrey L. 2002. "Disaster Medicine in the 21st Century: Future Hazards, Vulnerabilities, and Risk." *Prehospital and Disaster Medicine* 17 (1): 3–11.

Arthur, W. Brian, Steven N. Durlauf, and David A. Lane. 1997. "Introduction." In *The Economy as an Evolving Complex System II,* ed. W. Brian Arthur, Steven N.

Durlauf, and David A. Lane. Proceedings vol. 27, Santa Fe Institute Studies in the Science of Complexity. Reading, MA: Addison-Wesley, 1–14.

Atkinson, Anthony B. 2012. "Optimum Population, Welfare Economics, and Inequality." Oxford Martin School Seminar Paper. Revised version, January. University of Oxford, Oxford, UK.

———. Forthcoming. "Optimum Population, Welfare Economics, and Inequality." In *Is the Planet Full?*, ed. Ian Goldin. Oxford, UK: Oxford University Press.

Atlas. 2013. "Who Exports Electronic Integrated Circuits?" *The Observatory of Economic Complexity* (Map App). Accessed 7 February. http://atlas.media.mit.edu/.

Axelrod, Robert, and Robert O. Keohane. 1985. "Achieving Cooperation under Anarchy: Strategies and Institutions." *World Politics* 38 (1): 226–254.

Bair, Jennifer. 2008. *Frontiers of Commodity Chain Research.* Stanford, CA: Stanford University Press.

Baldwin, Richard E., and Martin, Philippe. 1999. "Two Waves of Globalization: Superficial Similarities, Fundamental Differences." NBER Working Paper 6904. National Bureau of Economic Research, Cambridge, MA. Accessed 4 January 2013. http://www.nber.org/papers/w6904.pdf.

Barker, David. 2012. "Is Deregulation to Blame for the Financial Crisis?" *Bank & Lender Liability* (a Westlaw Journal), 18 June. (Also in *Thomson Reuters News and Insight*, July 7.)

Barnett, Emma. 2009. "How Did Michael Jackson's Death Affect the Internet's Performance?" *Telegraph*, 26 June. Accessed 17 July 2013. http://www.telegraph .co.uk/technology/5649500/How-did-Michael-Jacksons-death-affect-the -internets-performance.html.

Barrett, Christopher B., Lawrence E. Blume, John G. McPeak, Bart Minten, Festus Murithi, Bernard N. Okumu, Alice Pell, Frank Place, Jean Claude Randrianarisoa, and Jhon Rasambainarivo. 2002. "Poverty Traps and Resource Degradation." *Basis Brief 6*, January. Accessed 26 January 2013. http://pdf.usaid.gov/pdf_docs/ PNACP283.pdf.

Barro, Robert J., and Xavier Sala-i-Martín. 1992. "Convergence." *Journal of Political Economy* 100 (2): 223–251.

Battiston, Stefano, Domenico Delli Gatti, Mauro Gallegatti, Bruce Greenwald, and Joseph E. Stiglitz. 2007. "Credit Chains and Bankruptcy Propagation in Production Networks." *Journal of Economic Dynamics and Control* 31 (6): 2061–2084.

BBC. 1999. "Lightning Knocked Out Brazil Power." BBC World Service, 13 March. Accessed 25 January 2013. http://news.bbc.co.uk/1/hi/world/americas/296038 .stm.

———. 2010. "Snow and Ice Leads to Travel Delays and School Closures." *BBC News*, 5 January. Accessed 25 January 2013. http://news.bbc.co.uk/1/hi/8440601 .stm.

———. 2012a. "Apple Paid Only 2% Corporation Tax Outside U.S." *BBC News*, 4 November. Accessed 6 February 2013. http://www.bbc.co.uk/news/ business-20197710.

———. 2012b. "Starbucks, Google, and Amazon Grilled over Tax Avoidance." *BBC News*, 12 November. Accessed 6 February 2013. http://www.bbc.co.uk/news/business-20288077.

———. 2012c. "Starbucks 'Paid Just £8.6m UK Tax in 14 Years.'" *BBC News*, 16 October. Accessed 6 February 2013. http://www.bbc.co.uk/news/business-19967397.

———. 2013a. "Local Elections: Nigel Farage Hails Results as a 'Game Changer.'" *BBC News*, 3 May. Accessed 24 July. http://www.bbc.co.uk/news/uk-politics-22382098.

———. 2013b. "Teenager's Death Sparks Cyber-Blackmailing Probe." *BBC News*, 16 August. Accessed 5 September. http://www.bbc.co.uk/news/uk-scotland-edinburgh-east-fife-23712000.

Beck, Ulrich. 2002. "The Terrorist Threat: World Risk Society Revisited." *Theory Culture Society* 19 (4): 39–55.

Bell, David M. 2012. "Global Trade Security Depends on Implementation of the Revised International Health Regulations." PowerPoint presentation. Centers for Disease Control and Prevention, Atlanta. Accessed 25 August. http://iom.edu/~/media/Files/Activity%20Files/Global/USandGlobalHealth/Bell.pdf.

Bell, David M., Isaac B. Weisfuse, Mauricio Hernandez-Avila, Carlos del Rio, Xinia Bustamante, and Guenael Rodier. 2009. "Pandemic Influenza as 21st Century Urban Public Health Crisis." *Emerging Infectious Diseases* 15 (12): 1963–1969.

Belson, Ken. 2008. "'03 Blackout Is Recalled, amid Lessons Learned." *New York Times*, 13 August. Accessed 1 February 2013. http://www.nytimes.com/2008/08/14/nyregion/14blackout.html?_r=0.

Bhagwati, Jagdish. 2007. *In Defense of Globalization.* New York: Oxford University Press.

Boeing. 2011. *Current Market Outlook: 2011–2030.* Seattle: Boeing Airplanes Market Analysis. Accessed 4 February 2013. http://www.boeing.com/commercial/cmo/pdf/Boeing_Current_Market_Outlook_2011_to_2030.pdf.

BOI (Board of Investment, Thailand). 2012. "Vibrant Thai Automotive Industry Shattering Performance Records." *Thailand Investment Review* 28 (8): 6. Accessed 17 January 2013. http://www.boi.go.th/tir/issue/201208_22_8/TIR-201208_22_8.pdf.

Borio, Claudio. 2010. "Implementing a Macroprudential Framework: Blending Boldness and Realism." Keynote speech at the Hong Kong Institute for Monetary Research and the Bank for International Settlements conference Financial Stability: Towards a Macroprudential Approach, Hong Kong, 5–6 July. Accessed 1 February 2013. http://www.bis.org/repofficepubl/hkimr201007.12c.pdf.

Bounds, Andrew. 2013. "Two Arrested after Cyber Attack on Manchester Internet Company." *Financial Times*, 8 August. Accessed 29 October. http://www.ft.com/cms/s/0/47878080-0050-11e3-9c40-00144feab7de.html#axzz2j7yEXNAT.

Bourguignon, François. 2012. *La Mondialisation de l'inégalité.* Paris: Editions du Seuil et La Republique des Idees.

Bourguignon, François, and Christian Morrisson. 2002. "Inequality among World Citizens: 1820–1992." *American Economic Review* 39 (4): 727–744.

Bouwer, Laurens M., Ryan P. Crompton, Eberhard Faust, Peter Höppe, and Roger A. Pielke Jr. 2007. "Confronting Disaster Losses." *Science* 318 (5851): 753.

BP (British Petroleum). 2011. *BP Statistical Review of World Energy, June 2011*. London: British Petroleum. Accessed 4 February 2013. http://www.bp.com/assets/bp_internet/globalbp/globalbp_uk_english/reports_and_publications/statistical_energy_review_2011/STAGING/local_assets/pdf/statistical_review_of_world_energy_full_report_2011.pdf.

Braithwaite, John, and Peter Drahos. 2000. *Global Business Regulation*. Cambridge, UK: Cambridge University Press.

Brandt, Loren, and Thomas G. Rawski. 2008. *China's Great Economic Transformation*. Cambridge, UK: Cambridge University Press.

Brilliant, Larry. 2006. "Larry Brilliant Wants to Stop Pandemics." *TED Talks*, February. Accessed 27 January 2013. http://www.ted.com/talks/larry_brilliant_wants_to_stop_pandemics.html.

Brintrup, Alexandra, Tomomi Kito, Felix Reed-Tsochas, and Steve New. 2011. "Mapping the Toyota Supply Network: Emergence of Resilience." Saïd Business School Working Paper 2011-05-012. University of Oxford, Oxford, UK.

Brock, William A., Cars H. Hommes, and Florian O. O. Wagener. 2008. "More Hedging Instruments May Destabilize Markets." CeNDEF Working Paper 08-04. Center for Nonlinear Dynamics in Economics and Finance, University of Amsterdam, Amsterdam.

Brockmann, Dirk, Lars Hufnagel, and Theo Geisel. 2005. "Dynamics of Modern Epidemics." In *SARS: A Case Study in Emerging Infections*, ed. Angela McLean, Robert May, John Pattison, and Robin Weiss. New York and London: Oxford University Press, 81–91.

Brogger, Tasneem, and Helga Kristin Einarsdottir. 2008. "Iceland Gets $4.6 Billion Bailout from IMF, Nordics (Update3)." Bloomberg website, 20 November. Accessed 5 February 2013. http://www.bloomberg.com/apps/news?pid=news archive&sid=a3Zf1f9IBUWg&refer=europe.

Brunnermeier, Markus K. 2008. "Deciphering the Liquidity and Credit Crunch, 2007–08." NBER Working Paper 14612. National Bureau of Economic Research, Cambridge, MA. Accessed 21 January 2013. http://www.nber.org/papers/w14612.

Butler, Paul. 2010. "Visualising Friendships." *Facebook*, 13 December. Accessed 27 January 2013. http://www.facebook.com/notes/facebook-engineering/visualizing-friendships/469716398919.

Byerly, Carol R. 2010. "The U.S. Military and the Influenza Pandemic of 1918–1919." *Public Health Reports* 125 (3): 82–91.

Caballero, Ricardo J., and Alp Simsek. 2009. "Fire-Sales in a Model of Complexity." MIT Department of Economics Working Paper 09-28. Massachusetts Institute of Technology, Cambridge, MA. Accessed 3 September 2013. http://dspace.mit.edu/bitstream/handle/1721.1/63625/firesalesinmodel00caba.pdf?sequence=1.

Carter, Helen. 2010. "Sub-zero Spell to Continue as Grit Supplies Reach the End of the Road." *Guardian*, 10 January. Accessed 28 January 2013. http://www .guardian.co.uk/uk/2010/jan/10/sub-zero-grit-supplies-snow?INTCMP=SRCH.

Castles, Stephen, and Mark J. Miller. 2009. *The Age of Migration: International Population Movements in the Modern World*. New York: Palgrave Macmillan.

CDC (Centers for Disease Control and Prevention). 2013. "Final Maps and Data for 1999–2012." Centers for Disease Control and Prevention. Accessed 19 July. http://www.cdc.gov/westnile/statsMaps/final.html.

Central Bank of Iceland. 2008a. "Economic Indicators," September, 2. Accessed 24 January 2013. http://www.sedlabanki.is/lisalib/getfile.aspx?itemid=6451.

———. 2008b. "Economic Indicators," November. Accessed 24 January 2013. http:// www.sedlabanki.is/lisalib/getfile.aspx?itemid=6628.

———. 2013. "Exchange Rate." Accessed 11 July. http://www.cb.is/exchange-rate/.

Chang, Ha-Joon. 2002. *Kicking Away the Ladder*. London: Anthem.

Chang, Ha-Joon, and Ilene Grabel. 2004. *Reclaiming Development: An Alternative Economic Policy Manual*. London: Zed Books.

Changxin, Gai. 2011. "CEIBS Calls for More MBA Programs." *China Daily*, 11 April. Accessed 7 July 2012. http://www.chinadaily.com.cn/business/2011-04/11/ content_12305897.htm.

Chen, Lincoln C., Tim G. Evans, and Richard A. Cash. 1999. "Health as a Global Public Good." In *Global Public Goods: International Cooperation in the 21st Century*, ed. Inge Kaul, Isabelle Grunberg, and Marc A. Stern. New York: Oxford University Press for the United Nations Development Programme, 284–304.

CII (Chartered Insurance Institute). 2012. *Future Risk: How Technology Could Make or Break Our World*. Centenary Future Risk Series, Report 4. London: Chartered Insurance Institute.

Cisco. 2011a. "Cisco Visual Networking Index: Global Mobile Data Traffic Forecast Update, 2010–2015." Cisco White Paper, 1 February. Accessed 7 January 2013. http://newsroom.cisco.com/ekits/Cisco_VNI_Global_Mobile_Data_Traffic_ Forecast_2010_2015.pdf.

———. 2011b. "Entering the Zettabyte Era." Article no longer available from http:// www.cisco.com.

———. 2012. "The Zettabyte Era." White paper, May. Accessed 4 February 2013. http://www.cisco.com/en/US/solutions/collateral/ns341/ns525/ns537/ns705/ ns827/VNI_Hyperconnectivity_WP.html.

Clark, David A., ed. 2012. *Adaptation, Poverty, and Development: The Dynamics of Subjective Well-being*. Basingstoke, UK: Palgrave Macmillan.

Clark, Gordon L., Adam D. Dixon, and Ashby H. B. Monk, eds. 2009. *Managing Financial Risks: From Global to Local*. Oxford, UK: Oxford University Press.

Cole, Matthew A., and Robert J. R. Elliott. 2003. "Determining the Trade–Environment Composition Effect: The Role of Capital, Labor, and Environmental Regulations." *Journal of Environmental Economics and Management* 46: 363–383.

Compass Worldwide Logistics. 2012. "Weather Closes All Italian Motorways." 10 September. Accessed 25 January 2013. http://www.cwwl.co.uk/2012/02/weather-closes-all-italian-motorways/.

Copeland, Brian R., and M. Scott Taylor. 2004. "Trade, Growth, and the Environment." *Journal of Economic Literature* 42 (1): 7–71.

Courbage, Cristophe, and Walter R. Stahel, eds. 2012. "Extreme Events and Insurance: 2011 Annus Horribilis." *Geneva Reports* 5 (May): 121–132.

Cro Forum. 2011. "Power Blackout Risks: Risk Management Options." Emerging Risk Initiative Position Paper, November. Accessed 25 January 2013. http://www.agcs.allianz.com/assets/PDFs/Special%20and%20stand-alone%20articles/Power_Blackout_Risks.pdf.

CSIS (Center for Strategic and International Studies). 2012. "Europe Economic Crisis and the Rise of Populism, Nationalism, and Extremism." CSIS Global Security Forum 2012, Washington, DC. Federal News Service transcript. Accessed 3 February 2013. http://csis.org/files/attachments/120413_EuropeEconomicCrisis_GSF_Transcript_0.pdf.

Daily Wireless. 2011. "Cisco's Traffic Forecast." 1 June. Accessed 7 February 2013. http://www.dailywireless.org/2011/06/01/ciscos-traffic-forecast/.

Dattels, Peter, and Laura Kodres. 2009. "Further Action Needed to Reinforce Signs of Market Recovery: IMF." *IMF Survey Magazine: IMF Research,* 21 April. Accessed 8 January 2013. http://www.imf.org/external/pubs/ft/survey/so/2009/RES042109C.htm.

Davis, Joshua. 2007. "Hackers Take Down the Most Wired Country in Europe." *Wired Magazine* 15 (9). Accessed 25 January 2013. http://www.wired.com/politics/security/magazine/15-09/ff_estonia?currentPage=all.

Dawood, Fatimah S., A. Danielle Luliano, Carrie Reed, Martin I. Meltzer, David K. Shay, Po-Yung Cheng, Don Bandaranayake, Robert F. Breiman, W. Abdullah Brooks, Philippe Buchy, et al. 2012. "Estimated Global Mortality Associated with the First 12 Months of 2009 Pandemic Influenza A H1N1 Virus Circulation: A Modelling Study." *Lancet Infectious Diseases* 12 (9): 687–695.

Day, Richard H. 2010. "On Simplicity and Macroeconomic Complexity." In *Handbook of Research on Complexity,* ed. J. Barkley Rosser Jr. Cheltenham, UK: Edward Elgar.

De Jong, Perro. 2006. "Louisiana Studies Dutch Dams." *BBC News,* 13 January. Accessed 30 October 2013. http://news.bbc.co.uk/1/hi/world/europe/4607452.stm.

De Nicolo, Gianni, and Myron L. Kwast. 2002. "Systemic Risk and Financial Consolidation: Are They Related?" *Journal of Banking and Finance* 26 (5): 861–880.

Delli Gatti, Domenico, Mauro Gallegati, Bruce C. Greenwald, Alberto Russo, and Joseph E. Stiglitz. 2009. "Business Fluctuations and Bankruptcy Avalanches in an Evolving Network Economy." *Journal of Economic Interaction and Coordination* 4 (2): 195–212.

Dewatripont, Mathias, and Jean-Charles Rochet. 2010. "The Treatment of Distressed Banks." In *Balancing the Banks: Global Lessons from the Financial Crisis,* ed. Mathias Dewatripont, Jean-Charles Rochet, and Jean Tirole. Princeton, NJ: Princeton University Press, 107–130.

Diamandis, Peter H., and Stephen Kotler. 2012. *Abundance: The Future Is Better Than You Think*. New York: Free Press.

Diamond, Jared. 2005. *Guns, Germs and Steel: The Fate of Human Societies*. London: Vintage.

DiJohn, Joseph, and Karen Allen. 2009. "The Burnham Transportation Plan of Chicago: 100 Years Later." Transport Research Forum, 16–18 March. Accessed 25 January 2013. http://www.trforum.org/forum/downloads/2009_32_BurnhamTransportation_paper.pdf.

Directorate of Labour (Iceland). 2013a. "Unemployment 9.3 in February 2010." *Directorate of Labour News*, 10 March. Accessed 24 January. http://english.vinnumalastofnun.is/about-directorate-of-labour/news/nr/1031/.

———. 2013b. "Unemployment 9.3 in March 2010." *Directorate of Labour News*, 20 April. Accessed 24 January. http://english.vinnumalastofnun.is/about-directorate-of-labour/news/nr/1061/.

Donnelly, Laura. 2013. "British Airways and Heathrow in Blame Game over Snow Chaos." *Telegraph*, 19 January. Accessed 6 February. http://www.telegraph.co.uk/topics/weather/9813427/British-Airways-and-Heathrow-in-blame-game-over-snow-chaos.html.

Doshi, Peter. 2011. "The Elusive Definition of Pandemic Influenza." *Bulletin of the World Health Organization* 89 (7): 532–538.

Dua, André, and Daniel C. Esty. 1997. *Sustaining the Asia Pacific Miracle: Environmental Protection and Economic Integration*. Washington, DC: Peterson Institute.

Dufrénot, Gilles, Valérie Mignon, and Théo Naccache. 2009. "The Slow Convergence of Per Capita Income between the Developing Countries: Growth Resistance and Sometimes Growth Tragedy." CREDIT Research Paper 09/03. Centre for Research in Economic Development and International Trade, Nottingham, UK. Accessed 3 February 2013. http://www.nottingham.ac.uk/credit/documents/papers/09-03.pdf.

Duplat, Patrick, and Emile Pare. 2010. "Haiti from the Ground Up." *Refugees International Field Report*, March. Accessed 30 January 2013. http://www.refugeesinternational.org/sites/default/files/030210_haiti_groundup.pdf.

Dustmann, Christian, Francesca Fabbri, and Ian Peter Preston. 2011. "Racial Harassment, Ethnic Concentration, and Economic Conditions." *Scandinavian Journal of Economics* 113 (3): 689–711.

ECB (European Central Bank). 2009. "The Concept of Systemic Risk." *Financial Stability Review*, December. European Central Bank, Frankfurt, 134–142.

———. 2010. "Analytical Models and Tools for the Identification and Assessment of Systemic Risks." *Financial Stability Review*, June. European Central Bank, Frankfurt, 138–146.

Economist. 2006. "When the Chain Breaks: Being Too Lean and Mean Is a Dangerous Thing." 15 June. Accessed 23 January 2013. http://www.economist.com/node/7032258.

———. 2012a. "Six Degrees of Mobilisation." 1 September. Accessed 28 January 2013. http://www.economist.com/node/21560977.

———. 2012b. "The Euro Crisis: An Ever-Deeper Democratic Deficit." 26 May. Accessed 28 January 2013. http://www.economist.com/node/21555927.

———. 2012c. "The Greek Election: Democracy in Action." 2 June. Accessed 28 January 2013. http://www.economist.com/node/21556302.

———. 2012d. "Wall Street Bonuses." 3 March. Accessed 4 February 2013. http://www.economist.com/node/21548981.

EEF (The Manufacturers' Organisation, UK). 2011. "Industry Looks to Re-shore Production in Response to Supply Risks." The Manufacturers' Organization. Accessed 31 January 2013. http://www.eef.org.uk/releases/uk/2011/Industry-looks-to-re-shore-production-in-response-to-supply-risks-.htm.

EIA (Energy Information Administration). 2008. "U.S. Natural Gas Pipeline Compressor Stations Illustration." Energy Information Administration. Accessed 4 February2013.http://www.eia.gov/pub/oil_gas/natural_gas/analysis_publications/ngpipeline/compressorMap.html.

Einarsdottir, Helga Kristin, and Tasneem Brogger. 2008. "Icelanders Take to Streets to Protest Policy Makers' Failures." *Bloomberg,* 15 November. Accessed 5 February 2013. http://www.bloomberg.com/apps/news?pid=newsarchive&sid=a0r9Lfo7mSUw&refer=europe.

Elamin, Mahmoud, and William Bednar. 2012. "How Is Structured Finance Doing?" Cleveland Federal Reserve Bank, 10 February. Accessed 5 February 2013. http://www.clevelandfed.org/research/trends/2012/0312/01finmar.cfm.

EPA (Environmental Protection Agency). 2010. *Climate Change Indicators in the United States.* Washington, DC: U.S. Environmental Protection Agency, 12. Accessed 5 February 2013. http://www.epa.gov/climatechange/pdfs/CI-full-2010.pdf.

Epstein, Larry G., and Tan Wang. 1994. "Intertemporal Asset Pricing under Knightian Uncertainty." *Econometrica* 62 (3): 283–322.

Escaith, Hubert, and Fabian Gonguet. 2009. "International Trade and Real Transmission Channels of Financial Shocks in Globalized Production Networks." Staff Working Paper ERSD-2009-06. Economics and Statistics Division, World Trade Organization. Accessed 1 February 2013. http://www.wto.org/english/res_e/reser_e/ersd200906_e.pdf.

Escaith, Hubert, Nannette Lindenberg, and Sébastien Miroudot. 2010. "International Supply Chains and Trade Elasticity in Times of Global Crisis." Staff Working Paper ESRD-2010-08. Economics and Statistics Division, World Trade Organization. Accessed 1 February 2013. http://www.wto.org/english/res_e/reser_e/ersd201008_e.pdf.

Espenilla, Nestor A. Jr. 2009. "Regulatory Factors That Contributed to the Global Financial Crisis." *Asia-Pacific Social Science Review* 9 (1): 35–40.

Esty, Daniel C. 2001. "Bridging the Trade–Environment Divide." *Journal of Economic Perspectives* 15 (3): 113–130.

EUI (European University Institute). 2011. "Indignados / Occupy Movement: A Global Phenomenon—A Round Table." European University Institute, 22 November. Accessed 1 June 2012. http://www.eui.eu/SeminarsAndEvents/Live.aspx.

Evans, Alex, Bruce Jones, and David Steven. 2010. *Confronting the Long Crisis of Globalization: Risk, Resilience, and International Order.* New York: Brookings Institute and Center on International Cooperation, New York University. Accessed 9 January 2013. http://www.brookings.edu/~/media/research/files/reports/2010/1/26%20globalization%20jones/01_globalization_evans_jones_steven.pdf.

Falk, Armin, Andreas Kuhn, and Josef Zweimüller. 2011. "Unemployment and Right-Wing Extremist Crime." *Scandinavian Journal of Economics* 113 (2): 260–285.

Federal Reserve Bank of St. Louis. 2012. "Debt Outstanding Domestic Financial Sectors." Board of Governors of the Federal Reserve System. Accessed 7 December. http://research.stlouisfed.org/fred2/data/DODFS.txt.

Fenner, Frank, Donald A. Henderson, Isao Arita, and Zdeněk Ježek. 1988. *Smallpox and Its Eradication.* Geneva: World Health Organization.

Financial Crisis Inquiry Commission. 2011. *Financial Crisis Inquiry Report: Final Report of the National Commission on the Causes of the Financial and Economic Crisis in the United States.* Washington, DC: U.S. Public Affairs.

Findlay, Ronald. 2008. "Comparative Advantage." In *The New Palgrave Dictionary of Economics,* vol. 1, 2nd ed., ed. Steven N. Durlauf and Lawrence E. Blume. Basingstoke, UK: Palgrave Macmillan, 514–517.

Fine, Charles K. 2005. "Are You Modular or Integral? Be Sure Your Supply Chain Knows." *Strategy+Business* 39 (23 May). Accessed 1 February 2013. http://www.strategy-business.com/article/05205?pg=all.

Fleck, Fiona. 2003. "How SARS Changed the World in Less Than Six Months." *Bulletin of the World Health Organization* 81 (8): 625–626.

Foreman, Tom. 2008. "Culprits of the Collapse—#7 Phil Gramm." CNN website, 14 October. Accessed 22 January 2013. http://ac360.blogs.cnn.com/2008/10/14/culprits-of-the-collapse-7-phil-gramm/.

Fourati, Khaled. 2009. "Half Full or Half Empty? The Contribution of Information and Communication Technologies to Development." *Global Governance* 15 (1): 37–42.

Frankel, Jeffrey A., and Andrew K. Rose. 2005. "Is Trade Good or Bad for the Environment? Sorting Out the Causality." *Review of Economics and Statistics* 87 (1): 85–91.

Freixas, Xavier, Gyöngyi Lóránth, and Alan D. Morrison. 2007. "Regulating Financial Conglomerates." *Journal of Financial Intermediation* 16: 479–514.

French, Shaun, Andrew Leyshon, and Nigel Thrift. 2009. "A Very Geographical Crisis: The Making and Breaking of the 2007–2008 Financial Crisis." *Cambridge Journal of Regions, Economy, and Society* 2 (2): 287–302.

G8 (Group of Eight). 2013. "Lough Erne Declaration." 18 June. Lough Erne Summit, Northern Ireland. Accessed 23 July. http://www.g8.utoronto.ca/summit/2013lougherne/Lough_Erne_Declaration_130618.pdf.

G20 (Group of Twenty). 2013. "OECD Presents Its Action Plan on Base Erosion and Profit Shifting." 19 July. Accessed 23 July. http://www.g20.org/news/20130719/781655012.html.

G30 (Group of Thirty) Working Group. 1997. *Global Institutions, National Supervision, and Systemic Risk*. Report. Washington, DC: Group of Thirty.

Gai, Prasanna, and Sujit Kapadia. 2010. "Contagion in Financial Networks." Bank of England Working Paper 383. Bank of England, London. Accessed 22 January 2013. http://www.bankofengland.co.uk/publications/Documents/workingpapers/wp383.pdf.

Gai, Prasanna, Andrew Haldane, and Sujit Kapadia. 2011. "Complexity, Concentration, and Contagion." *Journal of Monetary Economics* 58 (5): 453–470.

Gaidet, Nicolas, Julien Cappelle, John Y. Takekawa, Diann J. Prosser, Samuel A. Iverson, David C. Douglas, William M. Perry, Taej Mundkur, and Scott H. Newman. 2010. "Potential Spread of Highly Pathogenic Avian Influenza H5N1 by Wildfowl: Dispersal Ranges and Rates Determined from Large-Scale Satellite Telemetry." *Journal of Applied Ecology* 47 (5): 1147–1157.

Geissbauer, Reinhard, and Shoshanah Cohen. 2008. "Globalization in Uncertain Times: How Leading Companies Are Building Adaptable Supply Chains to Reap Benefits and Manage Risk." Reprinted from *PRTM Insight* 4. Accessed 2 February 2013. http://www.gsb.stanford.edu/sites/default/files/documents/PRTM_Globalization_In_Uncertain_Times.pdf.

Genesis Forwarding News. 2010. "Guarulhos Airport Congestion Chaos." Accessed circa 2010; article no longer available on website. http://www.genesis-forwarding.com/News/Guarulhos-Airport-Congestion-Chaos.aspx.

Gennaioli, Nicola, Andrei Shleifer, and Robert W. Vishny. 2012. "Neglected Risks, Financial Innovation, and Financial Fragility." *Journal of Financial Economics* 104 (3): 452–468.

Georg, Co-Pierre. 2011. "The Effect of the Interbank Network Structure on Contagion and Financial Stability." Discussion Paper Series 2: Banking and Financial Studies 12/2011. Deutsche Bundesbank, Frankfurt. Accessed 1 February 2013. http://econstor.eu/bitstream/10419/52134/1/671536869.pdf.

Georg, Co-Pierre, and Manjana Milkoreit. 2013. "Similarities in Complexity—Lessons from Finance and Climate Change." Mimeo. Oxford and Waterloo, UK.

Georg, Co-Pierre, and Jenny Poschmann. 2010. "Systemic Risk in a Network Model of Interbank Markets with Central Bank Activity." Jena Economic Research Paper 2010-33. Friedrich Schiller University and the Max Planck Institute of Economics, Jena, Germany. Accessed 1 February 2013. http://pubdb.wiwi.uni-jena.de/pdf/wp_2010_033.pdf.

George, Michael L., David T. Rowlands, and Bill Kastle. 2003. *What Is Lean Six Sigma?* New York: McGraw-Hill Professional.

Giddens, Anthony. 1991. *The Consequences of Modernity.* Stanford, CA: Stanford University Press.

Gigerenzer, Gerd. 2010. *Rationality for Mortals: How People Cope with Uncertainty.* New York: Oxford University Press.

Gigerenzer, Gerd, Ralph Hertwig, and Thorsten Pachur, eds. 2011. *Heuristics: The Foundations of Adaptive Behavior.* Oxford, UK: Oxford University Press.

Gladwell, Malcolm. 2002. *The Tipping Point: How Little Things Can Make a Big Difference.* London: Abacus.

GMAC (Graduate Management Admission Council). 2011. *Application Trends Survey.* Reston, VA: Graduate Management Admission Council. Accessed 4 February 2013. http://www.gmac.com/~/media/Files/gmac/Research/admissions-and -application-trends/applicationtrends2011_sr.pdf.

Goldin, Ian. 2010. "Managing and Mitigating Global Risks." In *Global Redesign: Strengthening Cooperation in a More Interdependent World,* ed. Richard Samans, Klaus Schwab, and Mark Malloch-Brown. Geneva: World Economic Forum, 429–442.

———. 2011. "Globalisation and Risks for Business: Implications for an Increasingly Connected World." *Lloyd's 360° Risk Insight.* London: Lloyds, and Oxford, UK: James Martin 21st Century School. Accessed 9 January 2013. http://www .lloyds.com/~/media/Lloyds/Reports/360/360%20Globalisation/Lloyds_360_ Globalisaton.pdf.

———. 2013. *Divided Nations: Why Global Governance Is Failing, and What We Can Do about It.* Oxford, UK: Oxford University Press.

———, ed. Forthcoming. *Is the Planet Full?* Oxford, UK: Oxford University Press.

Goldin, Ian, and Kenneth Reinert. 2012. *Globalization for Development: Meeting New Challenges,* new ed. Oxford, UK: Oxford University Press.

Goldin, Ian, and Tiffany Vogel. 2010. "Global Governance and Systemic Risk in the 21st Century: Lessons from the Financial Crisis." *Global Policy* 1 (1): 4–15.

Goldin, Ian, and L. Alan Winters, eds. 1992. *The Economics of Sustainable Development.* Cambridge, UK: Cambridge University Press.

Goldin, Ian, Geoffrey Cameron, and Meera Balarajan. 2011. *Exceptional People: How Migration Shaped Our World and Will Define Our Future.* Princeton, NJ: Princeton University Press.

Goldin, Ian, Halsey F. Rogers, and Nicholas H. Stern. 2002. "The Role and Effectiveness of Development Assistance: Lessons from World Bank Experience." Research paper, Development Economics Vice Presidency of the World Bank, Washington, DC.

Golob, Thomas F., and Amelia C. Regan. 2001. "Impacts of Information Technology on Personal Travel and Commercial Vehicle Operations: Research Challenges and Opportunities." *Transportation Research Part C* 9: 87–121.

Goodwin, Matthew. 2011. "Right Response: Understanding and Countering Populism and Extremism in Europe." Chatham House report, September. Chatham House, London. Accessed 5 February 2103. http://www.chathamhouse.org/sites/ default/files/r0911_goodwin.pdf.

Google. 2013. "The 1,000 Most Visited Sites on the Web" (as of July 2011). Accessed 26 January. http://www.google.com/adplanner/static/top1000/.

Google Ngram. 2012. "Google Books Ngram Viewer." Accessed 2012. http://books .google.com/ngrams.

Gorton, Garry B., and Andrew Metrick. 2010a. "Regulating the Shadow Banking System." *Brookings Papers on Economic Activity* 41 (2): 260–312. Accessed 5 February 2013. http://www.brookings.edu/~/media/projects/bpea/fall%202010/ 2010b_bpea_gorton.pdf.

———. 2010b. "Securitized Banking and the Run on Repo." NBER Working Paper 15223. National Bureau of Economic Research, Cambridge, MA. Accessed 21 January 2013. http://www.nber.org/papers/w15223.

Green, Manfred S., Tiberio Swartz, Elana Mayshar, Boaz Lev, Alex Leventhal, Paul E. Slater, and Joshua Shemer. 2002. "When Is an Epidemic an Epidemic?" *Israel Medical Association Journal* 4: 3–6.

Greenough, Gregg, Michael McGeehin, Susan M. Bernard, Juli Trtanj, Jasmin Riad, and David Engelberg. 2001. "The Potential Impacts of Climate Variability and Change on Health Impacts of Extreme Weather Events in the United States." *Environmental Health Perspectives* 109 (2): 191–198.

Gribben, Roland. 2011. "BT Power Breakdown Leaves 275,000 Customers without Internet." *Telegraph*, 4 October. Accessed 26 January 2013. http://www.telegraph .co.uk/finance/newsbysector/mediatechnologyandtelecoms/telecoms/8804971/ BT-power-breakdown-leaves-275000-customers-without-internet.html.

Guerin, Emmanuel, and Laurence Tubiana. 2012. "Preparing for the Green Exit." *Project Syndicate,* 30 May. Accessed 1 June. http://www.project-syndicate.org/ print/preparing-for-the-green-exit.

Guérot, Ulrike, and Thomas Klas. 2012. "After Merkozy: How France and Germany Can Make Europe Work." Policy Brief ECFR56, May. European Council on Foreign Relations, London. Accessed 3 February 2013. http://ecfr.eu/page/-/ ECFR56_FRANCE_GERMANY_BRIEF_AW.pdf.

Haldane, Andrew G. 2009. "Rethinking the Financial Network." Speech delivered to the Amsterdam Student Association, April. Accessed 21 January 2013. http:// www.bankofengland.co.uk/archive/Documents/historicpubs/speeches/2009/ speech386.pdf.

———. 2012. "The Dog and the Frisbee." Speech delivered at the Federal Reserve Bank of Kansas City's 36th Economic Policy Symposium, The Changing Policy Landscape, Jackson Hole, WY, 31 August. Accessed 31 January 2013. http://www .bankofengland.co.uk/publications/Documents/speeches/2012/speech596.pdf.

Haldane, Andrew G., and Robert M. May. 2011. "Systemic Risk in Banking Ecosystems." *Nature* 469: 351–355.

Hallegatte, Stéphane. 2011. "How Economic Growth and Rational Decisions Can Make Disaster Losses Grow Faster Than Wealth." Policy Research Working Paper 5617, March. Office of the Chief Economist, World Bank, Washington,

DC. Accessed 26 January 2013. http://elibrary.worldbank.org/docserver/download/5617.pdf?expires=1359224528&id=id&accname=guest&checksum=5458C4B0507F2486E4C5D04C90C973DE.

Hammond, Ross A. 2009. "Systemic Risk in the Financial System: Insights from Network Science." Insights from Network Science Briefing Paper 12. Pew Charitable Trust, Washington, DC. Accessed 28 January 2013. http://www.pewtrusts.org/uploadedFiles/wwwpewtrustsorg/Reports/Financial_Reform/Pew-Hammond-Systemic-Risk-and-Insights-from-Network-Science.pdf.

Hammond, Ross A., and Laurette Dubé. 2012. "A Systems Science Perspective and Transdisciplinary Models for Food and Nutrition Security." *Proceedings of the National Academy of Sciences (PNAS)* 109 (31): 12356–12363.

Hartmann, Philipp, Oliver De Bandt, and José Luis Peydró-Alcalde. 2009. "Systemic Risk in Banking: An Update." In *The Oxford Handbook of Banking*, ed. Allen N. Berger, Philip Molyneux, and John O. S. Wilson. Oxford, UK: Oxford University Press.

Haxel, Gordon B., James B. Hedrick, and Greta J. Orris. 2002. "Rare Earth Elements—Critical Resources for High Technology." Fact Sheet 087-02, U.S. Geological Survey. Accessed 4 February 2013. http://pubs.usgs.gov/fs/2002/fs087-02/.

Helbing, Dirk. 2013. "Globally Networked Risks and How to Respond." *Nature* 497: 51–59.

Held, David, Antony G. McGrew, David Goldblatt, and Jonathan Perraton. 1999. *Global Transformations: Politics, Economics, Culture*. Cambridge, UK: Polity Press.

Heshmati, Almas. 2004. "The Relationship between Income Inequality, Poverty, and Globalisation." IZA Discussion Paper 1277. Institute for the Study of Labour, Bonn. Accessed 3 February 2013. http://ftp.iza.org/dp1277.pdf.

Hidalgo, Cesar, Bailey Klinger, Albert-Laszlo Barabasi, and Ricardo Hausmann. 2007. "The Product Space Conditions the Development of Nations." *Science* 317 (5837): 482–487.

Hinduja, Sameer, and Justin W. Patchin. 2013. "Social Influences on Cyberbullying Behaviors among Middle and High School Students." *Journal of Youth and Adolescence* 42 (5): 711–722.

Hook, Leslie. 2012. "China's Rare Earth Stranglehold in Spotlight." *Financial Times*, 13 March. Accessed 23 January 2013. http://www.ft.com/cms/s/0/b3332e0a-348c-11e2-8986-00144feabdc0.html#axzz2DVY78Spi.

Hopkins, Donald R. *Smallpox: The Greatest Killer in History*. London: University of Chicago Press, esp. 313 ff.

Horan, Ruaidhri. 2012. "Frankfurt Airport Strike Causes Air Freight Chaos." *Emerald Freight Express*, 17 February. http://www.emeraldfreight.com/news/frankfurt-airport-strike-causes-air-freight-chaos.

Horgan, John. 1997. *The End of Science: Facing the Limits of Knowledge in the Twilight of the Scientific Age*. New York: Broadway Books.

Hufnagel, Lars, Dirk Brockmann, and Theo Geisel. 2004. "Forecast and Control of Epidemics in a Globalized World." *Proceedings of the National Academy of Sciences (PNAS)* 101 (42): 15124–15129.

Hummels, David. 2007. "Transportation Costs and International Trade in the Second Era of Globalization." *Journal of Economic Perspectives* 21 (3): 131–154.

Hunter, William C., George G. Kaufman, and Thomas H. Krueger, eds. 1999. *The Asian Financial Crisis: Origins, Implications, and Solutions.* Norwell, MA: Kluwer Academic.

IMF (International Monetary Fund) Staff. 2009. "Guidance to Assess the Systemic Importance of Financial Institutions, Markets, and Instruments." Report to G20 Finance Ministers and Governors. International Monetary Fund, Bank for International Settlements, and Financial Stability Board, October. Accessed 1 February 2013. http://www.financialstabilityboard.org/publications/r_091107c.pdf.

———. 2010. "The Financial Crisis and Information Gaps." Progress report. International Monetary Fund, Bank for International Settlements, and Financial Stability Board, May. Accessed 1 February 2013. http://www.imf.org/external/np/g20/pdf/053110.pdf.

Iori, Giulia, Saqib Jafarey, and Francisco G. Padilla. 2006. "Systemic Risk on the Interbank Market." *Journal of Economic Behavior and Organization* 61: 525–542.

Jackson, Robert. 2008. "The Big Chill." *Financial Times,* 15 November. Accessed 20 January 2013. http://www.ft.com/intl/cms/s/0/8641d080-b2b4-11dd-bbc9-0000779fd18c.html#axzz2Cn5IKHoa.

Jamieson, Alastair. 2009. "Google: 'Human Error' Brings Internet Chaos for Millions." *Telegraph,* 31 January. Accessed 26 January 2013. http://www.telegraph.co.uk/technology/google/4414452/Google-Human-error-brings-internet-chaos-for-millions.html.

Janardhanan, Arun. 2011. "Air Cargo Piles Up Due to Administrative Problems." *Times of India,* 29 April. Accessed 25 January 2013. http://articles.timesofindia.indiatimes.com/2011-04-29/chennai/29487072_1_cargo-handling-chennai-air-cargo-cargo-operations.

Jarzemsky, Matthew. 2012. "'Fat-Finger' Error Caused Oil-Stock Price Swings." *Wall Street Journal,* 19 September. Accessed 21 January 2013. http://blogs.wsj.com/marketbeat/2012/09/19/fat-finger-error-caused-oil-stock-price-swings/?KEYWORDS=Oilwell+Varco.

Jaumotte, Florence, Subir Lall, and Chris Papageorgiou. 2008. "Rising Income Inequality: Technology, or Trade and Financial Globalization?" IMF Working Paper 185. International Monetary Fund, Washington, DC. Accessed 3 February 2013. http://www.imf.org/external/pubs/ft/wp/2008/wp08185.pdf.

Jervis, Robert. 1997. *System Effects.* Princeton, NJ: Princeton University Press.

Johnson, Neil. 2009. *Simply Complexity: A Clear Guide to Complexity Theory.* Oxford, UK: Oneworld Publications.

Johnson, Simon. 2009. "The Quiet Coup." *Atlantic Magazine*, May. Accessed 16 October 2012. http://www.theatlantic.com/magazine/archive/2009/05/the-quiet-coup/307364/.

Jorgenson, Andrew K., J. Kelly Austin, and Christopher Dick. 2009. "Ecologically Unequal Exchange and the Resource Consumption / Environmental Degradation Paradox: A Panel Study of Less-Developed Countries, 1970–2000." *International Journal of Comparative Sociology* 50 (3–4): 263–284.

Kanatas, George, and Jianping Qi. 1998. "Underwriting by Commercial Banks: Incentive Conflicts, Scope Economies, and Project Quality." *Journal of Money, Credit, and Banking* 30: 119–133.

———. 2003. "Integration of Lending and Underwriting: Implications of Scope Economies." *Journal of Finance* 58 (3): 1167–1191.

Kaplan, Eben. 2007. "America's Vulnerable Energy Grid." *Council on Foreign Relations Backgrounders*, 17 April. Accessed 20 March 2012. http://www.cfr.org/energy-security/americas-vulnerable-energy-grid/p13153.

Kaufman, George G. 1995. "Comment on Systemic Risk." In *Research in Financial Services: Banking, Financial Markets, and Systemic Risk*, vol. 7, ed. George G. Kaufman. Greenwich, CT: JAI Press, 47–52.

Kaufman, George G., and Kenneth E. Scott. 2003. "What Is Systemic Risk, and Do Bank Regulators Retard or Contribute to It?" *Independent Review* 7 (3): 371–391.

Keegan, William. 2012. "Bank Deregulation Leads to Disaster: Shout It from the Rooftops." *Observer*, 6 May. Accessed 21 January 2013. http://www.guardian.co.uk/business/2012/may/06/shout-rooftops-bank-deregulation-leads-to-disaster.

Kennedy, John F. 1959. "Education: United Negro College Fund." Speech to the United Negro College Fund, Indianapolis, Indiana, 12 April, 2. Accessed 10 July 2013. http://www.jfklibrary.org/Asset-Viewer/Archives/JFKCAMP1960-1029-036.aspx.

Keohane, Robert O., and Joseph S. Nye Jr. 1977. *Power and Independence: World Politics in Transition*. Boston: Little, Brown.

Kerwer, Dieter. 2005. "Rules That Many Use: Standards and Global Regulation." *Governance* 18 (4): 611–632.

Khan, Kamran, Julien Arino, Wei Hu, Paulo Raposo, Jennifer Sears, Felipe Calderon, Christine Heidebrecht, Michael Macdonald, Jessica Liauw, Angie Chan, and Michael Gardam. 2009. "Spread of a Novel Influenza A (H1N1) Virus via Global Airline Transportation." *New England Journal of Medicine* 361 (2): 212–214.

Khondker, Habibul H. 2011. "Role of the New Media in the Arab Spring." *Globalizations* 8 (5): 675–679.

Kilbourne, Edwin D. 2006. "Influenza Pandemics of the 20th Century." *Emerging Infectious Diseases* 12 (1): 9–14.

Kilpatrick, A. Marm. 2011. "Globalization, Land Use, and the Invasion of West Nile Virus." *Science* 334 (6054): 323–327.

Knight, Frank H. 1921. *Risk, Uncertainty, and Profit.* Boston: Hart, Schaffner, and Marx.

Kochan, Thomas A., Russell D. Lansbury, and John P. MacDuffie, eds. 1997. *After Lean Production: Evolving Employment Practices in the World Auto Industry.* Ithaca, NY: Cornell University Press.

Korea Net. 2013. "Overview." Accessed 2 February. http://www.korea.net/AboutKorea/Economy/Overview.

Krauss, Clifford. 2012. "Shippers Concerned over Possible Suez Canal Disruptions." *New York Times,* 2 February. Accessed 1 February 2013. http://www.nytimes.com/2011/02/03/world/middleeast/03suez.html.

Krugman, Paul R. 2009. *The Conscience of a Liberal.* New York: Penguin.

Kunreuther, Howard, and Michael Useem. 2010a. "Preface." In *Learning from Catastrophes: Strategies for Reaction and Response,* ed. Howard Kunreuther and Michael Useem. Upper Saddle River, NJ: Prentice Hall, xv–xvii.

———. 2010b. "Principles and Challenges for Reducing Risks from Disasters." In *Learning from Catastrophes: Strategies for Reaction and Response,* ed. Howard Kunreuther and Michael Useem. Upper Saddle River, NJ: Prentice Hall, 1–17.

Laframboise, Nicole, and Boileau Loko. 2012. "Natural Disasters: Mitigating Impact, Managing Risks." IMF Working Paper 12/245. International Monetary Fund, Washington, DC. Accessed 12 February 2013. http://www.imf.org/external/pubs/ft/wp/2012/wp12245.pdf.

Lan, Tang, and Zhang Xin. 2010. "Can Cyber Deterrence Work?" In *Global Cyber Deterrence: Views from China, the U.S., Russia, India, and Norway,* ed. Andrew Nagorski. New York: EastWest Institute, 1–3.

Latour, Bruno. 2005. *Reassembling the Social: An Introduction to Actor-Network-Theory.* Oxford, UK: Oxford University Press.

Lederberg, Joshua. 1997. "Infectious Disease as an Evolutionary Paradigm." *Emerging Infectious Diseases* 3 (4): 417–423.

Lee, Hau L. 2004. "Triple-A Supply Chains." *Harvard Business Review,* 1 October, 102–112.

Lehar, Alfred. 2005. "Measuring Systemic Risk: A Risk Management Approach." *Journal of Banking and Finance* 29 (10): 2577–2603.

Lerner, Eric. 2003. "What's Wrong with the Electric Grid?" *Industrial Physicist* 9: 8–13.

Levin, Simon A., and Jane Lubchenco. 2008. "Resilience, Robustness, and Marine Ecosystem–Based Management." *Bio Science* 58 (1): 27–32.

Liker, Jeffrey. 2004. *The Toyota Way: 14 Management Principles from the World's Greatest Manufacturer.* New York: McGraw-Hill Professional.

Look, Anne. 2012. "Mali, ECOWAS Not on Same Page on Military Intervention." *Voice of America,* 18 September. Last accessed 1 February 2013. http://www.voanews.com/content/mali-ecowas-military-intervention/1510417.html.

Lorenz, Edward N. 1963. "Deterministic Nonperiodic Flow." *Journal of the Atmospheric Sciences* 20 (2): 130–141.

Lounibos, L. Philip. 2001. "Invasions by Insect: Vectors of Human Disease." *Annual Review of Entomology* 47: 233–266.

Lynn, Jonathan. 2010. "WHO to Review Its Handling of H1N1 Flu Pandemic." *Reuters,* 12 January. Accessed 25 August 2012. http://www.reuters.com/article/2010/01/12/us-flu-who-idUSTRE5BL2ZT20100112.

Mabey, Nick, and Richard McNally. 1998. *Foreign Direct Investment and the Environment: From Pollution Havens to Sustainable Development.* WWF-UK report, July. World Wide Fund for Nature. Accessed 27 January 2013. http://www.wwf.org.uk/filelibrary/pdf/fdi.pdf.

Maer, Lucinda, and Nida Broughton. 2012. "Financial Services: Contribution to the UK Economy." SN/EP/06193. House of Commons Library (Economics, Politics, and Statistics Section). Accessed 22 January 2013. http://www.parliament.uk/briefing-papers/SN06193.pdf.

Magee, David. 2008. *How Toyota Became #1: Leadership Lessons from the World's Greatest Car Company.* New York: Portfolio.

Maraia, Vincent. 2006. *The Build Master: Microsoft's Software Configuration Management Best Practices.* Upper Saddle River, NJ: Addison-Wesley.

Mariathasan, Mike, and Ouarda Merrouche. 2013. "The Manipulation of Basel Risk-Weights." CEPR Discussion Paper 9494. Centre for Economic Policy Research, London. May.

Markillie, Paul. 2006. "The Physical Internet." *Economist,* 15 June. Accessed 1 February 2013. http://www.economist.com/node/7032165.

Markowitz, Harry M. 1952. "Portfolio Selection," *Journal of Finance* 7: 77–91.

Marsh and McLennan. 2012. "Supply Chain." Marsh USA website. Accessed 1 August. http://usa.marsh.com/RiskIssues/SupplyChain/lapg-5776/2.aspx.

Marshall, Brent. 1999. "Globalisation, Environmental Degradation, and Ulrich Beck's Risk Society." *Environmental Values* 8: 253–275.

Martell, Luke. 2010. *The Sociology of Globalization.* Cambridge, UK: Polity Press.

Mason, Rowena. 2009. "David Oddsson's Ascent to Iceland's Editor in Chief Splits Opinion as Bloggers Gain Ground." *Telegraph,* 29 September. Accessed 1 February 2013. http://blogs.telegraph.co.uk/finance/rowenamason/100001134/david-oddssons-ascent-to-icelands-editor-in-chief-splits-opinion-as-bloggers-gain-ground/.

Maurer, Andreas, and Christophe Degain. 2010. "Globalization and Trade Flows: What You See Is Not What You Get!" Staff Working Paper ESRD-2010-12. Economics and Statistics Division, World Trade Organization. Accessed 2 February 2013. http://www.wto.org/english/res_e/reser_e/ersd201012_e.pdf.

May, Robert M., Simon A. Levin, and George Sugihara. 2008. "Complex Systems: Ecology for Bankers." *Nature* 451 (21 February): 893–895.

Mayor, Susan. 2000. "Flu Experts Warn of Need for Pandemics Plan." *British Medical Journal* 321 (7265): 852.

McAusland, Carol. 2008. "Globalisation's Direct and Indirect Effects on the Environment." Paper presented at the Organization for Economic Co-operation and Development's Global Forum on Transport and Environment in a Globalising World, Guadalajara, Mexico, 10–12 November, 6. Accessed 21 January 2013. http://www.oecd.org/env/transportandenvironment/41380703.pdf.

McIlvaine Company. 2006. "Storm Halts Refining at ConocoPhillips in Hartford, IL." Refinery update, August. Accessed 26 January 2013. http://www.mcilvainecompany.com/industryforecast/refineries/Updates/2006%20updates/aug%2006%20update.htm.

McKinsey. 2008. "McKinsey Global Survey Results: Managing Global Supply Chains." *McKinsey Quarterly*, August. Accessed 28 January 2013. http://www.mckinseyquarterly.com/McKinsey_Global_Survey_Results_Managing_global_supply_chains_2179.

Merriam-Webster Inc. 2004. *The Merriam-Webster Dictionary*, new ed. Merriam-Webster Mass Market Paperbacks.

Milanović, Branko. 2009. "Global Inequality Recalculated: The Effect of New 2005 PPP Estimates on Global Inequality." Policy Research Working Paper 5061. World Bank, Washington, DC. Accessed 19 July 2013. http://www-wds.worldbank.org/external/default/WDSContentServer/WDSP/IB/2009/09/22/000158349_20090922160230/Rendered/PDF/WPS5061.pdf.

———. 2011. "Global Inequality from Class to Location, from Proletarians to Migrants." Policy Research Working Paper 5820. World Bank, Washington, DC. Accessed 3 February 2013. http://www-wds.worldbank.org/servlet/WDSContentServer/WDSP/IB/2011/09/29/000158349_20110929082257/Rendered/PDF/WPS5820.pdf.

Milanović, Branko, and Lynn Squire. 2007. "Does Tariff Liberalization Increase Wage Inequality? Some Empirical Evidence." In *Globalization and Poverty*, ed. Ann Harrison. London: University of Chicago Press, 143–181.

Milford, Jana, John Nielsen, Vickie Patton, Nancy Ryan, V. John White, and Cindy Copeland. 2005. *Clearing California's Coal Shadow from the American West*. Environmental Defense. Accessed 18 July 2013. http://www.westernresourceadvocates.org/energy/pdf/CA%20Coal%20Shadow.pdf.

Miller, Rich. 2010. "How Many Servers Does Facebook Have?" *Data Center Knowledge*, 27 September. Accessed 26 January 2013. www.datacenterknowledge.com/the-facebook-data-center-faq-page-2.

———. 2011 [2009]. "Who Has the Most Servers?" *Data Center Knowledge*, 14 May 2009, updated April 2011. Accessed 26 January 2013. www.datacenterknowledge.com/archives/2009/05/14/whos-got-the-most-web-servers.

Minkenberg, Michael. 2011. "The Radical Right in Europe Today: Trends and Patterns in East and West." In *Is Europe on the "Right" Path? Right-Wing Extremism and*

Right-Wing Populism in Europe, ed. Nora Langenbacher and Britta Schellenberg. Berlin: Friedrich Ebert Stiftung Forum, 37–55.

Montreuil, Benoit. 2011. "Towards a Physical Internet: Meeting the Global Logistics Sustainability Grand Challenge." CIRRELT Working Paper 2011-03. Interuniversity Research Centre on Enterprise Networks, Logistics, and Transportation, University of Montreal, Montreal, Canada. Accessed 25 January 2013. https://www.cirrelt.ca/DocumentsTravail/CIRRELT-2011-03.pdf.

Moore, Gordon E. 1965. "Cramming More Components onto Integrated Circuits." *Electronics Magazine* 38 (19 April). Accessed 8 July 2013. http://download.inte-l.com/museum/Moores_Law/Articles-Press_Releases/Gordon_Moore_1965_Article.pdf.

———. 1975. "Progress in Digital Integrated Electronics." *Electron Devices Meeting* 27: 11–13.

Morelle, Rebecca. 2013. "Working Gun Made with 3D Printer." *BBC News,* 6 May. Accessed 21 July. http://www.bbc.co.uk/news/science-environment-22421185.

Morens, David M., and Anthony S. Fauci. 2007. "The 1918 Influenza Pandemic: Insights for the 21st Century." *Journal of Infectious Diseases* 195: 1018–1028.

Morens, David M., Gregory K. Folkers, and Anthony S. Fauci. 2009. "What Is a Pandemic?" *Journal of Infectious Diseases* 200 (7): 1018–1021.

Morgenthau, Hans. 1948. *Politics among Nations: The Struggle for Power and Peace.* New York: Knopf.

Nagurney, Anna. 2006. *Supply Chain Network Economics: Dynamics of Prices, Flows, and Profits.* Cheltenham, UK: Edward Elgar.

New York Times. 1999. "Wide Power Failure Strikes Southern Brazil." 12 March. Accessed 17 October 2012. http://www.nytimes.com/1999/03/12/world/wide-power-failure-strikes-southern-brazil.html?n=Top/Reference/Times%20Topics/Subjects/B/Blackouts%20and%20Brownouts%20.

Nier, Erlend, Jing Yang, Tanju Yorulmazer, and Amadeo Alentorn. 2007. "Network Models and Financial Stability." *Journal of Economic Dynamics and Control* 31 (6): 2033–2060.

Nordhaus, William D. 1994. *Managing the Global Commons: The Economics of Climate Change.* Cambridge, MA: MIT Press.

———. 2008. *A Question of Balance: Weighing the Options on Global Warming Policies.* New Haven, CT, and London: Yale University Press.

Nordqvist, Christian. 2009. "What Is a Pandemic? What Is an Epidemic?" *Medical News Today,* 5 May. Accessed 25 August 2012. http://www.medicalnewstoday.com/articles/148945.php.

Nuttall, Nick. 2004. "Overfishing: A Threat to Marine Biodiversity." *Ten Stories.* United Nations website. Accessed 14 April 2012. http://www.un.org/events/tenstories/06/story.asp?storyID=800.

Obama, Barack. 2009. "Remarks by the President on a New Beginning." White House website, 4 June. Accessed 12 August 2012. http://www.whitehouse.gov/the-press-office/remarks-president-cairo-university-6-04-09.

OECD (Organisation for Economic Co-operation and Development). 2003a. *Emerging Risks in the 21st Century: An Agenda for Action.* Paris: Organisation for Economic Cooperation and Development. Accessed 26 January 2013. http://www.oecd.org/futures/globalprospects/37944611.pdf.

———. 2003b. "History of the 0.7% ODA Target." *OECD Journal on Development* 3 (4): III-9–III-11.

———. 2011a. *Divided We Stand: Why Inequality Keeps Rising.* Paris: OECD Publishing.

———. 2011b. *Growing Income Inequality in OECD Countries: What Drives It and How Can Policy Tackle It?* OECD Forum on Tackling Inequality, Paris, 2 May. Accessed 3 February 2013. http://www.oecd.org/els/socialpoliciesanddata/47723414.pdf.

———. 2013. "2012 Producer Support Estimates by Country." *OECD.Stat Extracts*, accessed 6 February. http://stats.oecd.org/.

Oesch, Daniel. 2008. "Explaining Workers' Support for Right-Wing Populist Parties in Western Europe: Evidence from Austria, Belgium, France, Norway, and Switzerland." *International Political Science Review* 29 (3): 349–373.

O'Hara, Phillip A. 2006. *Growth and Development in the Global Political Economy.* London: Routledge.

Ohno, Taiichi. 1988. *Toyota Production System: Beyond Large-Scale Production.* Portland, OR: Productivity Press.

Ormerod, Paul. 2012. *Positive Linking: How Networks Can Revolutionise the World.* London: Faber and Faber.

Oxford Economics. 2010. *The Economic Impacts of Air Travel Restrictions Due to Volcanic Ash.* Report prepared for Airbus. Oxford, UK: Oxford Economics.

Oxford Martin Commission for Future Generations. 2013. *Now for the Long Term: The Report of the Oxford Martin Commission for Future Generations.* Oxford, UK: Oxford Martin School, University of Oxford. October. Accessed October 29. http://www.oxfordmartin.ox.ac.uk/downloads/commission/Oxford_Martin_Now_for_the_Long_Term.pdf.

Paddock, Catherine. 2012. "H5N1 Bird Flu Pandemic Potential Revealed." *Medical News Today,* 24 June. Accessed 24 August. http://www.medicalnewstoday.com/articles/246964.php.

Paillard, Christophe-Alexandre. 2010. "Russia and Europe's Mutual Energy Dependence." *Journal of International Affairs* 63 (2): 65–84.

Palmer, Tim. 2009. "Edward Norton Lorenz, 23 May 1916–16 April 2008." *Biographical Memoirs of Fellows of the Royal Society* 55: 139–155.

———. 2011. "A CERN for Climate Change." *Physics World,* March, 14–15. Accessed 24 July 2013. http://www.oxfordmartin.ox.ac.uk/downloads/press/climate-Palmer.pdf.

Pappaioanou, Marguerite. 2009. "Highly Pathogenic H5N1 Avian Influenza Virus: Cause of the Next Pandemic?" *Comparative Immunology, Microbiology, and Infectious Diseases* 32 (4): 287–300.

Pehe, Jiří. 2005. "Populism's Short March in Central Europe." *Project Syndicate*, 10 November. Accessed 1 June 2012. http://www.project-syndicate.org/print/populism-s-short-march-in-central-europe.

Perrow, Charles. 2009. "Modeling Firms in the Global Economy: New Forms, New Concentrations." *Theory and Society* 38 (3): 217–243.

Peters, Kai, and Narendra Laljani. 2009. "The Evolving MBA." *Global Study Magazine* 4 (3): 36–49.

Pongsiri, Monitira J., Joe Roman, Vanessa O. Ezenwa, Tony L. Goldberg, Hillel S. Koren, Stephen C. Newbold, Richard S. Ostfeld, Subhrendu K. Pattanayak, and Daniel J. Salkeld. 2009. "Biodiversity Loss Affects Global Disease Ecology." *BioScience* 59 (11): 945–954.

Prasad, Eswar S., Kenneth Rogoff, Shang-Jin Wei, and M. Ayan Kose. 2003. "Effects of Financial Globalization on Developing Countries: Some Empirical Evidence." IMF Occasional Paper 220. International Monetary Fund, Washington, DC.

Pritchett, Lant. 1997. "Convergence, Big Time." *Journal of Economic Perspectives* 11 (3): 3–17.

Pushpam, Kumar, ed. 2012. *The Economics of Ecosystems and Biodiversity: Ecological and Economic Foundations.* London: Routledge.

Raduege, Harry D. Jr. 2010. "The View from the United States: Fighting Weapons of Mass Disruption; Why America Needs a 'Cyber Triad.'" In *Global Cyber Deterrence: Views from China, the U.S., Russia, India, and Norway,* ed. Andrew Nagorski. New York: EastWest Institute, 3–5.

Rajan, Raghuram G. 2005. "The Greenspan Era: Lessons for the Future." Speech delivered at Financial Markets, Financial Fragility, and Central Banking, a symposium sponsored by the Federal Reserve Bank of Kansas City, Jackson Hole, Wyoming, 27 August. Accessed 21 January 2013. http://www.imf.org/external/np/speeches/2005/082705.htm.

———. 2011. *Fault Lines: How Hidden Fractures Still Threaten the World Economy.* Princeton, NJ: Princeton University Press.

Rama, Martin. 2003. "Globalization and Workers in Developing Countries." Policy Research Working Paper 2958. World Bank, Washington, DC. Accessed 3 February 2013. http://www-wds.worldbank.org/external/default/WDSContentServer/WDSP/IB/2003/02/07/000094946_03013004074424/Rendered/PDF/multi0page.pdf.

Ravallion, Martin, and Shaohua Chen. 2004. "Learning from Success: Understanding China's (Uneven) Progress against Poverty." *Finance and Development* 41 (4): 16–19.

Reader, Daniel, and John All. 2008. "Sustainability with Globalization: A Chilean Case Study." Paper presented at the Association of American Geographers (AAG) Conference, Boston, 15–19 April.

Reed-Tsochas, Felix. 2005. "From Biology to Business and Beyond." *Business at Oxford* (Magazine of the Saïd Business School) 8 (Winter): 4–5. Accessed

9 January 2013. http://www.sbs.ox.ac.uk/Documents/bao/BusinessatOxford Winter2005.pdf.

Renn, Ortwin. 2008. *Risk Governance: Coping with Uncertainty in a Complex World.* London: Earthscan.

Ricardo, David. 1817. *On the Principles of Political Economy, and Taxation.* London: John Murray.

Rochet, Jean-Charles. 2010. "The Future of Banking Regulation." In *Balancing the Banks: Global Lessons from the Financial Crisis,* ed. Mathias Dewatripont, Jean-Charles Rochet, and Jean Tirole. Princeton, NJ: Princeton University Press, 78–103.

Rodrigue, Jean-Paul, Claude Comtois, and Brian Slack. 2009. *The Geography of Transport Systems.* New York: Routledge.

———. 2012. "World Air Travel and World Air Freight Carried, 1950–2011." In *The Geography of Transport Systems.* New York: Routledge, chap. 3. Accessed 19 October. http://people.hofstra.edu/geotrans/eng/ch3en/conc3en/evolairtransport .html.

Rodrik, Dani. 2002. "Globalization for Whom?" *Harvard Magazine,* July–August, 29–31. Accessed 31 January 2013. http://harvardmagazine.com/2002/07/ globalization-for-whom.html.

———. 2011. *The Globalization Paradox: Democracy and the Future of the World Economy.* New York and London: W. W. Norton.

———. 2012. "Global Poverty amid Global Plenty: Getting Globalization Right." *Americas Quarterly,* Spring. Accessed 4 January 2013. http://www .americasquarterly.org/node/3560.

Roeller, Lars-Hendrik, and Leonard Waverman. 2001. "Telecommunications Infrastructure and Economic Development: A Simultaneous Approach." *American Economic Review* 91 (4): 909–923.

Rosner, David. 2010. "'Spanish Flu, or Whatever It Is . . .': The Paradox of Public Health in a Time of Crisis." *Public Health Reports* 125 (3): 38–47.

Rosser, J. Barkley Jr. 2009a. "Computational and Dynamic Complexity in Economics." In *Handbook of Research on Complexity,* ed. J. Barkley Rosser Jr. Cheltenham, UK: Edgar Elgar, 22–25.

———. 2009b. "Introduction." In *Handbook of Research on Complexity,* ed. J. Barkley Rosser Jr. Cheltenham, UK: Edgar Elgar, 3–11.

Roxburgh, Charles, Susan Lund, and John Piotrowski. 2011. *Updated Research: Mapping Global Capital Markets.* New York: McKinsey, August. Accessed 21 January 2013. http://www.mckinsey.com/insights/mgi/research/financial_markets/ mapping_global_capital_markets_2011.

Roxburgh, Charles, Susan Lund, Charles Atkins, Stanislas Belot, Wayne W. Hu, and Moira S. Pierce. 2009. *Global Capital Markets: Entering a New Era.* New York: McKinsey and Company, September. Accessed 21 January 2013. http://www.mckinsey.com/insights/mgi/research/financial_markets/global_ capital_markets_entering_a_new_era.

Runde, Jochen. 1998. "Clarifying Frank Knight's Discussion of the Meaning of Risk and Uncertainty." *Cambridge Journal of Economics* 22 (5): 539–546.

Rydgren, Jens. 2008. "Immigration Sceptics, Xenophobes or Racists? Radical Right-Wing Voting in Six West European Countries." *European Journal of Political Research* 47: 737–765.

Schich, Sebastian, and Sofia Lindh. 2012. "Implicit Guarantees for Bank Debt: Where Do We Stand?" *OECD Journal: Financial Market Trends* 2012 (1). Accessed 22 January 2013. http://www.oecd.org/finance/financialmarkets/Implicit -Guarantees-for-bank-debt.pdf.

Sen, Amartya K. 1999. *Development as Freedom.* Oxford, UK: Oxford University Press.

Senate Banking Committee. 1999. "Gramm's Statement at Signing Ceremony for Gramm-Leach-Bliley Act." Senate Banking Committee Press Release, 12 November. Accessed 21 January 2013. http://banking.senate.gov/prel99/1112gbl.htm.

Serrano, M. Ángeles, Marián Boguñá, and Alessandro Vespignani. 2007. "Patterns of Dominant Flows in the World Trade Web." *Journal of Economic Interaction and Coordination* 2 (2): 111–124.

Shaffer, Paul. 2008. "New Thinking on Poverty: Implications for Globalisation and Poverty Reduction Strategies." DESA Working Paper 65. United Nations Department of Economic and Social Affairs, New York. Accessed 3 February 2013. http://www.un.org/esa/desa/papers/2008/wp65_2008.pdf.

Shen, Junyi. 2008. "Trade Liberalization and Environmental Degradation in China." *Applied Economics* 40: 997–1004.

Simsek, Alp. 2011. "Speculation and Risk Sharing with New Financial Assets." NBER Working Paper 17506. National Bureau of Economic Research, Cambridge, MA. Accessed 21 January 2013. http://www.nber.org/papers/w17506.

Slaughter, Matthew J. 1998. "International Trade and Per Capita Income Convergence: A Difference-in-Differences Analysis." NBER Working Paper 6557. National Bureau of Economic Research, Cambridge, MA. Accessed 3 February 2013. http://www.nber.org/papers/w6557.pdf.

Small, Michael, and Chi K. Tse. 2005. "Small World and Scale Free Model of Transmission of SARS." *International Journal of Bifurcation and Chaos* 15 (5): 1745–1755.

Smith, Gavin J. D., Dhanasekaran Vijaykrishna, Justin Bahl, Samantha J. Lycett, Michael Worobey, Oliver G. Pybus, Siu Kit Ma, Cheung Chung Lam, Jayna Raghwani, Samir Bhatt, et al. 2009. "Origins and Evolutionary Genomics of the 2009 Swine-Origin H1N1 Influenza A Epidemic." *Nature* 459: 1122–1126.

Solow, Robert M. 1956. "A Contribution to the Theory of Economic Growth." *Quarterly Journal of Economics* 70 (1): 65–94.

Soramäki, Kimmo, Morten L. Bech, Jeffrey Arnold, Robert J. Glass, and Walter Beyeler. 2007. "The Topology of Interbank Payment Flows." *Physica A: Statistical Mechanics and Its Applications* 379 (1): 317–333.

Sorman, Guy. 2012. "Back to Utopia?" *Project Syndicate,* 14 May. Accessed 1 June. http://www.project-syndicate.org/commentary/back-to-utopia.

Stafford, James. 2012. "Tom Murphy Interview: Resource Depletion Is a Bigger Threat Than Climate Change." *Oilprice.com,* 22 March. Accessed 18 August. http://oilprice.com/Interviews/Tom-Murphy-Interview-Resource-Depletion-is-a-Bigger-Threat-than-Climate-Change.html.

Starr, Randy, Jim Newfrock, and Michael Delurey. 2003. "Enterprise Resilience: Managing Risk in the Networked Economy." *Booz Allen Hamilton Strategy and Business Magazine* 30: 1–10. Accessed 23 January 2013. http://www.boozallen.com/media/file/139766.pdf.

Stern, Nicholas H. 2010. *A Blueprint for a Safer Planet: How We Can Save the World and Create Prosperity.* London: Vintage.

Stiglitz, Jospeh E. 2006. *Making Globalization Work.* London: W. W. Norton.

———. 2012. *The Price of Inequality.* London: Allen Lane.

Stock, James H., and Mark W. Watson. 2002. "Has the Business Cycle Changed and Why?" In *NBER Macroeconomics Annual,* vol. 17, ed. Mark Gertler and Kenneth Rogoff. Cambridge, MA: MIT Press, 159–218.

Strasburg, Jenny, and Jacob Bunge. 2012. "Loss Swamps Trading Firm: Knight Capital Searches for Partner as Tab for Computer Glitch Hits $440 Million." *Wall Street Journal,* 2 August. Accessed 21 January 2013. http://online.wsj.com/article/SB10000872396390443866404577564772083961412.html.

Suez Canal Authority. 2011. *Yearly Report.* Ismailia, Egypt: Suez Canal Authority. Accessed 25 January 2013. http://www.suezcanal.gov.eg/Files/Publications/73.pdf.

Swing, Kelly. 2013. "Conservation: Inertia Is Speeding Fish-Stock Declines." *Nature* 494: 314.

Swiss Re. 2002. *Opportunities and Risks of Climate Change.* Zurich: Swiss Re Publications. Accessed 26 January 2013. http://stephenschneider.stanford.edu/Publications/PDF_Papers/SwissReClimateChange.pdf.

Tabb, William K. 2004. *Economic Governance in the Age of Globalization.* New York: Columbia University Press.

Tarullo, Daniel K. 2008. *Banking on Basel: The Future of International Financial Regulation.* Washington, DC: Peterson Institute for International Economics.

TEEB (The Economics of Ecosystems and Biodiversity). 2010. *The Economics of Ecosystems and Biodiversity: Mainstreaming the Economics of Nature; A Synthesis of the Approach, Conclusions, and Recommendations of TEEB.* United Nations Environment Programme. Malta: Progress Press.

Tirole, Jean. 2010. "Lessons from the Crisis." In *Balancing the Banks: Global Lessons from the Financial Crisis,* ed. Mathias Dewatripont, Jean-Charles Rochet, and Jean Tirole. Princeton, NJ: Princeton University Press, 10–77.

Topping, Alexandra. 2013. "Hannah Smith Suicide: MPs Call for Education in Social-Media Awareness." *Guardian,* 7 August. Accessed 5 September. http://www

.theguardian.com/society/2013/aug/07/hannah-smith-suicide-cyberbullying -ask-fm-twitter.

UCPSOTF (U.S.–Canada Power System Outage Task Force). 2004. *Final Report on the August 14, 2003, Blackout in the United States and Canada: Causes and Recommendations.* U.S.–Canada Power System Outage Task Force, April. Accessed 16 July 2013. http://energy.gov/sites/prod/files/oeprod/DocumentsandMedia/BlackoutFinal-Web.pdf.

UIC (International Union of Railways). 2010. *High Speed around the World,* 15 December. Paris: High Speed Department, International Union of Railways.

UN (United Nations). 2003. *Water for People, Water for Life—The United Nations World Water Development Report.* World Water Development Report 1. Barcelona: United Nations Educational, Scientific, and Cultural Organization and Berghahn Books. Accessed 11 January 2013. http://www.unesco.org/new/en/natural-sciences/environment/water/wwap/wwdr/wwdr1-2003/.

UNEP (United Nations Environment Programme). 2011. *UNEP Year Book 2011: Emerging Issues in Our Global Environment.* Nairobi: United Nations Environment Programme. Accessed 25 January 2013. http://www.unep.org/yearbook/2011/pdfs/UNEP_YEARBOOK_Fullreport.pdf.

UNFPA (United Nations Population Fund). 2011. *State of World Population 2011: People and Possibilities in a World of Seven Billion.* New York: United Nations Population Fund. Accessed 7 January 2013. http://www.unfpa.org/public/home/publications/pid/8726.

UNISDR (United Nations Office for Disaster Risk Reduction). 2004. "Note on Terminology from the WCDR Conference Secretariat to the Drafting Committee (18/11/2004)." United Nations Office for Disaster Risk Reduction, Geneva. Accessed 15 October 2012. http://www.unisdr.org/2005/wcdr/intergover/drafting -committe/terminology.pdf.

USDHHS (U.S. Department of Health and Human Services). 2012a. "About Pandemics." U.S. Department of Health and Human Services. Accessed 21 August. http://www.flu.gov/pandemic/about/index.html.

———. 2012b. "Pandemic Flu History." U.S. Department of Health and Human Services. Accessed 21 August. http://www.flu.gov/pandemic/history/#.

Useem, Michael. 2011. "Deutsche Bank Case Study: Catastrophic Risk Management during the Fukushima Earthquake in March 2011." Presentation at the Sasin Bangkok Forum: Asia in Transformation, Royal Méridien Hotel, Bangkok, 8–9 July.

USGS (U.S. Geological Survey). 2000. "Volcanic Ash Fall—A 'Hard Rain' of Abrasive Particles." Fact Sheet 0027–00. U.S. Geological Survey. Accessed 15 July 2013. http://pubs.usgs.gov/fs/fs027-00/fs027-00.pdf.

Valdimarsson, Omar. 2009. "Iceland Parliament Approves Debt Bill." *Reuters,* 28 August. Accessed 25 January 2013. http://www.reuters.com/article/2009/08/28/businesspro-us-iceland-debts-idUSTRE57R3B920090828.

Verhoeven, Harry. 2011. "Climate Change, Conflict, and Development in Sudan: Global Neo-Malthusian Narratives and Local Power Struggles." *Development and Change* 42 (3): 679–707.

Verseck, Keno. 2012. "Eastern Europe Swings Right." *Spiegel Online,* 18 January. Accessed 1 June. http://www.spiegel.de/international/europe/poor-and-prejudiced -eastern-europe-swings-right-a-809827-druck.html.

Vitali, Stefania, James B. Glattfelder, and Stefano Battiston. 2011. "The Network of Global Corporate Control." *PLoS ONE* 6 (10). Accessed 4 February 2013. http:// www.plosone.org/article/info%3Adoi%2F10.1371%2Fjournal.pone.0025995.

Walker, Brian, C. S. Holling, Stephen R. Carpenter, and Ann Kinzig. 2004. "Resilience, Adaptability, and Transformability in Social-Ecological Systems." *Ecology and Society* 11 (1): 5. Accessed 9 January 2013. http://www.ecologyandsociety .org/vol9/iss2/art5/print.pdf.

Waltz, Kenneth. 1979. *The Theory of International Politics.* Boston: McGraw–Hill.

Watts, Duncan J. 2002. "A Simple Model of Global Cascades on Random Networks." *Proceedings of the National Academy of Science (PNAS)* 99 (9): 5766–5771.

WEF (World Economic Forum). 2012a. "Impact of Thailand Floods 2011 on Supply Chain." Mimeo, World Economic Forum.

———. 2012b. *Global Risks 2012.* Geneva: World Economic Forum.

White, Lawrence J. 1997. "Technological Change, Financial Innovation, and Financial Regulation in the U.S.: The Challenges for Public Policy." Presentation at the Conference on Performance of Financial Institutions, Wharton Financial Institutions Center, University of Pennsylvania, Philadelphia, May 8–10. Accessed 21 January 2013. http://fic.wharton.upenn.edu/fic/papers/97/white.pdf.

White House. 2012. "National Strategy for Global Supply Chain Security." White House, Washington, DC. Accessed 2 February 2013. http://www.whitehouse.gov/ sites/default/files/national_strategy_for_global_supply_chain_security.pdf.

———. 2013. "Statement by Deputy National Security Advisor for Strategic Communications Ben Rhodes on Syrian Chemical Weapons Use." Office of the Press Secretary, White House, Washington, DC, 13 June. Accessed 21 July. http://www.whitehouse.gov/the-press-office/2013/06/13/statement-deputy -national-security-advisor-strategic-communications-ben-.

Whitney, Lance. 2010. "With Legal Nod, Microsoft Ambushes Waledac Botnet." *CNET News,* 26 February. Accessed 17 July 2013. http://news.cnet.com/8301 -1009_3-10459558-83.html.

WHO (World Health Organization). 2003. "WHO Scientific Research Advisory Committee on Severe Acute Respiratory Syndrome." Report of the First Meeting, Geneva, Switzerland, WHO/CDS/CSR/GAR/2004.16, 20–21 October, 2. Accessed 3 February 2013. http://www.who.int/csr/resources/publications/SRAC -CDSCSRGAR2004_16.pdf.

———. 2004a. "China's Latest SARS Outbreak Has Been Contained, but Biosafety Concerns Remain—Update 7." Global Alert and Response, World Health

Organization, 18 May. Accessed 28 January 2013. http://www.who.int/csr/don/2004_05_18a/en/index.html.

———. 2004b. "WHO Guidelines for the Global Surveillance of Severe Acute Respiratory Syndrome: Updated Recommendations." WHO/CDS/CSR/ARO/2004.1, October, 6. Accessed 3 February 2013. http://www.who.int/csr/resources/publications/WHO_CDS_CSR_ARO_2004_1.pdf.

———. 2011a. "Annex 5—Reported Number of People Receiving Antiretroviral Therapy in Low- and Middle-Income Countries by Sex and by Age, and Estimated Number of Children Receiving and Needing Antiretroviral Therapy and Coverage Percentages, 2010." In *Global HIV/AIDS Response: Epidemic Update and Health Sector Progress Towards Universal Access.* Progress report. Geneva: WHO, UNAIDS, and UNICEF. Accessed 2 February 2013. http://www.who.int/hiv/data/tuapr2011_annex5_web.xls.

———. 2011b. "Annex 8—HIV and AIDS Statistics, by WHO and UNICEF Regions, 2010." In *Global HIV/AIDS Response: Epidemic Update and Health Sector Progress Towards Universal Access.* Progress report. Geneva: WHO, UNAIDS, and UNICEF. Geneva. Accessed 2 February 2013. http://www.who.int/hiv/data/tuapr2011_annex8_web.xls.

———. 2011c. "Avian Influenza." *WHO Factsheet,* April. Accessed 3 February 2013. http://www.who.int/mediacentre/factsheets/avian_influenza/en/index.html.

———. 2011d. *Global Status Report on Noncommunicable Diseases 2010.* Geneva: World Health Organization. Accessed 3 February 2013. http://whqlibdoc.who.int/publications/2011/9789240686458_eng.pdf.

———. 2012a. "10 Facts on Climate Change and Health." *Fact File.* Accessed 30 August. http://www.who.int/features/factfiles/climate_change/facts/en/index.html.

———. 2012b. "Current WHO Phase of Pandemic Alert (Avian Influenza H5N1)." *Influenza.* Accessed 21 August. http://www.who.int/influenza/preparedness/pandemic/h5n1phase/en/.

———. 2013. "Global Outbreak Alert and Response Network." Network website. Accessed 3 February. http://www.who.int/csr/outbreaknetwork/en/.

Williams, Alan P. O. 2010. *The History of UK Business and Management Education.* Bingley, UK: Emerald Group.

Wilson, Dominic, and Raluca Dragusanu. 2008. "The Expanding Middle: The Exploding World Middle Class and Falling Global Inequality." Global Economic Papers 170. Goldman Sachs, New York. Accessed 3 February 2013. http://www.ryanallis.com/wp-content/uploads/2008/07/expandingmiddle.pdf.

Withers, Paul. 2012. "iPhone 5 Production Delayed as Foxconn Staff Walk Out." *Mobile News,* 8 October. Accessed 16 October. http://www.mobilenewscwp.co.uk/2012/10/08/iphone-5-production-delayed-as-foxconn-staff-walk-out/.

Witzel, Morgen. 2011. *A History of Management Thought.* New York: Routledge.

World Bank. 2012a. "GDP per Capita (Current US$)." *Data.* Accessed 3 September. http://data.worldbank.org/indicator/NY.GDP.PCAP.CD/countries.

World Bank. 2012b. "Poverty and Equity Data." Accessed circa late 2012. http://povertydata.worldbank.org/poverty/home.

———. 2013. *World Development Indicators.* World DataBank. Accessed 7, 26, and 31 January, 12 February, and 19 July. http://databank.worldbank.org/data/home.aspx.

World Health Assembly. 2003. "Severe Acute Respiratory Syndrome (SARS)." *Fifty-Sixth World Health Assembly Resolution WHA56.29,* 26 May. Accessed 2 February 2013. http://www.who.int/csr/sars/en/ea56r29.pdf.

WTO (World Trade Organization). 2013a. "OECD–WTO Database on Trade in Value-Added: Preliminary Results." *OECD–WTO Brochure.* World Trade Organization, 17 January. Accessed 23 January. http://www.wto.org/english/res_e/statis_e/miwi_e/tradedataday13_e/oecdbrochurejanv13_e.pdf.

———. 2013b. *Statistics Database.* World Trade Organization. Accessed 4 February. http://stat.wto.org/Home/WSDBHome.aspx?Language=E.

———. 2013c. "The Multilateral Trading System and Climate Change," World Trade Organization. Accessed 1 December. http://www.wto.org/english/tratop_e/envir_e/climate_change_e.pdf.

Wynne, Brian, and Kerstin Dressel. 2001. "Cultures of Uncertainty: Transboundary Risks and BSE in Europe." In *Transboundary Risk Management,* ed. Joanne Linneroth-Bayer, Ragnar Löefstedt, and Gunnar Sjöestedt. London: Earthscan, 126–154.

Yuichi, Ono, and Luis G. Aranda. 2011. *Economic and Social Impact of Volcanic Eruptions.* World Economic Forum Report, December. Geneva: World Economic Forum.

Zhao, Jie, Peiquan Jin, and Guorui Huang. 2011. "A Survey on Detecting Public Emergencies from Web Pages." *Advances on Information Sciences and Service Sciences* 3 (3): 56–63.

Zittrain, Jonathan. 2009. *The Future of the Internet—And How to Stop It.* London: Penguin.

Index

Page numbers for entries occurring in boxes are followed by a *b*; those for entries in figures, by an *f*; those for entries in notes, by an *n*; and those for entries in tables, by a *t*.